Effective Writing Skills for Public Relations

WITHDRAWN

Third Edition

KU-525-566

John Foster

CIPR

CHARTERED INSTITUTE OF PUBLIC RELATIONS

First published in 1998
Second edition published in 2001
Third edition published in 2005
Reprinted in 2005

Kogan Page Limited
120 Pentonville Road
London N1 9JN
UK
www.kogan-page.co.uk

Kogan Page US
525 South 4th Street, #241
Philadelphia, PA 19147
USA

© John Foster 1998, 2001, 2005

British Library Cataloguing in Publication Data

A CIP record for this book is available from the British Library

ISBN 0 7494 4381 2

Library of Congress Cataloging-in-Publication Data

Foster, John, 1926-
    Effective writing skills for public relations / John Foster. -- 3rd ed.
        p. cm.
    ISBN 0-7494-4381-2
    1. Business writing--Handbooks, manuals, etc. 2. Public
relations--Handbooks, manuals, etc. I. Title.
HF5718.3.F67 2005
808'.066659--dc

                            2005000863

Typeset by Jean Cussons Typesetting, Diss, Norfolk
Printed and bound in Great Britain by Bell & Bain, Glasgow

Contents

Contents

PR in Practice Series

Published in association with the Chartered Institute of Public Relations
Series Editor: Anne Gregory

Kogan Page has joined forces with the Chartered Institute of Public Relations to publish this unique series, which is designed specifically to meet the needs of the increasing numbers of people seeking to enter the public relations profession and the large band of existing PR professionals. Taking a practical, action-oriented approach, the books in the series concentrate on the day-to-day issues of public relations practice and management rather than academic history. They provide ideal primers for all those on CIPR, CAM and CIM courses or those taking NVQs in PR. For PR practitioners, they provide useful refreshers and ensure that their knowledge and skills are kept up to date.

Anne Gregory is one of the UK's leading public relations academics. She is Director of the Centre for Public Relations Studies at Leeds Business School, a faculty of Leeds Metropolitan University. Before becoming an academic, Anne spent 12 years in public relations practice and has experience at a senior level both in-house and in consultancy. She remains involved in consultancy work and is a non-executive director of South West Yorkshire Mental Health NHS Trust with special responsibility for financial and communication issues. Anne is Consultant Editor of the PR in Practice series and edited the book of the same name and wrote *Planning and Managing Public Relations Campaigns*, also in this series. She was President of the CIPR in 2004.

Other titles in the series:

Creativity in Public Relations by Andy Green
Effective Internal Communication by Lyn Smith and Pamela Mounter
Effective Media Relations by Michael Bland, Alison Theaker and David Wragg
Managing Activism by Denise Deegan
Online Public Relations by David Phillips
Planning and Managing Public Relations Campaigns by Anne Gregory
Public Relations: A practical guide to the basics by Philip Henslowe
Public Relations in Practice edited by Anne Gregory
Public Relations Strategy by Sandra Oliver
Risk Issues and Crisis Management in Public Relations by Michael Regester
    and Judy Larkin
Running a Public Relations Department by Mike Beard

Forthcoming:

Introduction to Public Affairs by Stuart Thompson and Dr Steve John

The above titles are available from all good bookshops. To obtain further information, please go to the CIPR website (www.cipr.co.uk/books) or contact the publishers at the address below:

Kogan Page Ltd
120 Pentonville Road
London N1 9JN
Tel: 020 7278 0433   Fax: 020 7837 6348
www.kogan-page.co.uk

About the author

John Foster spent several years in journalism with weekly trade papers, finally as assistant editor of a leading printing industry magazine and as editor of a quarterly journal on platemaking for print production.

He subsequently held public relations posts with Pira International, the technology centre for the printing, paper, packaging and publishing industries, and with the Institute of Practitioners in Advertising (IPA) which represents the interests of UK advertising agencies.

He has written, edited and produced a variety of printwork, from house journals and books to posters, brochures and leaflets plus writing news releases, speeches, film scripts, slide presentations and exhibition panels. As a specialist freelance journalist, he has written on management and technical issues in the printing industry. He has also undertaken public relations projects in the field of healthcare.

A keen advocate of good, consistent style in the written and spoken word, John Foster is a regular contributor to the CIPR magazine *Profile*. He is a Fellow of the CIPR and holds the CAM Diploma in Public Relations. A member of the Institute since 1954, he has served on the Council, Board of Management and

Membership Committee, and was Programme Director 1979–81. He is an honorary member of the IPA, a member of the CAM Education Foundation, a Fellow of the Royal Society of Arts and an Associate (journalist) member of the Foreign Press Association.

In July 2003, John Foster was awarded the Stephen Tallents Medal by the then President of the CIPR, John Aspery, for 'his contribution and commitment to the effective use of the written word'. The Tallents Medal, presented annually, recognises exceptional achievement in, and contribution to, the development of public relations practice by a member of the Institute.

Foreword

Writing good English must be one of the most difficult jobs in the world. The tracking of a developing language that is rich, diverse and constantly evolving in use and meaning is not an easy task. Today's rules and uses quickly become outdated, but this book captures English as it should be used now.

There have always been books on grammar and most of us, if we are honest, have to sneak the occasional look to check whether an apostrophe is in the right place or where a quote mark goes.

This book by John Foster gives invaluable advice, not only on the rules of English grammar, but on how to make the language come alive. How do you make people excited by your writing style and keep them reading on? How do you delight and surprise them, even if the topic is essentially dull?

Of course there's writing and there's writing. Writing for the press is very different from writing for the office. John takes us through the basics of style for all occasions, right down to pronunciation.

Also included in this third edition are four useful appendices: definitions of grammar with good practical examples, similar pairs of words that are often confused, a short glossary of everyday terms in IT and publishing, and some tips for when you are lost for words.

The book is written in a lively, imaginative style and is suited not only for the new practitioner who is eager to improve his or her mastery of the English language, but for the more experienced practitioner who needs a quick checklist of the essentials of grammar and some hints on how to pep up their writing style.

Effective Writing Skills for Public Relations is intended to be a no-nonsense guide for busy practitioners. It avoids the traps of being so comprehensive and detailed that it confuses, or so superficial as to be of no use at all. It covers all the major grammatical constructions that we use day-to-day with the one objective in mind: writing good readable English. Every PR practitioner should have one. Its potential readership extends to the wider reaches of the communications industry – in fact to anyone interested in words and their usage.

Anne Gregory
Series Editor

Acknowledgements

I wish to thank the many friends and colleagues who helped in the preparation of this book. In particular, grateful appreciation is recorded to Nigel Ellis, former CIPR president, who read the early drafts of every chapter of the first edition and made many helpful suggestions for improvements.

Special thanks are also due to Pat Bowman, former head of PR at Lloyds Bank, to Don Billett, former public affairs director, Du Pont de Nemours International, to Robin Paterson, formerly senior public affairs specialist, DuPont (UK), and to Peter Jackson, editor and communications consultant, all of whom read individual chapters or sections and made helpful comments and alterations to the original text.

I would like to express my gratitude to a number of friends and colleagues who have helped me with subsequent editions. I would particularly like to record my sincere thanks to Ian Arnison, former head of press and publications at the British Standards Institution; Branislav Bokan, IT consultant; David Lowe, marketing consultant; Steve Sawyer, Web Consultant, Computer Software Group (CSG) Integra; Philip Spink, head of information services, the Advertising Association; Roy Topp, creative services consultant and public-speaking coach; Susan Wright, freelance technology journalist, and Feona McEwan, communications director of WPP Group PLC.

For this third edition, I would particularly like to thank Pat Bowman and Robin Paterson who read, respectively, the chapters on editing skills and tone in writing; Peter Prowse, Executive Chairman of Prowse & Co, and David Ames of accountants Gibbons & Mannington for checking the chapter on annual reports; and Philip Circus, Legal Affairs Director of the Institute of Sales Promotion and Legal Adviser to the British Promotional Merchandise Association, for his guidance and help with the law chapter.

I also wish to thank the British Association of Communicators in Business for providing examples of winning entries in their 2004 awards. Photography: Trident Photographic Services for the CiB. The *Mail Made Easy* leaflet shown in Chapter 6 is copyright © Royal Mail Group Plc 2004. Reproduced by kind permission of Royal Mail. All rights reserved. Internet usage statistics were provided by Computer Industry Almanac (www.c-i-a.com/pr0904.htm).

Grateful acknowledgement must go to Professor Anne Gregory, Director, Centre for PR Studies, Leeds Metropolitan University and President of the CIPR in 2004, the first editor of this series of textbooks for the Institute, for her constant support and encouragement and for letting me get on with it as I wished.

I have referred to several titles published by Oxford University Press in the preparation of this work and thank them for permission to quote information, references and examples from *Fowler's Modern English Usage*, *The Oxford Guide to English Usage*, *The Oxford Dictionary of Grammar*, and *The Oxford Style Manual*. Acknowledgement is also given to Headline Book Publishing Ltd for permission to quote examples from *Debrett's Correct Form*.

JF

Introduction

Style is the crucial ingredient for everything we say and do: in writing, it is the way sentences are structured, the choice of words and the way they are used, plus punctuation. If the style is outmoded and all over the place, the reader will soon lose interest and might not even get beyond the first few lines. Style calls for clarity, brevity coupled with the use of plain language, and the avoidance of clichés and jargon. It means making sure spellings are correct and that words are not misused. Above all it means consistency.

This book has been designed for students and others entering the communications industry, in particular for those intending to follow a career in public relations. It will also be helpful for those already employed in the public relations profession either in consultancies or as in-house practitioners – in fact for all those earning their living by their writing skills.

The advice in these pages is based on the authority of established style guides, in particular the *Oxford Guide to English Usage* and the *Oxford Style Manual*, which embraces the *Oxford Dictionary for Writers and Editors* and the *Oxford Guide to Style*, itself replacing the classic reference source, *Hart's Rules for Compositors and Readers*, and also on personal experience. This has covered many years of close involvement in writing, editing and producing publications of several kinds; from technical and scientific material to professional and trade journals, news releases, and general printwork including booklets, brochures, manuals and leaflets.

Effective Writing Skills deals not only with the printed but also the spoken word: for messages to be properly communicated and understood, clarity of speech is essential and a chapter is included for those giving audio-visual presentations and taking on public-speaking assignments.

While readers will benefit from reading this book from cover to cover, some will doubtless wish to dip into individual chapters as needs dictate. If some sections, such as the positioning of apostrophes, appear to be elementary, there will always be someone not far away who is getting it wrong!

This is not a book of grammar, but does serve as a reminder of some of the basic principles. The emphasis throughout is on those style points which are frequent causes of argument and disagreement: for example when and where to put capitals, how to deal with figures and abbreviations, plus the skills of hyphenating, punctuating and paragraphing. A new chapter on editing skills discusses what editors and subeditors look for and why they change your hard-crafted copy. The fewer corrections they make, the better for you, the writer.

Further new chapters in this third edition cover tone of voice, the essential ingredient for every message, annual reports, Americanisms and the legal issues facing all writers. The reader will find help on language of information technology and the skills needed for successful presentations. The technicalities of presentations, and the equipment needed, are not covered since these are beyond the scope of this book. Also covered are the essential requirements for handling headlines and captions, as well as the basics of news releases, and the need for concise language coupled with the readability of the printed word.

These and other chapters will provide practitioners with a useful reference source for their day-to-day work. Most chapters in the first and second editions have been updated and expanded, with new material added where appropriate.

Every organisation should have a house style, and that very often calls for a 'style police officer' to make sure that the rules are followed by everyone, from director and manager to all support staff. If that is achieved, and if as a result there is closer interest in and awareness of style, then this book will have met its objective.

For this edition, a number of style changes have been agreed with the publishers. Chief among these are the adoption of lower case for internet, web and website as one word, and no hyphen in email and online. Readers in North America may notice that words with -ize in them have been changed to -ise since this is the style generally favoured in the UK both in style guides and in the media. The author hopes that those readers will appreciate the reasons for adopting this style in the current edition.

1

The importance of style: an overview

Effective communication demands clear, consistent style. Everyone in public relations – whether in-house or a consultancy practitioner – should put style at the top of their priority list. This book is about the various characteristics of the written and spoken word, or the manner of writing and speaking; in other words the style, the ultimate hallmark of professionalism. It is not about English grammar, although it touches upon some of the hotly argued rules that tend to be the territory of the pedant. The basic terminology of grammar is explained in Appendix 1 to enable the reader to check upon the technicalities and to provide a refresher if needed.

The following chapters enlarge upon the topics discussed in my regular column in the *IPR Journal* since 1993 and in the CIPR's *Profile* magazine from November 1999. The interest generated by these articles led me to embark upon this work which, it is hoped, will lead to a greater awareness of the importance of style. First, pay close attention to what newspapers and magazines do, and also to developments in book publishing. As soon as a new book comes out on style and usage, get a copy and start a collection. This will be invaluable when you want to establish a set of house rules, to update an existing one, or just for day-to-day reference. Set up a library of books on English style and usage that is accessible to everyone – not just to your own department but to all who use a keyboard. A list of such books will be found in the Further Reading section at the end. Some newspaper style guides, for example those issued by *The Guardian* and *The Times*, can be viewed online.

STYLE ON THE MOVE

Style changes fast. Compare, for instance, a magazine or newspaper of today with one printed only a few decades ago: overuse of capitals, stilted phraseology and solid slabs of type unrelieved by subheadings were all commonplace in the 1950s and 1960s. Even now, it is not hard to find press releases ridden with banalities, boring headlines, 'label' headings devoid of verb and verve, poorly punctuated reports and letters; and, probably worst of all, inconsistencies in spelling (let alone howlers like 'one *foul* swoop' from a BBC newcaster early in 1997).

The ignorance which surrounds modern style trends emanates through lack of interest in the subject. For young people entering the competitive world of communications it is essential to have a grasp of the basics: to know, for instance, that *media* and *data* are plural nouns, to understand the difference between a colon and a semi-colon, to appreciate that a dash and a hyphen are not the same thing. (It was this last point, incidentally, which led to the first 'Verbals' column in the *IPR Journal,* later titled *Profile.*)

Some will no doubt wonder what all the fuss is about. But the hyphen masquerading as a dash is symptomatic of the lax attitude towards style; few word-processor and computer typists bother whether style is consistent, or even know what it means. So it is up to the public relations practitioner – in fact all professional communicators – to get the message across that style matters in everything an organisation does.

The way we all write has changed dramatically over the last few years, often without our even noticing it. Information technology has brought scores of new words. Newspapers and magazines have led style changes: hyphens are dropped to make one word, two-word phrases become one. All this reduces clutter, speeds up the copy and helps the reader. Unless we keep up with style trends we soon become outdated, out of step with everyone else. And a reminder: make sure you edit your copy and watch for those style points as you go along. They are just as important as those facts and figures.

APPRECIATING STYLE

Acquiring a grounding in grammar is not enough: the finer points of style and presentation will often make all the difference between a good and a mediocre publication – between a stodgy leaflet or complex, wordy brochure and one which is lively and appealing. This means printwork that promotes a product or service and turns a glancer into a reader; that tells a story succinctly and in plain language; and is consistent in every respect. If this is achieved then the style has worked, communication has done its job and the public relations effort has paid off.

It is essential for everyone in PR and communications to have an appreciation of style so that the reader, or receiver of the message, is on the side of the sender from the outset. Just as important is visual presentation style: well-crafted slides where the logo is always the same size and colour, and text mirroring the typeface, are but two essential requirements for a corporate identity – the hallmark of a successful and profitable company or organisation.

Packs and display panels with a recognisable type style are instantly identified with the company and product. If that happens, the PR effort has worked and produced tangible results. Clear, unambiguous, concise copy written like a front-page news story is usually the best means of getting your message across and making it work for you, your company or your client. There are other times, however, when a more measured style is appropriate – much depends on the target audience and the marketing objectives.

It is important when looking at your style that you take tone of voice into account. As discussed more fully in Chapter 19, the tone you adopt for printwork, correspondence and all other communications must be warm, friendly, easily understood and free of jargon and technospeak. How you go about this is, of course, a matter for management decision, but once agreed it should be followed rigorously and should be included as a major item in your rules for house style.

YOUR ORGANISATION'S STYLE

Style extends beyond the confines of publications and the printed word in packaging. It applies to the livery for your delivery van or lorry; to news releases; to film; to audio-visuals; to video news releases (VNRs); to radio and TV broadcasts; to how your story is put over in speeches at conferences and seminars; the platform arrangements; product labelling and design; office stationery; the layout and wording of the website; and even to the way your receptionist answers the telephone. Stick to the style you have adopted in absolutely everything concerning your company or your client's products and services. Think about it in all the tasks you perform. Is it consistent? Is it doing justice to your endeavours? Is it, in fact, good PR?

There are a number of style guides to assist you and some of the best known are mentioned in later chapters. They deal mainly with the printed word, for that is where style is most important and where guidance is often needed. Journalists are inculcated with a sense of style from the moment they join a newspaper or magazine, and it is helpful to see how newspapers and magazines treat the printed word. Most newspapers produce style guides for their editorial staff and it is worthwhile asking for copies.

There is, for instance, wide variation between one newspaper or magazine and another in the use of titles, the way dates are set out, and how abbreviations are handled. When writing articles for the press you should preferably type the copy in the publication's style, so check on the way figures are set; how names are written; when and where capitals are used; how quotes are dealt with; whether copy is set ragged right or justified with both edges aligned; whether *-ise* or *-ize* endings are used. A public relations executive who writes material specifically for a target medium and follows its style has a far better chance of getting material published than one who ignores it.

Press releases should follow the general style adopted by newspapers for the treatment of quotations, for example double quote marks rather than single, with short sentences and paragraphs. If points like these are all followed then the sub-editor will be on the writer's side, and your copy is less likely to be changed. A bonus for the public relations executive if the chairman's favourite phrase remains unaltered!

PR practitioners must also keep abreast of style trends in broadcasting: radio and TV stations usually have their own rules for scripts. The BBC has its own style guide for presenters and contributors; to take a current example, they are told that it is memorandums not memoranda, an argument with listeners that was settled in a flash on Radio Four's *Broadcasting House*.

KEEP IT CONSISTENT

There is nothing sacrosanct about style: it is constantly changing, with spellings, 'vogue' words and phrases falling into disuse, to be replaced smartly by new ones. Favourite sayings become clichés, and myths that infinitives must not be split, that sentences must never end with a preposition, and that words that once were capitalised can now be lower-cased with abandon, are now mainly discarded.

On the other hand, some style rules like never starting a sentence with a figure, or numbers up to and including ten always being spelt out unless they are part of a table or figure, are still firmly established in style books. But whatever you decide on, keep it consistent throughout the whole piece.

POINTS TO WATCH

Be on your guard against repetition, or using the wrong word and putting your reader off for good. Perhaps it won't be noticed, but mostly it will. *Imply* is not the same as *infer*; there are no degrees of uniqueness (something is either unique or it isn't); *fewer than* is often used for *less than* and vice versa (*fewer* is not interchangeable with *less*); and so on. Keep it simple and understandable: use short rather than long words, write snappy sentences, cut out jargon and over-worked words, and leave foreign words to the specialist journal. But don't hesitate, occasionally, to launch into 'Franglais' (*le Channel Tunnel*) or German-English (*Die Teenagers*) or even *ein steadyseller* (for the bookshop) to provide a breather and a spot of humour.

Usage differs enormously: English is spoken as a first language by over 377 million people throughout the world (226 million in the United States alone, 56 million in the UK), while almost as many speak it as a second language. As a percentage of the world's population, 6.2 per cent use English as their mother tongue, second only to Chinese. English is the official language of over 70 countries.

Writers have at their command more than half a million words (there are some 640,000 in the latest edition of the *Oxford English Dictionary* (*OED*)), yet it has been estimated that most people go through life with only some 2000 words at their command. This limit on the average person's vocabulary shows there is good reason for avoiding long or little-used words: not only do they fail to communicate, but the writer is felt to 'talk down' to the reader.

A number of rules for style and usage have been proposed by journalists, lexicographers and others, but few are set in stone; the advice and examples given in this book are based on current best practice, although allowance must be made for individual taste. English is a living language always on the move: today's style will soon be yesterday's.

When you are thinking about your company's style and following the rules that have been established, it is crucial not to be pedantic and over-zealous with your corrections. But what is the difference between being pedantic and being correct? Pedantic is being over-fussy, like never ending a sentence with a preposition; on the other hand, there are shades of correctness depending on constantly changing style tenets.

However, there are some points of grammar like verb agreeing with subject on which there can be no argument: they are either correct or they are not. The overriding rule is, follow trends but keep the grammar right.

Language must never get in the way of the message. It is therefore important to be aware of the significant style differences existing between American English and ours, particularly now that so many websites and press releases are targeted to the United States. For instance, while it is acceptable to write 'shop' for 'store' on both sides of the Atlantic it is wrong for a motoring journalist over there to talk about a 'bonnet' when he should say 'hood', or put 'boot' for 'trunk'.

The question of whether or not to adopt Americanisms such as in spelling or vocabulary for communications to US and global markets is discussed in a later chapter.

The guidance in these pages will help public relations practitioners and other communicators to lay down effective style rules for their own companies and organisations. Once these have been established, they should be rigorously followed. If they are not, then style becomes inconsistent and that is always as bad as not having any rules at all. All the work that has gone into establishing the style will be wasted. But not for long: it will be revision time again before you know it!

GOOD STYLE IS GOOD MANNERS

Good style means good work. It also means good manners: letters being answered promptly, returning telephone calls, sincerity in everything you say and do. If you cannot do something, say so – don't just leave it and hope that the problem will go away. And when Christmas comes, don't send out an unsigned card, even if your company's name and address is printed inside.

Style is just as important with the spoken word. Few speakers at a conference would think of muttering and mumbling their way through a talk. Carefully enunciated speech without clichés or jargon is essential for avoiding slipshod presentation and ensuring effective communication.

Some hints and tips on pronunciation style will be found in Chapter 16. And as Sir Trevor McDonald, the TV presenter and newscaster, confirms, well-articulated speech can raise someone from humble origins to the very top. McDonald advises young people aiming for wider horizons to speak their language well. Diction and grammar really do matter. This is particularly true when most people entering the PR profession soon find themselves making presentations – sometimes to packed conferences – and frequently appearing in radio and TV interviews.

Appreciate the need for style – be aware of style trends – and follow it through relentlessly and consistently. This book will help you to do that.

AT A GLANCE

- Make good, consistent style your priority.
- Follow style trends. Don't be old-fashioned.
- Good style means clear, plain, lively, concise language.
- An instantly recognisable style helps to get your message across.
- Build a library of style guides accessible to all.
- Adopt the right tone of voice for your audience.
- Distinguish between being pedantic and correct.
- Never let language get in the way of the message.
- Good style, good manners mean good work.

2

Trouble with plurals and possessives

How many times have you seen attempts to make words ending in -y into plurals just by adding an 's' and ending up with *daisys*? Or even worse – *tomato's*, a familiar notice in the high street? Errors like these would be immediately spotted by professional communicators, and staff in PR departments making them would not last for long. But there are plenty of difficult plurals and it is not always easy to tell from the office dictionary how to deal with them. Similarly, there is often confusion about how to handle possessives: not just to know whether an apostrophe should be there, but where to place it. Again, how frequently have you seen the possessive *its* with an apostrophe shouting at you, pretending that *it's* is OK?

PLURAL MATTERS

Common problems

Most nouns require an 's' to make them plural. Because of the needs of pronunciation, with some words it is necessary to put in an 'e' to give an extra vowel (branches), with different rules for changing vowel sounds (stomachs). Particular difficulty is encountered with words ending in -o: embargoes but mementos. A useful rule here is that -e is never inserted when another vowel comes before -o: an instant answer to any thought of putting an 'e' in ratios. Note that there are roofs, not rooves; wharves but dwarfs; scarves but turfs.

Compound words made up of a noun and adjective, or two nouns connected by a preposition, form plurals by a change in the main word as in courts martial, heirs presumptive, poets laureate and in sons-in-law, hangers-on, runners-up, passers-by and men-of-war. Note, however, that there are brigadier-generals and sergeant-majors. And there are run-throughs, set-ups and forget-me-nots, handfuls, stand-bys and spoonfuls.

Care is needed with plurals for words of foreign origin and it must be noted here that media/data are plural nouns and take a plural verb. However, the new edition of *Fowler's Modern English Usage* says 'we are "still at the debating table" on the question of the media is/are', but nevertheless recommends the use of the plural when in doubt. (In informal writing, or speech, only the purist will object to the media is/data is.) Misuse of criteria and phenomena is common as they are mistaken for being collective, singular nouns: the singular forms are criterion and phenomenon. It should be noted that graffiti is the plural of graffito, termini of terminus, viruses of virus and bacteria of bacterium.

Some other plurals: analyses, appendices, basis/es, bureaux (but often Anglicised to bureaus), indexes (but indices in mathematics), memorandums (but memoranda in a collective sense), moratoriums, referendums, quorums (but addenda, curricula), stadiums (try saying stadia/syllabi and you are in danger of being pedantic and bowing to the purist); also synopses, syllabuses, theses. An extensive list of foreign words in their singular and plural forms will be found in *The Oxford Guide to Style*, the successor to *Hart's Rules*.

Singular or plural for collective nouns?

There is a problem for the writer using a collective noun: should it take a singular or plural verb? The choice will depend on whether the noun is considered as a single entity or as a group of people or things. Thus, whether to write the committee is or are, agrees or agree can be answered simply by saying to yourself does it refer to the committee as a whole or to the views of separate members? Similarly, the mass noun audience can take either the singular or plural as in 'the *audience* was seated, ready for the speaker' or as in 'the audience were all clapping madly'. The same applies to other mass nouns like board, cast (of actors), committee, company, family, group, government, staff.

It is important to decide if the emphasis lies on the individual or the group with a word like *board*, to take one example. If it lies on the individual members of the board, then write the board *'who* broke off for lunch' but if the sense is collective, the construction would be 'the board *which* made a decision'. When we use the singular word majority we write 'the majority of people are'. That is because it is people being talking about, thus the noun takes the plural. But if it's the majority itself that is being discussed then it needs a singular verb (the majority is smaller). Again, if number is the subject then it takes the singular, but plural if 'of people' is added. The singular always follows if the noun has a qualifier like this, that, every as in 'every manager has a part to play'.

As a general rule, it is better to have a singular verb with a collective noun, and to treat names of companies and organisations as singular entities. The plural form tends to smack of informality: 'XYZ company are announcing' is a relaxed and friendly style, but loses crispness. Avoid a mixed style of singular verb and plural pronoun as in 'the committee *has* made *their* decision' ('the committee *has* made *its* decision is preferable). In the end, however, house style will decide – another reason for every company to have a set of rules for basic style points such as this.

Whether to write *is* or *are* for companies with more than one name, such as Legal & General, is somewhat of a conundrum, and one faced sooner or later by everyone. While it is largely a matter of house style, Marks & Spencer and the multi-name styles for PR consultancies and advertising agencies mostly take the singular verb, thus adhering to the general rule of 'keep it singular'.

Watch out for company or brand names ending in 's'. They will invariably be singular as in Boots is, PG Tips makes – again a matter of house style. The same applies to organisations, such as the United Nations and US Congress, which always takes the singular, and this is so even in the case of the United States.

Note, however, that a pair and a couple take the plural, as do two singular nouns linked by *and* unless the conjoined words form a single idea as in wining and dining. Conversely, note that the number *is*, public relations *is*. Other nouns taking a singular verb include advice, equipment, furniture, knowledge, machinery, stationery, traffic. There are a number of nouns which only take the plural: people, police, clergy and some others recognisable by their -s endings, notably briefs, clothes, congratulations, glasses, goggles, outskirts, pants, pliers, remains, riches, scissors, thanks, tights. Nouns with a plural form which do take a singular verb are billiards, measles, news. Trousers, on the other hand, have not always been a plural. Gone are the days when the assistant in a menswear shop might have declared 'A good *trouser*, Sir'.

The crucial point in any singular/plural dispute is to maintain consistency throughout the piece as a whole, through each sentence and each paragraph. If that consistency is lost, news releases may be rubbished, and printed documents and contact reports will mostly fail to command the reader's respect.

Communication or communications?

Difficulty also arises in distinguishing between the terms communication and communications. Even public relations practitioners have a problem with this and argument rages: both refer to the act of communicating, the latter relating to the technicalities or the hardware of communicating – email, faxes, telephones and so on. Confusion is compounded by the fact that there are courses in communication management, and that communications can be managed. In reality, there is little difference in meaning. So, take your pick!

It is relevant to note that the titles communications manager/consultant have largely replaced the title public relations officer, which has now become somewhat outdated. But whatever the title – whether for undertaking the mechanics of communications or for advising how a company communicates with its public – the context will usually clarify job descriptions. Again, consistency is the watchword.

APOSTROPHE PROBLEMS

Trouble with possessives

The missing or misplaced apostrophe was once dubbed by a news-paper columnist 'that errant tadpole'. True enough. It seems that knowing where to put the apostrophe in possessives – indicating possession or ownership – causes as much difficulty as any other mark. Kingsley Amis in *The King's English* says that if it hasn't been mastered by the age of 14 then the chances are that there will always be the possibility of error. There is often confusion between *its* (in the possessive) and *it's*, the shortened form of *it is*. And the apostrophe is further misused when denoting the plural – the so-called greengrocer's apostrophe as in *potato's* (or perhaps even *potatoe's*!) – or when letter(s) have been omitted.

First, take the basic rules for positioning the apostrophe for a possessive. When the thing or person is in the singular then the apostrophe goes before the 's' as in the *boy's tie*. If, however, there is more than one boy, the apostrophe goes after the 's' as in the *boys' ties*. Another example: in *the cat's paws* there is one cat and as the paws belong to the cat it is the cat that is in the possessive, and since it is one cat the apostrophe goes before the 's'. You talk about the *campaign's objective* (where there is one campaign and one or more objectives); *John's brother* (or *brothers*, it doesn't matter) there is one John and the name is in the singular. When there are several journalists, you talk about *journalists' needs*.

For singular words ending in 's', just add 's as in the *boss's office*. To form the plural possessive, add 'es' apostrophe after the 's' as in *the bosses' bonus, the Joneses' dog*. With plural words that end with an 's', simply add the apostrophe as in the *ladies' room*, the *Smiths' house*. For nouns that are already plural as in *children, men, women* add an apostrophe 's' in the same way: *children's, men's, women's, people's*. Never write childrens', mens', womens' or peoples' or leave out the apostrophe altogether, even though you might be tempted to do so.

It is quite common to see *four weeks holiday* wrongly written without an apostrophe as a matter of course. While the clumsy *holiday of four weeks* would be pedantic in the extreme, it is far better to write *four weeks'* holiday with the apostrophe correctly positioned than not having one at all and risk offending the reader. And, of course, you go on a *fortnight's cruise*. In distinguishing the difference between *its* and *it's*, two examples will help: *its* in the possessive – the dog wagged *its* tail; *it's* as the shortened version of *it is* – the client said *'it's* a good presentation'.

Many other purposes, but don't put one if not needed

The apostrophe is a multi-purpose mark: it can signify omitted characters as in isn't, doesn't, and the verbal elisions I'm, I'll, you'll, we'll. It indicates the plural of single letters: *A's* and *B's*, *p's* and *q's*. Note that the apostrophe is omitted in the plurals of groups of letters and numbers as in *MPs*, *1990s* and in *whys* and *wherefores*. It would, however, be used to show an omission as in the *'90s*.

There is, of course, no apostrophe in *hers, ours, yours* or *theirs* (an apostrophe is needed in *one's*), but care is needed in distinguishing between the relative pronoun *whose* and *who's*, the shortened version of *who is*.

Leaving it out when it should be there is bad enough, but putting one in when it is not needed is worse still: not only is there the illiterate use of the apostrophe for plurals as in the greengrocers' signs for *carrot's* and *pea's* – there are now 'garage' apostrophes in advertisements for *Fiesta's* and *Mondeo's* and there are headlines for *Suzuki's* but, curiously, they advertise at the same time *Range Rovers* and *Cavaliers*, while cafés have notices for *tea's* and *coffee's*, and roadside restaurants displaying signs for *lunch's* and *dinner's*. Ouch! It happens more often than you might think.

Much of the problem comes from designers who either don't know or don't care whether there should be an apostrophe: *Grannys* (a shop), *Henrys Table* (a restaurant); but it is gratifying to see that *Sainsbury's* has stuck with tradition. And the apostrophe is often at the mercy of the designer who readily turns it into a dagger, pen or heart without a qualm, diminishing its importance and contributing if not to its demise, to uncertainty about positioning.

It is a tenet of 'netiquette' to drop the apostrophe, along with capitals where they are normally needed. Such disdain for usual practice can mean trouble: an important yet pedantic client could deliver a sharp rebuke in return for a sloppy message!

Inconsistencies to watch for

Organisations drop their apostrophes without hesitation, perhaps in an attempt at making them user- and customer-friendly. Thus we see *Chambers English Dictionary, Debenhams* and *Barclays Bank*; or *Queens' College* (Cambridge) but *Queen's College* and *All Souls* (Oxford), which all add to the inconsistencies. Some of the above can easily be checked in telephone directories, but where writers struggle is in knowing where to put the apostrophe in words ending in -s in names like Charles. *The Oxford Guide to Style* says: 'Use 's for the possessive case whenever possible.'

The guidance here is that the 's should appear in all monosyllables and in longer words accented on the next to last syllable as in *Jones's, Thomas's, St James's Square.* Another striking inconsistency is Earls Court which does not have an apostrophe according to style books. Yet it is given one by London Transport for the Tube station and by the exhibition centre. And in addition there is a long tradition of the possessive apostrophe being dropped from some proper names, Boots, Harrods and Horlicks.

I would prefer to keep this 'aerial comma' or 'errant tadpole', call it what you will, if only for reasons of consistency. But as in everything else, there's a contrary view, and that says the mark just causes clutter. There's even the opinion that the apostrophe in Earl's Court should go after the 's' simply because there were a number of earls who were part of the original courthouse. So you could be right whatever you do.

In multi-syllable words like Nicholas, it is equally acceptable to put the apostrophe alone as in *Nicholas'* or *Nicholas's,* but if in doubt always add the 's. For *goodness' sake* always think where it should go.

It would be unwise to put *public relations* in the possessive. Try it, and the result it awful if not a tongue-twister: public relations' or public relations's are equally ugly; a better way would be to treat public relations as an adjective and so achieve, for example, the *public relations objective,* or the wordier *objective of public relations.*

While no apostrophe is needed when writing 'He will be taken to the cleaners,' it should appear in such constructions as 'He is going to the butcher's' when there is ellipsis of the word 'shop'. However, to say (or write) 'I am going to the doctor's' with the ellipsis of the word 'surgery' would offend many an ear or eye. In these and similar examples, it would be better to omit the 's' altogether.

There are, shown above, a number of inconsistencies in the use of the apostrophe, and it seems that incorrect usage is increasing both where the apostrophe is omitted or where it is included when it shouldn't be. The *Oxford Guide to English Usage*, as well as *Fowler's* and other style guides should be consulted whenever in doubt. Dictionaries do not help much for dealing with these matters.

Responding to an appeal for its abolition by *Guardian* columnist Matthew Engel, the Queen's English Society points out that the apostrophe aids clarity. 'If we had no apostrophes someone reading Mr Engel's article would not know if he was Engel or Engels', says Dr Bernard Lamb of the QES. Linguists agree that the apostrophe does have a purpose and should be retained so long as we have possessives.

Further help on whether and where to place an apostrophe will be found in the excellent and intellectually vigorous handbook *Eats, Shoots & Leaves* by journalist Lynne Truss. Of all the points she makes, it is the unnecessary apostrophe in *it's* when in the possessive that disturbs her most.

AT A GLANCE

- Watch the spelling when adding 's' for plurals.
- Plural noun/adjective compounds need special care.
- Misuse of Latin plurals easily occurs.
- Collective nouns take singular or plural verbs but singular is usually best.
- Some nouns only take the plural.
- The apostrophe goes after the 's' for plural possessives, before the 's' when singular.
- Don't confuse the possessive *its* (no apostrophe) with *it's* for it is.
- The apostrophe can signify omitted characters.
- Look out for inconsistencies: Sainsbury's but Harrods.

3

Making your mark

Taking care over punctuation shows that the writer has the reader in mind. Putting the correct marks – and making sure there are no unnecessary ones – aids understanding and avoids ambiguity. The comma, stop, colon and interrogation mark are not there just to satisfy the rules of construction. They have a real and active purpose: to give the reader a breather, to give a pause and, at intervals, to provide a change of pace or thought. They are like traffic signs to take and guide the reader along a piece of written work. The full stop, if you like, is the red light to stop you moving forward and to bring the sentence to an end, the comma a yellow to provide a pause.

Too many people think that punctuation is just another chore: get on with the words, never mind the irritations of having to bother with brackets, dashes or hyphens, let alone using quote marks properly or typed the right way round. On the other hand, it is easy to over-punctuate and end up with complicated, obscure sentences and a 'spotty' page. Look now at the various marks and how they should be used and presented.

BASIC PUNCTUATION

'Style is the template of the times, not an irrevocable rule', declares *The Times Style and Usage Guide*. Nevertheless, there are some basic rules of punctuation to help the reader understand and follow the work: they are there not to show how clever you are at placing commas and dashes, but to provide a structure for whatever you have written. Correct and properly placed punctuation gives style and presence to any news story or feature article, brochure or report. And if it is misused it can spoil the message, even give it the opposite meaning.

Let's now look at the marks one by one.

The full stop

This is the writer's best aid to crisp, clear copy. That, after all, is what the public relations practitioner should aim for when writing for the press, and indeed for most forms of communication. But that does not mean that a piece of copy should be littered with stops like currants in a pudding. A full stop (or full point to the printer) brings a sentence to an abrupt halt, ready for the next one and an expansion of thought. No stop is needed when ending a sentence with a question mark, exclamation mark or if ending a sentence with a quotation which itself ends with a full stop.

But there are other uses: for instance, a set of three is used to show an omission (use three and only three, but if they come at the end of a sentence insert a concluding one). It will soon be noticed when the incorrect number has been used – there are plenty of examples of the writer not having the faintest idea of how many stops to put and sometimes finishing up with a line of them! Full stops are rarely seen these days in sets of initials for organisations (put them between the initials CIPR – or for any other organisation you can think of – and it will immediately look old-fashioned).

Stops are fast disappearing from initials of company names, but they can be used with great effect and impact in advertisement display heads. They should not appear in headings for press release stories for the simple reason that they are hardly ever seen in newspaper or magazine headlines. Do not put them after abbreviations like Mr, Mrs, Ms, or in lb or ft, unless of course they come at the end of a sentence.

The comma

This is one of the most common marks, but often misused: either it is put in when not needed or it is in the wrong place. Typically, the comma is used to encase a job title or descriptive phrase after a name. But a very usual mistake is just to put an opening comma, leaving the rest of the description dangling and yelling out for a companion comma.

The comma separates adjectives qualifying a noun as in 'a small, profitable consultancy', but there is no comma when one adjective qualifies another, for example 'a bright red tie'. They are useful for breaking up a long sentence, but take care not to put in too many and cause greater confusion than having none at all.

Some do's and don'ts. A comma would only go before *and* in a list of items if one of the items includes another *and*. Do not put commas in dates or round adverbs and adverbial phrases unless special emphasis is required. They do not normally go before or after *therefore* and *accordingly*, but they always encase *however* when there is a change of thought. And do not, at least in copy for press or printwork, put a comma before a direct quote – a colon should be used here.

It is easy to go mad with commas and put them where they're not needed, or leave one out and completely change the meaning. This is illustrated well by the title chosen for Lynne Truss's book. Remove the comma in *Eats, Shoots & Leaves* and it's saying something else entirely: it thus makes the point in a striking way that commas and their placing are critical elements in any writing.

It is worth noting that commas should be kept inside quote marks when you insert 'he said' in a passage, as in 'The figures are good,' he said, 'but the year ahead will be difficult.' *The Times* guide advises that the comma should be omitted before *if, unless, before, since, when* unless sense demands it. Journalists are also advised that the so-called 'Oxford comma' before *and* should be avoided in, for example, 'he ate bread, butter, and jam.' The reader will find further help on positioning of quotes in relation to punctuation later in this chapter.

But for me, my firm rule is that if there are three commas in a sentence there's probably one too many. Just look at any newspaper front page and you will see what I mean. Unless it's an unedited quote, there'll be only one or two in most sentences.

The colon

The colon is used to amplify or explain something. This is a useful mark for the writer of news releases, and copy for articles and house journals. It is normal journalistic practice to use a colon to introduce a quote, as in Joe Bloggs said: 'This is the best way of doing it.' (Teachers and college instructors, who seldom have any knowledge of, or interest in typography, usually insist upon a comma before the quote – perhaps this is why this style is seen so often.) The colon is useful for starting a list, but do not put a dash after it as in :– where the dash is superfluous. It is also handy for leading the reader to fresh fact or thought or to follow these expressions: such as, for example, namely, the following.

The semicolon

This little-used mark deserves greater awareness of its attributes. While in no sense a substitute for the comma, the semicolon provides a far stronger break and a longer pause, and it can perform some of the comma's functions. It can separate two or more clauses of equal importance and is useful for listing words and phrases that cannot neatly be separated by commas. In a lengthy sentence, it can bring a thought to a halt, enabling a new one to be started, so aiding clarity. Some writers will prefer to use a full stop instead; perhaps this is why the semicolon is falling into disuse. Certainly, journalists hardly ever use them. It is rare these days for front-page news stories to carry a single semicolon. They are far more likely to be seen in feature articles. Semicolons slow down the copy and simply mean more words per sentence.

Exclamation and interrogation marks

These marks normally count as a concluding full stop and take a capital letter afterwards. But they are sometimes seen after a supporting clause in brackets within a sentence. Exclamation marks express surprise or dismay: don't use them for emphasising simple statements. Don't use an exclamation mark in a release unless it is a quote, and even then edit it out if you can. It is a perfectly valid rule to say never use one: it is hardly ever needed. They are out of place in printed publications and formal documents; the only time for them is for emails and the occasional headline in house magazines. And never, never put more than one.

The interrogation (question) mark never follows indirect speech, or statements that pose a question; only direct questions – as used in quotes.

Brackets, round and square

When using round brackets to enclose a complete sentence, put the full stop *inside* the closing bracket as in (This is the way to do it.). It goes *outside* only if the last part of the sentence is in brackets. The square bracket is used to denote comments or explanations added to the original text, usually by the editor or someone other than the author.

The dash

This is used to add an afterthought or, if used as a pair, to replace commas if there are already too many in the sentence. Some writers are getting into the habit of using a hyphen instead of a dash. This on the face of it seems to matter little, but there is a distinct difference between the two marks: the dash (known to the printer as the en-dash) is twice as long as the hyphen and when they are both used in the same piece – as very often happens – something is clearly amiss. The hyphen masquerading as the dash is a common fault, but seldom seen in newspapers and magazines and in well-designed house journals and printwork.

Today's keyboards do not always have a dash key and that is how the trouble starts. To print a dash with some computers two keys are usually needed, and reference should be made to the operating manual or to the software supplier for advice on achieving a proper en-dash. Don't take the easy way out and type, or even double-type, a hyphen when a little effort will show how to produce a dash. It's the sign of a professionally produced publication if your dashes are right!

Journalists are usually advised to avoid dashes, which can indicate that a sentence is badly constructed and needs rewriting. Too many, says Robert Thomson, Editor of *The Times*, can be 'ugly and disruptive'.

The hyphen

Hyphens indicate when two or more words should be read together and taken as one. A check with the dictionary will quickly tell whether a word is hyphenated or not. They will enable the reader to distinguish between, for example, *recover* (from an illness) and re-cover (with material). Modern style soon overturns established practice, and words that were once hyphenated are now seen as one: payphone, feedback, multinationals, wildlife for instance. Few in PR would think of writing lay-out or hand-out!

Once a hyphenated word assumes everyday usage, it is not long before the hyphen disappears. The closed up form usually looks and 'feels' better; a hyphen in the middle looks a touch pedantic and ugly to some eyes.

Hyphens are happiest when used in numbers (twenty-one) or as fractions (two-thirds). And they are useful for separating similar vowel sounds (co-ordinate/co-operate for instance). The main purpose of a hyphen is to avoid ambiguity as in five-year-old children. But always ensure that if you do use a hyphen it has a job to do. A consultancy once asked me whether its client should say 'state-of-the-art facility', followed by 'easy-to-use products' and even a further hyphenation 'to-the-point solutions'. Avoid such abominations: sets of compounds in the same sentence should be re-written. Do it once and once only.

Whether or not to hyphenate is hardly a subject of breathtaking importance. Study current style and decide for yourself.

If you adopt a rule which leans towards avoiding the hyphen whenever possible, that would have my vote. But for certain compounds, such as adjective/noun combinations, then the hyphen must be retained for sense and to make the meaning clear.

The apostrophe

The main use of the apostrophe is to denote the possessive case, a subject discussed at length in the previous chapter (see pages 16–19). It is also used as a mark of omission: it can signify omitted characters as in *isn't*, *doesn't*, *I'm*; it distinguishes between *its* and *it's*; it indicates the plural of single letters, A's and B's.

WHEN YOU ARE QUOTING...

Quotation marks often give trouble. The writer who knows that a word or phrase – for example a cliché – is not the right one gets over the problem by enclosing it in quotes; at other times, there may not be a need for quote marks at all. Further, there is often uncertainty about whether to use single or double quotes, and on the placing of punctuation within them. Consider now some of the pitfalls.

Try not to use them for facetious, technical or slang words. Their proper, and most usual place, is for direct speech quotations: hence the term quotes or quote marks. (The phrase 'inverted commas' is old-fashioned and not the way most journalists would describe them.) They should be used for words or phrases not yet in everyday use – but only sparingly. Include them for titles of articles in magazines or chapters of books, but again avoid over-use. Do not use them for house names as there is no logic or merit in doing so.

Single or double?

Most publishers nowadays use the single quote mark for direct quotations, inserting the double mark for quotes within a quote. This does not, however, apply to newspapers whose editors will favour double quotes for quoted speech and the single mark for quotes within. Consequently, the double quote style should be used for press releases and news-type publications. For example, a chairman's address to an AGM might contain a quote from the marketing director; in which case the release would be typed with double quotes for the main statement and with single quotes for the marketing director's comments inside it.

Misuse occurs when there are several paragraphs of quoted speech. Quotes get closed at the end of each paragraph and opened again at the next paragraph. But the opening quote marks should go at the beginning of each paragraph and only appear at the *end* of the quote. If the text reverts to reported speech at any point the quote should be closed, and only opened again when direct speech restarts.

Punctuation marks go *inside* the quote marks (single or double as style dictates) when they refer to the words quoted, as in the managing director said: 'When will dividends be sent out?' but *outside* if they are part of a longer sentence carrying the quotation: the chairman commented on the company's 'excellent year'. If the complete sentence is a quotation the final point goes *inside*, as follows: 'The marketing director wants greater effort by the sales staff.'

Guidance on the relative placing of punctuation and quotation marks will be found in most style books, with *The Oxford Style Manual* giving detailed advice and a variety of examples. And take a look to see how newspapers deal with this point; they provide an excellent guide to the treatment of quotations, and they are at your elbow every day.

Unless the piece contains a number of direct quotes, general guidance gives that quotations marks be used sparingly. You can often avoid them altogether by indenting the paragraph (or paragraphs) and setting the type in a smaller size. Take special care when using direct quotes: make sure they are verbatim. The last thing you want is the person to whom the quote was attributed later denying the words were ever said. And it goes without saying that the writer must be sure the quoted words were not in any way defamatory.

Finally, when proof-reading, ensure that the quote marks are the right way round. They are easy to spot and you will surprise yourself when you see how many word processor operators get them wrong. They can be corrected easily by typing the key twice and then deleting the unwanted one. The pity is that so many typists cannot be bothered to do that. But they usually remember that a capital letter follows all punctuation marks except a comma, colon, semicolon and quote marks within a sentence. When and when not to use capitals will be the subject of the next chapter.

Quotes in news releases

Journalists love quotes. Aim for one or two in a release to follow the first or second paragraph of a news story. Quotes can be inserted in feature articles to good effect – perhaps a series of them throughout the piece. These would give it pace and energy.

Speeches can give significant and newsworthy quotes. In a release, you can usually include a significant quote in the intro. But don't open with a quote: it will be written out by the subeditor or placed lower down where impact will be lost.

Above all, ensure accuracy. Unless you have a tape-recording, check the source every time. Once a release has gone out and you spot a mistake, there's little you can do. Except pray.

AT A GLANCE

- The full stop is your best friend. Use it liberally.
- Don't put stops in sets of initials, they look old-fashioned.
- Only three stops to show something left out, one more as a terminator.
- If you have more than three commas in a sentence you usually have one too many.
- The colon introduces a quote. Don't use a comma instead.
- Avoid semicolons in news stories.
- Exclamation marks are hardly ever needed.
- Don't use a hyphen or even two together for a dash.
- Drop hyphens when possible. The closed-up form often looks and 'feels' better.
- Double quotes are for direct quotations, single for quoted passages inside.
- Journalists love quotes. Include at least one in main news stories.

4

Down with capitalism!

Only journalists and those committed to style principles appear to know or care where or when initial capital letters should be used. Whether to capitalise a word or not is one of the most hotly argued points in any office, particularly when preparing copy for publication. The only rule that most people can remember is: capital letter for the particular, small for the general. That is all right as far as it goes, but where is the dividing line? Is there too much capitalisation anyway? What, if any, are the guidelines?

CONSISTENCY IS THE ESSENCE

Dictionaries are helpful when you are uncertain whether to capitalise, and they should be consulted before reaching for the style guide or entering into a heated discussion. Uncertainty exists over words that have dual meanings. For example, a few years ago it was fashionable to give the word 'press', when referring to the media, a capital 'P'. Current style now demands a small 'p' which is logical since context will always make the meaning clear.

Similarly, new technology has bred new terms and expressions. The word 'internet' began with a capital. Nowadays most newspapers and trade papers (including *PRWeek*) give it a small 'i' simply to follow the trend for lower-case whenever possible. A cleaner and less cluttered look results. See also Chapter 18 on styles for IT.

Consistency is of paramount importance. Nothing looks worse than a publication displaying irregular capitalisation; this looks haphazard. If the name of a firm's department is used first with a capital letter and soon after with a small initial letter, the reader is immediately confused. On top of that it looks as though an amateur has been at work. If you are unsure whether to use a capital, it is better to retain consistency rather than risk style absurdities with some words of similar meaning given a capital and others not.

Always aim to restrict capitals to a minimum. Too many spoil the appearance of the page, look old-fashioned and fail to follow modern style. Imagine a line of type with the 'up and down' look; the eye is quickly distracted, making reading difficult. Such was the style of many of the books and magazines published up to the 1950s and even the 1960s. Compare today's style, and the difference is staggering: a continuous flow of small characters is easy on the eye and modern-looking.

Problem words, particularly when it comes to preparing copy for desktop publishing, are those which sometimes take an initial capital and other times do not. It is important for every organisation to have firm rules for the capitalisation of commonly used words. The fewer the capitals, the easier it is to be consistent and the better looking the printed page. In short, down with the capitalists!

WHY LOWER CASE, UPPER CASE?

Another way to describe capitals is to call them 'upper case' and small letters 'lower case'. These terms are now universally accepted and derive from the time when printers' compositors kept their small type characters in low cases, close to hand, while those characters in less frequent use were stored in a higher (upper) case. Thus, if a line of type is set with a mixture of small and capital letters it is said by the printer to be in 'upper and lower case' and marked u&lc, as opposed to text set completely in capitals, or very rarely in lower case only (a style for just a few words for display purposes for example).

WHEN TO USE CAPITALS

A capital is used for the first word in every sentence. It follows a full stop, question and interrogation marks, is used at the opening of a quote if it begins a sentence, and also for months and days of the week. Capitals should be used for proper nouns or names (words referring to a particular person or place), for formal titles, names of companies and organisations, political parties, titles of newspapers and magazines, titles of newspaper and periodical articles, books, films, trade names, names of ships and aircraft types. They are usually used for abbreviations, although some organisations adopt a lower-case style in order to reflect advertising or product branding.

Don't be influenced by the dictum that says a word must have an initial capital letter because there is only one of it. There's only one world – and it always has a lower case 'w'.

WHERE DIFFICULTIES OCCUR

Job titles

This is where a lot of difficulty arises. The advice here is to follow newspaper style which generally uses lower case where the title is descriptive as in managing director, marketing director or communications manager. Some will no doubt find it hard to accept a lower case style for job titles, but once used to it the small letters look right and objections diminish. It is seen often enough in the press.

To follow each and every rule exactly is not always possible. But there are some instances where apparent inconsistencies must be observed. For example, you can talk about Miss Jones, the head teacher but if the title is put before the name it is usually capitalised, as in Head Teacher Miss Jones.

When referring back after first mention, it is usual practice to revert to lower case, as in Oriel College, your college. When writing about government ministers and officials, it is always best to see how they are styled in the broadsheet press. If you follow their style, you can hardly go wrong. Check with *Debrett's* or *Who's Who* when naming royalty and distinguished people.

For titles that are both formal and descriptive, such as President, use capitals for a full reference, as in John Smith, President, of XYZ Association. Subsequent mentions could just be John Smith, the president. The same applies to royalty: Prince Charles becomes 'the prince' and the Princess Royal 'the princess' in subsequent references. A following reference to Her Majesty the Queen should be written as either Her Majesty or the Queen. Check with *Debrett* and *Who's Who* when naming members of the Royal Family, the peerage and principal personages.

Capitals for a company?

Stockbrokers, thankfully, no longer refer to their partnerships as 'the Firm'. Nevertheless, many executives insist upon using a capital initial letter for 'company' in the mistaken belief that the capital somehow bestows importance. The only time for a capital is when the name of the firm or company is spelt out in full.

The Government

When you refer to the Government keep the capital to make it clear that you are referring to the Government of the country. However, Acts of Parliament only carry upper case when their full titles are used; the same applies to bills and white papers. Use lower case for the ministry and minister, but capitals when putting the title in full. Note that if office holders are referred to only by their office, the titles prime minister, chancellor of the exchequer, foreign secretary and so on are in lower case in some national newspapers. Most will use capitals when the complete name and formal title are given. You will never be criticised if you always put such titles in capitals. But you will soon be in trouble with the purists if you don't.

Use upper and lower case for the House of Commons, House of Lords, Department of Trade and Industry; but the department or

DTI in subsequent references. Put left/right (wing), the speaker, the opposition, the cabinet.

When referring to political parties, the name of the party should be in upper case as in 'the Labour Party', while retaining the capital for general references when the word 'party' is not used. However, when used as a normal adjective, write lower case as in conservative outlook, socialist objectives. Members of Parliament are capitalised to MPs, not MP's, and certainly not MsP.

The seasons

Some writers feel that somehow the seasons are so important that they must be capitalised. This is nonsense and is not supported by style guides. But note that religious festivals such as Easter take capitals. So does Christmas, but new year or new year's day need not.

Geographical regions

Recognisable regions such as Northern Ireland carry capitals, but are lower case if referring to northern England for example. Capitals are well established for the North-East, the North and the West Country, but here again it would scarcely cause offence if these regions lost their capital letters.

Derivatives

Adjectives derived from proper names carry capitals, for example Christian, Catholic. But note that you wear wellingtons (hence *wellies*) and a jersey; and that we have amperes and volts. Use lower case when connection with the proper name is remote, as in arabic (letters), french (chalk, polish, windows), italic (script), roman (numerals). Use lower case for gargantuan and herculean, but with less familiar words use a capital, as in draconian.

Events and periods

Names of events and periods of time should be capitalised: the First World War, Second World War (or World War I or II), but for general references use the 1914–18 war or the last war.

Trade names

All registered trade names must carry a capital letter. A frequent error is to give lower case 's' to Sellotape, an 'h' for Hoover, a 'k' for Kodak. Note capitals for Biro, Filofax, Marmite, Pyrex, Stilton, Vaseline, Xerox. To find out whether a word is, in fact, a trade name and needs a capital, check with the *Kompass Register of Industrial Trade Names*, available in public reference libraries, or with the Register of Trade Names held at the Patent Office in London, Newport and Manchester.

Committees

Names of committees, particularly those of an official nature, should be in capitals. Style will vary from one organisation to another, but so long as the writer is consistent and follows house style, there can be little argument.

Headings in publications

As a rule, use upper *and* lower case letters for headings. A line in full caps is not so easy to read as one in lower case. All-cap headings are seldom seen in newspapers these days, and less frequently in magazines and newsletters. Feel free, however, to use underlined and capitalised headings in news releases – they stand out much better.

THE TREND IS TO KNOCK IT DOWN

The above examples are included to show the narrow divide between choice of capital or small letter. Style is constantly changing and words that were once always capitalised will soon be lower-cased. Even if you don't notice the 'knock it down' trend, and still want to use capitals when no one else does, use lower case until to do so would look stupid and out of place. The general rule is to capitalise titles of organisations, not those of people.

Do not use capitals for words one after the other in a line. This is often done in the belief that a fully capitalised line will have added emphasis and the reader will take more notice of it. While a few capitalised words might stand out, too many or a line-full will be self-defeating: they will offend the eye and not be read.

AT A GLANCE

- Check dictionaries, style guides if doubtful whether to capitalise.
- Go for lower case when you can. Too many capitals are hard on the eye.
- Follow the 'knock it down' rule: it helps the reader and looks modern.
- Use capitals for proper nouns, names of companies and formal titles.
- Maintain consistency throughout.
- Don't use line after line of caps in a vain attempt at emphasis.
- Use lower case for headings where you can. Capitals are harder to read.
- Consult *Debrett's* or *Who's Who* when naming royalty and other personages.

5

Clichés, jargon and other worn words

Originality of expression is the keynote to good writing style. It is the stale, worn-out phase – the cliché – that can spoil otherwise well-written and crisp copy. Likewise, jargon words which are meaningless and unintelligible fail to communicate. Avoiding clichés and jargon is not always easy. In fact there are occasions when they can be used to good effect, so long as the reader knows they are deliberate. At other times they present the only way of getting over a specific point or idea.

The word cliché (French for a duplicate printing plate, stereotype or electrotype), means a hackneyed, overworked phrase or a saying that has lost vigour and originality. In fact the word 'stereotype' is itself a cliché as it is now taken to mean a role model (also a cliché). The difficulty for the writer is to identify such expressions and then to find others to take their places which won't turn out to be yet more clichés. Effort to express new ideas in a different way will be well rewarded. The writer will be refreshed, as will the reader.

It is important to cultivate sensitivity to the hackneyed phrase; if you can see that you have just written a cliché, this is a good sign for you can now replace it with a fresh thought. If a cliché is deliberate, or cannot be avoided, then one solution is to let the reader know you are aware of it: say so by putting the word or phrase in quotes.

Catchphrases and metaphors, many of which have become firmly embedded in the English language, soon become stale if overused. Yet there can still be room for the idiomatic expression to liven up otherwise dull text – if used sparingly.

RECOGNISING CLICHÉS

To help you recognise tired phrases, here are a few in current use: put on the back burner, bottom line, low/high profile, having said that, passed its sell-by date; stock similes like *as hard as nails*; pompous phrases including wind of change, or a sea-change development should all get *the blue pencil* treatment. Some sayings demand instant excision: address a problem, conventional wisdom, take on board, a wide range of issues, put on hold, a whole new ball game, lifestyle, in this day and age, when it comes to the crunch, quantum leap, up front money. These examples – they slip off the tongue *as easy as wink* – are only just *the tip of the iceberg*.

We have had Cool Britannia, a wake-up call, all over bar the shouting, level playing field, the great and the good, back to the drawing board, mind management, learning curve, ballpark figure, up to our ears. More recently there have been these horrors repeated with boring monotony: to be honest, behaviour pattern, with all due/great respect, I hear what you are saying/where you are coming from, let's touch base, winning hearts and minds, WMD, 'cool', quality time – the list is unending.

One of the most common expressions is 'at this point in time'; this is not only a tired phrase, but tedious when a perfectly good word for the same thing is *now*. Here, it should be noted that 'moment in time' is not so much a cliché as tautology since moment already means *point in time*. Other stock phrases to come from tongue or pen with ease are at the end of the day, no Brownie points, career girl, between a rock and a hard place, now for the good/bad news, not to mention some that have *stood the test of time* and make us as sick as a parrot. It's as simple as that, yer know what I mean? Ah right! Guard against what Sir Ernest Gowers in his *The Complete Plain Words* calls the 'Siamese twins' or part and parcel, to all intents and purposes, or swing of the pendulum.

But Gowers points out that writers would be 'needlessly handi-capped' if they were never allowed to use such phrases as strictly speaking, rears its ugly head or even essentially – the new basi-cally. Context coupled with judgement will indicate whether it is necessary to rewrite the sentence. But what is new is not neces-sarily better; the old saying that 'there's many a good tune played on an old fiddle' still holds true today. Be on constant guard against writing clichés: when you think you are radiantly happy by leaps and bounds or want to rule the roost, check with Eric Partridge's *A Dictionary of Clichés* or with Julia Cresswell's Penguin volume of the same title, for you will find these overused phrases listed among hundreds of other worn and tired expressions.

Business clichés are used extensively: some, like please find enclosed, are worn and faded and, thankfully disappearing. In public relations, a client presentation, new business pitch, account win, corporate hospitality, target audience, focus group, spin doctor, methodology (why not just method?), on/off message, sound bite, and overkill are stock expressions and hard to avoid. The dividing line between commonly used phrases and jargon is a fine one: both kinds are so frequently used that it is impossible to do without them.

Once you have heard a saying that strikes you as being clever, that's the danger signal: forget it. If you're tempted to use a slogan or catchphrase you've heard before, like the full Monty, to lay down the law, banging your head against a brick wall, stick with it, to ring a bell, like oil and water, I'm not getting any younger, think again. Start with a dictionary of synonyms, or better still the *Oxford Thesaurus*. Hit the delete key and find alternatives for those grind-ingly boring words issue and key.

The Plain English Campaign's website (www.plainenglish.co.uk) directs viewers to an A to Z guide to alternative words and free information CD. There's also an emailed weekly newsletter and monthly magazine. As a last check go to www.clichesite.com where you'll find hundreds of stale words. There's a cliché of the day, followed by 30 or more everyday sayings. But all this doesn't mean you must never use a cliché. Sometimes Hobson's choice can be useful.

JARGON: HELP OR HINDRANCE?

The word jargon was used in the late fourteenth century to mean 'the twittering of the birds' or as the latest edition of *Fowler's Modern English Usage* puts it: 'a term of contempt for something (including a foreign language) that the reader does not understand... any mode of speech abounding in unfamiliar terms... eg the specialised vocabulary or bureaucrats, scientists, or sociologists'.

Jargon is jargon when words are so technical or obscure that they defy comprehension. They contribute nothing to sense or meaning and might just as well not be written at all. Public relations and advertising jargon soon slide into the vernacular, as opposed to formal or literary English, and is used without hesitation just because everyone else speaks or writes it. That is all very well, but if it fails to communicate to those outside 'media village-speak', then there is a case for reducing it as much as possible.

There is little to choose between public relations jargon (networking, publics, press kit/pack, coverage, perception) and marketing idiom (positioning, conceptual, target, focus, strategic planning). It does not take long for jargon like this to drift into cliché and for readers quickly to tire of it: upmarket, downsizing, downshifting, niche marketing, layered management, interface/interact, state-of-the-art are all firmly in the language of communications. Phrases and words like in-depth, on-going, user-friendly, cutting edge, parameters, definitive and conceptual should be used sparingly or preferably avoided altogether.

Jargon is often embedded in public relations terminology. Take this example from a trade directory entry: 'Well researched communication messages, disseminated through appropriate influence channels to target professional audiences are the hallmark of an approach which...' Quite what the writer expected the reader to glean from that defies imagination.

A recent example of jargon getting out of hand is the use of upskilling to mean improving performance through training. Although understandable, this is jargon that is unlikely to last or ever find a place in a dictionary along with can-do, core business, critical mass and eye contact. But some jargon words can provide an element of fun and are likely to last longer, for example: yuppie, dinkies (double income, no kids), woolfie (well-off older person), wrinklie, along with bimbos, foodies and toyboys, all of which have earned a place in the English language. Soon we are to have mouse potatoes (computer addicts), netizens and cybernauts (regular internet surfers) as firm entries in the *OED*.

Here are some snappy acronyms from the advertising world: *Panses* (politically active, not seeking employment), *Sinbads* (single income, no boyfriend, absolutely desperate), *Yappies* (young affluent parents), *Sitcoms* (single income, two children and oppressive mortgage). We also hear about *Nipples* (New Irish professionals living in London), and *Puppies* (Punjabi upwardly mobile professionals). Few are, however, likely to attain *OED* status.

Apart from the specialised jargon of the legal fraternity, it is in the area of information technology where technical words are used freely in the belief that they will always be understood. For example, news releases on computer technology are notorious for being packed tight with jargon. That is acceptable for journalists from computer publications who know and understand the technical terms used, but those writing for the popular press or broadcasting will have difficulty in putting over the information and giving clear and unambiguous explanations.

Two contrasting examples of typical jargon illustrate the point: 'the stylistic expressiveness of vector based brush strokes with the speed and resolution independence of an advanced drawing application', and 'automatically generated site map using HotSauce MCF (Meta Content Format Files)'. The first assumes the reader knows exactly what is meant, but leaves room for mistake and misinterpretation, while the second makes an attempt at explanation within the body of the text, while also giving full details of the technical terms used as a footnote. If there is no alternative to a jargon word or phrase, then explain the terms in straightforward language, perhaps inserting a word or two of explanation in brackets.

Foreign words are also jargon to most readers; steer clear of them unless context demands their inclusion. The occasional foreign expression gives a lift to articles and speeches, but they should not, repeat not, go in releases. Examples are *Schadenfreude* (malicious enjoyment of other people's misfortunes), from the German *schade* (harm) and *freude* (delight), and *Zeitgeist* (spirit of the time). More familiar, perhaps, are *bête noire* (disliked person or thing) and *de rigueur* (required by custom). Words and phrases like these soon find their way into volumes of clichés. Use sparingly.

Jargon baffles the reader and specialist writers should never use it for audiences outside their own field. Unless the audience is steeped in the jargon of public relations, little sense can be made of ROI (return on investment) or CSR (corporate social responsibility). Such abbreviations must be explained at first reference, or perhaps later if there's a big gap in-between uses.

CATCHPHRASES QUICKLY BECOME STALE...

Like clichés, catchphrases quickly lose originality: the source of catchphrases is mostly the entertainment industry (films, radio and TV shows in particular), but some also come from advertising and public relations campaigns such as It's good to talk (BT), a diamond is forever (De Beers Consolidated Mines), one of the longest-running advertising campaigns this century, ... refreshes the parts that other ... cannot reach from the Heineken beer slogan described as 'PR wizardry to sell its message', We deliver you more (ASDA home delivery service), A to B it, we RAC to it (Royal Automobile Club).

These have only a limited life, but others like *virtual reality* are more likely to find a permanent place in the language. Popular catchphrases such as mindset, nice little earner, or have a nice day, and catchwords like loadsamoney and other permutations of loadsa should be avoided since any originality has long since vanished.

It is advisable, when drafting press releases and articles in particular, to watch out for the catchphrase that might be used unwittingly and lead to editorial deletion. If catchphrases are overdone, predictability takes over and the writer is not able to take the reader by surprise and attract attention.

... SO CAN METAPHORS AND SIMILES

A metaphor is a figure of speech, a way of describing an object or action imaginatively and without being directly related to it (a *glaring* error), enabling the writer to convey thoughts briefly and without having to resort to lengthy explanation. But they can easily be overworked. As Sir Ernest Gowers points out, 'sometimes they are so absurdly overtaxed that they become a laughing stock and die of ridicule'.

Avoid mixed or inappropriate metaphors, where incongruous and incompatible terms are used for the same object: We have the key to the 21st Century as quoted in the *Oxford Dictionary of English Grammar*. Gowers gives further explanation and examples.

A simile, also a figure of speech, compares one thing with another of a different kind and is usually identified by insertion of *as* or *like* (cold as charity, deaf as a post, blush like a schoolgirl, look like grim death). As with metaphors, guard against overuse.

MAKE ROOM FOR THE IDIOM

Readers soon become bored by dull, continuous text; there is always room for idiomatic expressions. Attempting to find a suitable idiomatic expression to fit the flow of thought is not easy and dictionaries are not much help. Useful collections will be found in the *Oxford Dictionary of English Idioms*, which contains 7,000 idioms and their variant forms plus examples in modern writing. Or there is the *Wordsworth Dictionary of Idioms*, which also has several thousand examples with meanings cross-referenced by head words and first words, in three distinct categories – formal, informal and slang. Lastly there is *Chambers Idioms*, which contains several thousand entries.

In the region of (formal), hit the headlines (informal) and pack it in (slang), offer a few examples. Often defying grammatical and logical rules, idioms can give colour and vitality to a piece of writing without risking faded and overused phrases. The English language is particularly rich in idiom, but use it sparingly – slang expressions are fine in speech but should be avoided in writing.

BEWARE OF SLANG

Slang can, however, offend. Most of it comes from cant, the jargon of a trade or business. If you say something is awesome when you mean very good or excellent, that is slang at its worst if used by a professional communicator. Snail mail is the emailer's slang for mail by post, but usage has put it in everyday vocabulary.

Nevertheless, there is no place for ginormous, coach potato, fab, must-have (a must-have bag) in any formal sense.

Much modern-day slang owes its popularity to the advertising copywriter. Night is spelt nite, you is U, clean becomes kleen, flow sides to flo. Slang has contributed to confusion about spelling and yet, despite the protestations of purists, much of it is finding its way into the language. Computer technology, multimedia, interactive television, even healthcare have all provided their own slang expressions, much of them pure jargon, intelligible only to those working in the field. Slang is for the voice, not for the pen. If you must use it, then keep it only for informal writing – the sales leaflet, correspondence or staff memos; but never for the release, the annual report or the corporate brochure.

Slangy words like punter, donned, luvvies are hated by journalists. But text messaging and attendant youth culture have been responsible for much of today's slang. We hear in speech gonna for going to, lippie for lipstick, terms that are simply soap opera solecisms.

Such abbreviations as gwp (gift with purchase item), lmk (let me know), nib (new in box) have no place in print simply because they do not communicate what is meant. On the other hand, speech writers might find inspiration in rhyming slang: mince pies (eyes), dog and bone (phone), dicky dirt (shirt), plates of meat (feet), if only to get a laugh. Hundreds of examples will be found in John Ayto's *Oxford Dictionary of Rhyming Slang* and in *The Oxford Dictionary of Modern Slang* by John Utah and John Simpson.

AT A GLANCE

- Cultivate sensitivity to clichés and jargon.
- Replace worn words and phrases with synonyms from thesauruses and dictionaries.
- Beware of jargon, the language of the specialist. It might not be understood.
- Use simple words instead if you can; if not, explain.
- Put short explanation afterwards in brackets.
- Catchphrases soon become stale.
- There's always room for idiom.
- Avoid slang in formal documents and print.
- Speechwriters can get a laugh from rhyming slang.

6

Is it easy to read?

The words are as you want them, you have got rid of clichés and jargon, the punctuation is right – in fact the style so far is just about spot on. But there is more to it than that. No matter how much effort has been put into the text, it will be wasted if it is hard to read. Readability is a complex subject and is the province of the designer and typographer. There are, nevertheless, some basic principles to be considered now that desktop publishing (DTP) is so widely used. And when the copy goes off to the printers for a publication or document you want to be sure that when the proof comes back it will be right both textually and visually.

Even if the work is going to an outside consultancy before printing, the copy must be prepared in such a way that the presentation style will be followed at the final stages of typographical design. For internal documents, too, care must be taken to see that the visual style is going to help the reader – in short, be easy on the eye. For if it isn't then there is an instant barrier to communication.

This section covers important factors in readability and concentrates on the overall appearance, whether you have a straightforward word-processed document or a print job from DTP origination. The pros and cons of one design against another will not be considered here, nor will guidance be offered on how print-work should be designed, as these are subjective and beyond the scope of this book.

EDIT WITH THE READER IN MIND

Always consider the appearance of the page when editing. Avoid the 'grey' look which results when slabs of typematter are unrelieved by paragraph breaks or subsidiary headings and illustrations. Depending on the subject matter, make headings as lively as possible so that they not only drive the text forwards but make the page look attractive.

One sure way of achieving interest is to start the text with a drop initial letter, usually larger and bolder than the rest of the copy. This can increase readership by as much as 10 per cent. Some designers specify fancy and seldom-used typefaces for the drop initial letter, but these are usually unnecessary – the text type will normally suffice unless it is an 'arty-crafty' publication. If the opening paragraph can be kept to a dozen or so words then interest is sharpened and the reader is on the writer's side from the start.

AIM FOR SHORT SENTENCES

Short sentences aid readability; anything up to 30 words is easy to follow and assimilate. There are obviously occasions when this can and should be exceeded, particularly for technical and scientific subjects; but even here, aim for brevity unless detailed explanation is required.

Keep your paragraphs short if you are writing for the popular and tabloid press. Five-word lines – sometimes even shorter – will be seen in *The Mirror* and *The Sun*, but for general publication work – leaflets, brochures and the like – the aim should be for perhaps three or four sentences in each paragraph. Even the occasional one-line sentence of a few words would not be out of place in a sales leaflet.

GUIDELINES ON PARAGRAPHING

One of the main factors affecting readability is the length of paragraphs and where they are placed in the text. Short paragraphs (pars or paras to journalists) attract and hold the reader's attention, while excessively long ones tend to be unreadable and fail to communicate. Just look at a page of typescript that is unrelieved by paragraph breaks: it immediately seems to be indigestible and stuffy. Compare that with a page broken up by lively headings which straightaway appears more interesting and inviting.

Paragraphs allow the writer to change tack or subject and, equally important, give the eye a rest. When the text moves from one point to another that is the time for a par break. However, much will depend on the style of the publication or document and on the column width. For news-style print jobs, using double or multi-column format, paragraph breaks are usually needed after every second or third sentence – say about every 50 to 70 words. At make-up stage, this will allow subheadings to be inserted and columns to be equalised or space filled with displayed quotes. For single-column reports, books, manuals, leaflets and brochures, it is usually better to have longer paragraphs with perhaps four or five sentences. There should be at least two par breaks per column, otherwise you are back to that grey look again.

Short paragraphs are best for news releases; if each has a significant fact, then the release will stand a much better chance of being used than a long, stodgy one. The same applies to speeches which may be issued along with the release. An occasional single-sentence paragraph can have an electrifying effect on the text, especially if it is a technical or heavy-going subject. But, on the other hand, too many jerky, staccato paragraphs can distract and confuse the reader. As with everything else, it is a case of moderation.

Where to place the par break? This requires some skill: it is no use hitting the return key and hoping for the best. A paragraph is a unit of thought, not of length, says Fowler. But in news-style publications and certainly in news releases, it is the other way round: the paragraph is essentially a unit of length with maybe six or seven par breaks per page of copy, possibly more in some cases.

The best place for a break is where the text can be neatly divided without upsetting the word flow, say three or four per page of typescript, with one linked to the other in a seamless way. If a natural link is not there, then use an appropriate conjunction like *but, moreover, however*; otherwise recast the sentence at the break and refer back. But you will usually be able to find suitable points to break the text without editing. Aim for a mix of short and slightly longer sentences to produce a change of pace and give colour to the copy. Too many short ones can irritate the reader, but too many long ones can bore and tire the eye.

Some final points in relation to computer typesetting: try to leave at least three words on the last line of a paragraph; avoid starting a new paragraph on the last line of a page. Indents for typescript and typesetting should not be more than three or four characters' width; if they go in too far the par break will be over-emphasised, although some designers may prefer to do this deliberately for special effect. Intros and first paragraphs after headings usually go full out (to the full column width) with subsequent par breaks indented. Don't leave a 'widow' with a few characters or words dangling at the top of a page: *-ed* or *-der* hanging overhead look awful. Try to fill the line out by adding words, or cutting and taking the overhang back.

LINE WIDTH AND TYPE SIZE

As for column width, try not to have more than 45 characters per line, including spaces and punctuation in double-column format; anything above that tends to give a 'stringy' look. If the copy is set across the page, aim for between 70 and 80 characters per line. But remember that lines with only a few characters, those that run round a photograph or display heading for example, will be awkward to read and look messy.

Be careful when considering the relationship between line length and type size. Much will depend on your design objectives and the purpose of your printwork. As a general guide for ease of reading, type should not be much smaller than 10pt, or perhaps 9pt at a pinch if well line-spaced. A line of 45 characters of 10pt Times, for example, gives a very readable 70mm column width.

8 Point
DESIGN AS APPLIED TO PRINTED MATTER IS THE MEANING
ful arrangement of the elements in a page or other visual area. The
arrangement serves as an invisible scaffolding or framework on which
to display meanings in print and picture. The contribution of the

9 Point
DESIGN AS APPLIED TO PRINTED MATTER IS THE
meaningful arrangement of the elements in a page or other
visual area. The arrangement serves as an invisible scaffolding
or framework on which to display meanings in print and pic

10 Point
DESIGN AS APPLIED TO PRINTED MATTER IS THE
meaningful arrangement of the elements in a page or
other visual area. The arrangement serves as an invis
ible scaffolding or framework on which to display

11 Point
DESIGN AS APPLIED TO PRINTED MATTER IS
the meaningful arrangement of the elements in
a page or other visual area. The arrangement
serves as an invisible scaffolding or framework on

12 Point
DESIGN AS APPLIED TO PRINTED MATT
er is the meaningful arrangement of the
elements in a page or other visual area. The
arrangement serves as an invisible scaffolding

14 Point
DESIGN AS APPLIED TO PRINTED
matter is the meaningful arrangement
of the elements in a page or other

16 Point
DESIGN AS APPLIED TO PRINT
ed matter is the meaningful arr
angement of the elements in a pa

18 Point
DESIGN AS APPLIED TO PRI

Figure 6.1 *Comparison between a serif type (Baskerville) and non-serif (Gill Sans) in medium and bold styles, 8pt to 32pt sizes*

20 Point

DESIGN AS APPLIED TO printed matter is the mean ingful arrangement of the

22 Point

DESIGN AS APPLIED T o printed matter is the meaningful arrangement

24 Point

DESIGN AS APPLIED to printed matter is the meaningful arrangeme

28 Point

DESIGN AS APPLI ed to printed matt er is the meaningfu

32 Point

DESIGN AS APP

Figure 6.1 *continued*

8 Point

DESIGN AS APPLIED TO PRINTED MATTER IS THE MEANING
ful arrangement of the elements in a page or other visual area. The
arrangement serves as an invisible scaffolding or framework on
which to display meanings in print and picture. The contribution

9 Point

DESIGN AS APPLIED TO PRINTED MATTER IS THE
meaningful arrangement of the elements in a page or other
visual area. The arrangement serves as an invisible scaf
folding or framework on which to display meanings in print

10 Point

DESIGN AS APPLIED TO PRINTED MATTER IS
the meaningful arrangement of the elements in a page
or other visual area. The arrangement serves as an
invisible scaffolding or framework on which to display

11 Point

DESIGN AS APPLIED TO PRINTED MATTER
is the meaningful arrangement of the elements
in a page or other visual area. The arrangement
serves as an invisible scaffolding or framework on

12 Point

DESIGN AS APPLIED TO PRINTED MAT
ter is the meaningful arrangement of the
elements in a page or other visual area. The
arrangement serves as an invisible scaffolding

14 Point

DESIGN AS APPLIED TO PRINTED
matter is the meaningful arrangement
of the elements in a page or other vis

16 Point

DESIGN AS APPLIED TO PRIN
ted matter is the meaningful arr
angement of the elements in a

18 Point

DESIGN AS APPLIED TO P

Figure 6.1 *continued*

20 Point

DESIGN AS APPLIED TO PRI
nted matter is the meaningful
arrangement of the element in

22 Point

DESIGN AS APPLIED TO P
rinted matter is the meanin
gful arrangement of the ele

24 Point

DESIGN AS APPLIED T
o printed matter is the
meaningful arrangement o

28 Point

DESIGN AS APPLIED
to printed matter is
the meaningful arrang

32 Point

DESIGN AS APPLI

Figure 6.1   *continued*

The eyes have it

Sadly, we do not all have the eyesight of youth, and for some, reading can be hard work. It is therefore crucial that the printed word can be read easily by the elderly as well by the young. David Coates of the company 'to the point', the CIPR's design consultants, says that the easiest print to read has good contrast against the background, and ideally that type should not be smaller than 11pt. 'An unfussy, plain typeface is preferable to an ornate one and should be printed black on a matt, off-white paper since shiny stock causes reflections and making reading difficult. And never allow line after line of capitals: they are almost unreadable.'

It is obvious that the bigger the type, the better the readability. But there are limits: if it is too big, say much above 12pt as recommended by the DTI in its leaflet *Read me*, the print begins to look like a child's big-print word book. The Royal Institute for the Blind advises that a minimum of 12pt should be used 'at all times'.

Doyen print journalist Pincus Jaspert says he is appalled by 'computer obsessed typographic dilettantes' who print green on blue or the reverse, even harder to read. 'A single blotch of colour designed to catch the eye instead confuses and irritates the reader.'

There is no single, clear-cut answer to what constitutes good legibility. So much depends on typeface, the size chosen, the column or page width and line spacing. It is the job of the designer to specify what is most appropriate for a given audience and print medium: magazine, book, leaflet or poster. It is the designer who is skilled in typographic principles and knows what the printer can do who knows best.

CROSSHEADS AND SUBHEADS

If you want to divide off copy into sections, if you are short of a line or two at the bottom of a page, or if there is a mass of grey text then you'll need the humble crosshead – probably several. For an A4 page in two columns, four or five are usually enough. But all depends on the style and layout.

Solid lumps of type will put the reader off. If for some reason you cannot break up the text with par breaks and/or illustrations, insert subheadings (also called crossheadings). These are of inferior weight to the main heading or title and give the eye a break from line after line of characters. They also add interest to the piece by flagging up new points the writer wishes to bring out.

Subheadings should be either in a larger size and/or perhaps in bold so as to stand out from the rest of the text. Make sure there are not too many on a page. If they are scattered about willy-nilly they look untidy, and might even look as if they are just there to fill space (which they might well be!). When you insert headings, balance them so as to avoid 'rivering' with one adjacent to another. In news-style publications, one-word subheadings look best, preferably of not more than seven or eight characters.

The best time to insert subheadings is at first proof stage; if they go in too early you will not know where they will fall when the type has been set and the layout completed. If the job carries a second colour, you can use it for crossheads at no extra cost.

Avoid having a subhead above the last line of a column: put it in higher up or cut it out. Headlines can also go in at proof stage. It is useful to have a working heading when the copy is written to help with identification later on.

LINE AND LETTER SPACING

Space between lines is called 'leading' (pronounced *ledding*) from the time when a strip of metal – usually a casting in lead – was inserted between each line of hand-composed type, or automatically added to the line in machine typesetting. Leading is said to increase readability by 12 per cent as it introduces what the designer calls 'air' into the solid text, making it easier on the eye.

But avoid too much space between lines: that can be as bad as not enough, for the text will be harder, not easier, to read. And the wider the text is set, the more leading is needed for good readability. Where there is no leading at all, the text is said to be 'set solid'. The spacing is specified in point sizes (for example, 1pt or 2pt, with 72 points to the inch). Make sure that this line-by-line spacing is consistent; this is particularly important when setting text for reproduction.

Software packages enable the computer operator to select line spacing leading in point sizes and to perform many other typographical settings like line justification and widths, variable type sizes and a wide selection of typefaces, as well as extended and condensed styles. Underlining is another option, but care is needed in order to avoid it 'colliding' with the line underneath.

Pay close attention to the spacing between characters, or what the printer would call letterspacing. This is another software option and some computers and word processors will insert letterspacing automatically in order to fill out the line, particularly when copy is set justified with both edges aligned. Letterspacing can be adjusted for readability and aesthetics or to fill a certain area, and is most often used for lines of capitals for display. Special typographic effects can be obtained by removing or adding space between characters to produce what is known as 'kerning'.

Figure 6.2   *Good, clean design for a Royal Mail leaflet. It communicates well; note the lower case, sans serif type throughout*

WHERE TO BREAK

End-of-line word division often causes trouble, and words can get misread if they are broken at the wrong place. Once the prerogative of the compositor, word breaks are now mostly computer controlled but they can still go wrong: at worst a single character gets turned over; at best a typographical eyesore. When the copy is keyed in, the operator tells the computer to hyphenate and take over a set number of characters for a given line width. Some software options allow the operator to override automatic hyphenation and insert word breaks manually.

Computers sometimes get it right but more often do not. And then the word processor operator shuts off the automatic mode and goes to hyphensearch, relying on fading memories of how to break words at the right place. Avoid word breaks if possible: one way is to set copy ranged left and ragged right; this will mean fewer word breaks than if the type matter is justified with both margins aligned and with the ends of the lines ranged with one another.

Unless you have lines ending with longish words (10 or more characters) there is seldom any need for a break when using ragged right setting. At proof stage avoid hyphenated line endings by simply taking a word over to the next line. Avoid uneven word spacing, when the computer struggles to complete a line and thus breaks where it can.

Where word breaks are unavoidable, etymology and pronunciation are the main determinants. Divide words at obvious syllable breaks, as in *atmo-sphere* or *trans-port*, or where two consonants come together like *forget-ting*, *minis-ter* and *estab-lish*. If there is one consonant at the break point, that character is normally taken over as with *Euro-pean*, *popu-lar*.

Do not divide two consonants forming one sound (*calm-est*, *fea-ther*). The endings *-ism*, *-ist*, and *-istic* are usually taken over and so are *-ing* present participles like *target-ing*. (But note *puz-zling*, *trick-ling*.) Do not carry over *-ted* or *-ded*. Be careful to reject divisions that could confuse or change the meaning: le-gends not leg-ends, re-adjust not read-just. A divided word should never end a page, especially a right hand one. A word should not be broken at the end of a paragraph to leave the last line with a hyphen and a few characters. Many more examples will be found in *The*

Oxford Style Manual and in the Collins Gem Dictionary of Spelling and Word Division.

CHOICE OF TYPEFACE

Choosing the appropriate typeface is quite complex as much depends on the subject matter and style of the work. However, here are some ground rules worth considering: one is that serif types (those where the letter strokes are finished off like Times or Bodoni) are easier to read line after line than sans serif typefaces like Gill and Helvetica.

Set type so that it reads with the minimum of effort and eyestrain; each job presents different problems depending on the type style being used. The professional designer or typographer will gauge the most appropriate typeface for any given job by taking into account the target audience and subjects covered.

PRINTING CONSIDERATIONS

Without going into the broad – and subjective – subject of design, it is important to remember that ideas that might look great on a visual sometimes fail to work when they get into print. For instance, it is next to useless reversing large amounts of text out of a solid colour (say white out of black) or out of a photograph as this guarantees non-readability. A few lines of display type set fairly large can be read without difficulty, but when it comes to lines of text set solid in 10pt or smaller, there will be an immediate switch-off.

Similarly, don't try to print a tinted typeface over a tinted page of equal strength. And don't try to print yellow type on white paper, or any pastel shades on white for that matter. Tinted papers often give readability problems and it is generally better to stick to black on white, using colour either as solids or as tints for headings and display panels.

INCLUDE ILLUSTRATIONS IF POSSIBLE

If the job if text-intensive and in danger of looking 'stodgy' it is advisable to include illustrations – either line drawings, photographs or perhaps explanatory panels which can be overprinted in colour. All illustrations should of course be captioned unless they are simply for decoration. The reader will often ignore the text and only look at the photograph or drawing. Captions are read twice as much as the text and turn glancers and page-flippers into readers. Annual reports are a typical example of this.

Break up the monotony of long blocks of copy by using the ornaments and symbols provided by most software packages. If there is a series of facts it is better to number them rather than trying to interconnect them. Always try to think of ways to attract the reader's eye, in ways appropriate to the content.

JUSTIFIED OR RAGGED RIGHT?

Both styles have their advantages, and all designers have their own ideas on whether the one is more readable than the other. It depends largely on the style of publication: if it is a 'newsy' one then the justified style would probably be better for that is the way most newspapers set their type. On the other hand, brochures and leaflets usually look more attractive and are easier for the reader to follow when set ragged right. But there are no firm rules and it is up to the designer to produce an acceptable style directed at the target audience and within the house style pattern of the publishing organisation.

PUTTING ON THE STRESS

Bold type helps the reader to identify subject changes and gives the printed page visual interest. It provides focal points among roman and non-bold typefaces. But again it is a case of everything in moderation: too much bold type destroys the impact of a few carefully positioned subheadings. As a general rule do not use bold type in any great quantity, except perhaps for a display panel. Nearly all typefaces will have fonts in boldface, and most computers and word processors will have the facility to change from 'plain' type to bold or italics, and to some other type styles as well.

Figure 6.3 *WPP Group wins the Platinum Award from League of American Communications Professionals for its 2003 annual report and accounts*

Individual words in a run of text should not be set in bold just for stress, for that is the job of italics. But if too many words are italicised, or even whole sentences or complete paragraphs, this method of providing emphasis ceases to work. Fowler is scornful of overuse: 'Printing a passage in italics, like underlining one in a letter, is a primitive way of soliciting attention', says the second edition.

Bold to the rescue

Likewise, boldface is easy to produce on your word processor or PC from any font. Use it to give weight to a quote or announcement. Put titles of seminars or conferences in roman (or plain) unless it's a promotional leaflet. Use bold for headings, captions and draw-down quotes. But over-bolding fails to add force. Its best use is for limited runs of text especially if reversed out of a strong colour. It is easiest to read when white out of black, worst when white out of a pale tint.

Main uses for italics

Long, italicised paragraphs are out of place and look dated. In a release, troubles start: subeditors will not attach more importance to passages in bold or italics. Let the words, not typographical tricks, make the point.

Too many italicised words together upset word-flow, and at worst, confuse the reader. An otherwise neat newsletter can easily be spoilt this way. Excessive use of underlining, too, fails to add stress or emphasis. Underlining is the traditional mark for italics and looks awful when printed.

Foreign words and phrases not fully naturalised in English are usually italicised, but commonly used phrases like ad hoc, de rigueur and en masse are set in roman type nowadays. Once a foreign word gains wide currency in English, italics usage diminishes. This is particularly noticeable in titles of foreign publications.

For media titles carrying the definite article, write *The Daily Telegraph, The Times, The Economist, The Mirror, The Sun* but *Daily Mail, Daily Express, Evening Standard*. If there is *The* in the masthead, italicise that too. If in doubt check your media guide. When used adjectivally, drop the definite article as in '*Telegraph* reporters investigated…'. For textual references to titles of house magazines, use italics; the same goes for releases. Use sparingly everywhere.

The main uses of italic include titles of books, names of ships, newspapers and magazines, titles of TV and radio programmes and films. Check for others in your style manuals. As a general guide, try to avoid overuse of italics and bold in texts simply because the more there is, the less the impact. When you want to use bold and italics, let your designer decide where they will work best.

USING THE DESIGNER TO THE BEST ADVANTAGE

Choice of designer is crucial: get the wrong one and you have wasted valuable time and probably spent money you could ill afford. Take two views on this important subject – one from a communications consultant and the other from an organisation with its own studio. The first comes from consultant and former *Profile* editor Peter C Jackson:

> Any editor worth their salt should have a basic knowledge of the most effective way to present their words to the reader. But sooner or later they must commit their precious sentences to the expert hand of the graphic designer.
>
> It is always worth taking time and trouble to seek out a designer who will be sympathetic to your overall objectives. There are those who have a purely visual approach to publication design; they see your deathless prose as merely slabs of grey matter to balance illustrations and white space. Use them at your peril.
>
> Seek out (by example or recommendation) those designers with a flair for words themselves. They will be able to meld words, pictures and display type into an imaginative and satisfying whole. There is no finer working partnership than a writer and a designer who each appreciates and respects the other's experience and skills. That is a combination worth pursuing.

Designers will tell you that before a single word is read, the layout, colours and typography must form an immediate impression that will entice and excite the eye. And it is that first impression that counts more than anything else.

It is crucial that the designer is properly briefed on the objective, tone of the message and target audience of the publication, brochure or leaflet – no matter what it is. If the typography and layout reflect and support the message conveyed then the text stands a much better chance of being read. A 'busy' layout, possibly with a combination of complementary typefaces, would be suitable for a leaflet describing a new product; whereas a brochure describing an expensive management training course would project a more 'upmarket' image by using a sans serif typeface printed on high quality paper with plenty of white space.

A page of text without headings is uninviting and disorientating to the reader. Signpost headings in a different typeface or bullet points are effective in directing the reader to changes of thought or subject.

Readability is probably the most important factor in the design of any publication no matter how it is printed. Paying attention to it is the communicator's first priority.

NOW IT'S PROOF MARKING TIME...

The job of the PR professional is to spot the mistake, or 'literal', everyone else misses. Diligent proof-reading spells well-produced, fault-free printwork. And that largely depends on using the proper correction marks. You can avoid printing errors, usually known as 'typos', by marking proofs in the standard way universally understood by printers and their keyboard operators. Non-standard corrections only confuse and lead to more errors. Follow the marks approved by the British Standards Institution (BS 5261) – see Figure 6.4.

Typical typos: misspellings, wrong punctuation and transposed words or sentences; end-of-line breaks where a hyphen wrongly divides a word; layout faults such as mispositioned text, headings, captions; style slips like italics or bold instead of roman, capitals instead of lower case.

Mark all corrections clearly in ink, preferably by ballpoint pen. Use different colours to distinguish between errors made by the printer and your own corrections – red for printer's errors and blue or black for yours. Printers usually charge heavily for alterations, or alts for short; ensure you are not charged for theirs!

Put the change in the adjacent margin and a text mark showing the position. Where there are several marginal marks these should go from left to right in the same order as the textual marks. Put a diagonal stroke (/) after each marginal mark to show the end of the correction.

Where new copy replaces existing text line-for-line, count the number of printed characters in a line (including spaces) for the number of typescript characters needed to fill it. Get someone to read the copy while you check and mark the proof. Mark alphabetically each additional item of copy; check cross-references and the contents lists against page numbers. Take special care with headings and captions.

For heavy corrections, retype and attach a separate sheet clearly marked for position. Read and re-read, checking as you go. Remember that you read what you want to read. The BSI marks and useful tips on proofing are in *Authors' corrections cost money and cause delay*, available free of charge from the British Printing Industries Federation (020 7915 8300). The more time you spend on proof-reading, the better. It pays to look at every piece of print you see to check if there are any typos or style faults. I bet you will find something wrong or that could be improved. The main marks follow.

Standard proof correction marks

Extracts from BS 5261 Part 2: 1976 (1995) are reproduced with permission of the British Standards Institution under licence number 2001SK/0003. Complete standards can be obtained from BSI Customer Services, 389 Chiswick High Road, London W4 4AL (tel: 020 8996 9001). These extracts are also reproduced by permission of the the British Printing Industries Federation.

	Textual Mark	Marginal Mark
Correction is concluded	None	/
Leave unchanged	------ under character to remain	(√)
Push down risen spacing material	Encircle blemish	⊥
Insert in text the matter indicated in the margin	⋏	New matter followed by ⋏
Insert additional matter identified by a letter in a diamond	⋏	⋏ Followed by for example ⟨A⟩
Delete	/ through character(s) or ⊢——⊣ through word(s) to be deleted	♂

Figure 6.4   *Standard symbols for correcting proofs (continued over)*

Instruction	Textual Mark	Marginal Mark
Delete and close up	through character or through character e.g. charaᶻcter chara⬛cter	⌒
Substitute character or substitute part of one or more word(s)	/ through character or ⊢——————⊣ through word(s)	New character or new word(s)
Wrong fount. Replace by character(s) of correct fount	Encircle character(s) to be changed	⊗
Change damaged character(s)	Encircle character(s) to be changed	✕
Set in or change to italic	———— under character(s) to be set or changed	⊔
Set in or change to capital letters	≡≡≡ under character(s) to be set or changed	≡
Set in or change to small capital letters	═══ under character(s) to be set or changed	═
Set in or change to capital letters for initial letters and small capital letters for the rest of the words	≡ under initial letters and ═══ under rest of word(s)	≣
Set in or change to bold type	∿∿∿∿ ·under character(s) to be set or changed	∿
Change capital letters to lower case letters	Encircle character(s) to be changed	≢
Change italic to upright type	Encircle character(s) to be changed	⊔

Figure 6.4 *continued*

Instruction	Textual Mark	Marginal Mark
Invert type	Encircle character to be inverted	↺
Substitute or insert full stop or decimal point	/ through character or ⋏ where required	⊙
Substitute or insert semi-colon	/ through character or ⋏ where required	;
Substitute or insert comma	/ through character or ⋏ where required	,
Start new paragraph	⌐	⌐
Run on (no new paragraph)	⌒	⌒
Centre	[enclosing matter to be centred]	[ ]
Indent	⌐	⌐
Cancel indent	←⌐	⌐
Move matter specified distance to the right	enclosing matter to be moved to the right →	[

Figure 6.4 *continued*

Instruction	Textual Mark	Marginal Mark
Take over character(s), word(s) or line to next line, column or page		
Take back character(s), word(s) or line to previous line, column or page		
Raise matter	over matter to be raised under matter to be raised	
Lower matter	over matter to be lowered under matter to be lowered	
Correct horizontal alignment	Single line above and below misaligned matter e.g. mi$_{sa}$lign_ed	
Close up. Delete space between characters or words	linking characters	
Insert space between characters	between characters affected	
Insert space between words	between words affected	
Reduce space between characters	between characters affected	
Reduce space between words	between words affected	
Make space appear equal between characters or words	between characters or words affected	

Figure 6.4 *continued*

AT A GLANCE

- Consider the appearance of the page when editing.
- Avoid long slabs of type and a 'grey' look.
- Go for short sentences and paragraphs.
- Edit out 'widows' with just a few words at top of page or column.
- Include plenty of crossheads and subheads to give 'air' in solid text.
- Try not to have too many word breaks at line-ends.
- Choose typefaces with care: the designer knows best.
- Think of older eyes: will print be legible? Keep to no smaller than 11 or 10pt size.
- Illustrations and photographs liven up dull text.
- Don't overuse bold or italics.
- Learn the proof-reading marks and always use them when marking up.
- The more time you spend checking your proofs the better.

7

Headlines: making them work

Headlines are a crucial element in printed communication. Short, punchy headings attract attention and take the eye to the text. However well the words have been crafted, they will not be read if the reader isn't encouraged to move on. That is the job of the headline: style will depend on the audience and type of publication. Newspaper format house journals and periodicals demand a brisk, urgent approach. Leaflets and brochures require a different kind of headline, as do internal and contact reports.

Whatever the type of publication or report, the headline must encapsulate the main points of the text in an interesting and eye-catching way. In fact, the livelier the better. Space will always be a limiting factor, and this is why it is often difficult to achieve a newsy yet informative headline within the constraints of the column or page widths. That, of course, is where skill and experience come in.

House journals must be in tune with the audience to which the publication is addressed. A study of the many journal styles to be seen today will help you when you edit and produce publications whether current or new. Newspaper and magazine headings

Figure 7.1 *Simplicity is the keynote for Hyde Housing Association report, a class winner in the Communicators in Business (CiB) Awards, 2004. Produced by The Grand Design*

reveal many contrasting forms, with the tabloids shouting the news and the 'heavies' taking a more staid and thoughtful line. The trade press, professional and scientific journals each adopts differing styles to reflect the varying needs and interests of their audiences.

There are no set rules for writing headlines, as every publication requires different treatment. The following basic guidelines for creating and presenting headlines will provide the foundation for a usable and flexible style, which can be adapted according to individual needs.

USE PRESENT TENSE, ACTIVE VERBS

The headline is essential for effective communication and to arrest the reader's attention. Its job is to take the eye to the story, to whet the appetite, to excite and inform. In-house newspaper or newsletter headlines should contain a present-tense verb, and thus generally follow newspaper style. Participle *-ing* endings should be avoided as in 'XYZ company is *launching* a new product.' It is much better to write 'XYZ company *launches*…' While the former is passive, slow and boring, the latter is vibrant and active. Most people read newspapers, and so it makes sense to follow their style whenever possible.

Headlines must be both impartial and accurate. They must give the news (or tell a story if a feature), not the opinions of the writer. They must not embellish the facts, but present them accurately and succinctly. If the story is about a person, name the person unless he or she is unknown to the audience. Brevity is your first priority, but don't sacrifice crucial detail on which the story hangs.

Headlines work best when they have an active, 'doing' verb, preferably single syllable ones like *calls, tells, says, goes*. The heading should say what the story is about in a few short words, enough to make the reader want to find out more, and there are plenty of examples of two- or three-word headlines that work well.

But there are occasions when just one word can have a dramatic effect and take the reader to the heart of the story like GOTCHA! (during the Falklands war) and GRABALOT (pay rises and bonuses for Camelot directors). Headlines like these, which appear regularly in the tabloid press, take much thought, but are extremely effective in telling a story in a punchy, pithy way.

It is important that headlines should stand on their own and not become part of the following copy; for example a house journal headline might read 'John Smith, new managing director of XYZ company,' with the first line of the copy running on directly from it saying 'Has plans for expansion…' Headlines should never do that.

QUESTIONS AND HUMOUR

Another way to spark interest is to write question headings from time to time, starting with *Who, Why, Where, What,* or constructions like *Is it, Was it.* For publications containing mostly feature material, take a softer line. You can use longer headings and perhaps even leave out the verb. Jokey headlines, like HELLO TO GOOD BUYS in women's pages, work best in tabloid-style newspapers and house journals, but can dilute the meaning of a serious message. If used sparingly, headings like PURRFECT ENDING for a story about cats about to use up their nine lives, and MONEY TO

Figure 7.2 *Category-winning tabloid staff newspaper for BT Wholesale in the 2004 CiB awards, 2004. Design by Chandler Gooding*

BYRNE for a news item announcing a two-million pound pools winner can get a story over far more effectively than a straightforward heading. Look for headings with a play on words, the *double entendre*. But avoid being facetious, and while there can be no objection to the occasional pun, attempts at being funny can cause a groan and be seen as a poor form of wit. It is all a question of balance, and fitting headlines to the audience and message. There is always room for humour.

AVOID 'LABEL' HEADINGS

'Label' headings make a bland statement without verb or verve and hold little interest for the reader. They produce an effect of dullness and monotony. A heading which announces the winners of an awards scheme SMITH WINS TOP AWARD is so much better than the bland statement AWARDS ANNOUNCED – a typical label heading.

Do not use label headings above feature articles in house magazines or in newsletters. They can, however, be used as signposts for sectioning off a publication: labels like 'Latest publications' or 'Future events' are quite acceptable for this purpose.

Sometimes a label is unavoidable, particularly if space is short. In this case, use key words that are potent in themselves: anger, big, career, cut, gain, job, profit, loss, lose, new, win work well. Look for words that will arrest – and keep the reader reading.

One trick is to insert the occasional play on words, the *double entendre*, in headlines. You will notice such headings in tabloids and popular magazines, but if overused they can be painful for the reader. Avoid clever-clever headings in press releases they are likely to backfire and cause unexpected problems.

HEADINGS IN SALES LEAFLETS AND BROCHURES

Sales leaflets, company brochures, catalogues and manuals require hard sell and persuasive messages. You can borrow a lot from the language of advertising. David Ogilvy, founder of the Ogilvy and Mather agency, writing in *Confessions of an Advertising Man*, says that five times as many people read the headline as the text. He goes on: 'The wickedest of all sins is to run an advertisement *without* a headline.' And then he adds something that could cause the writer of a sales leaflet to take a deep inward breath: 'If you haven't done some selling in your headline, you have wasted 80 per cent of your client's money.'

The two most powerful words in a headline are *free* and *new*. Other words and phrases useful for headlines are: advance, advice/help on, bargain, big/great/huge, development, easy, fast/quick, gain, hurry, important, just out, profit/loss, quality, says/tells, win, want/need. Avoid superlatives like amazing, magic, miraculous, revolutionary, sensational, superb, startling unless they are for an advertisement.

Emotion can play a significant part in a successful and memorable headline: Ogilvy suggests that headlines can be strengthened by words like darling, love, fear, proud, friend, baby. He quotes a headline of a few decades ago for a range of soaps and moisturisers with a girl talking to her lover on the telephone:

DARLING, I'M HAVING THE MOST EXTRAORDINARY EXPE-
RIENCE... I'M HEAD OVER HEELS IN DOVE as being one of the
most provocative headlines ever to come out of O&M. More recent
examples of memorable headlines include CATISFACTION
(Whiskas petfoods) and CHANNEL FUNNEL (P&O) and, more
recently, THE FUTURE'S BRIGHT, THE FUTURE'S ORANGE.

Figure 7.3 *Snappy headline for the Newspaper/Newsletter category of
the CiB Awards 2004. Metropolitcan Police Services* The Job, *produced
by Trident Communications*

For sales leaflets and other promotional material, a good headline
is one which makes a stated promise and a well-defined benefit, is
not set at an angle so that the reader gets neck-ache trying to read
it, and is set in easy-to-read type. Headlines using an unfamiliar
typeface and those that are buried in the text and printed upside
down just to satisfy a creative whim should be ruled out immediately.

STYLE AND PRESENTATION

While short, snappy headings are suitable for news-style publications, longer ones are sometimes more appropriate for sales leaflets and brochures. According to Ogilvy, when the New York University School of Retailing ran headline tests for a big department store, it found that headlines of 10 words or more, and containing news and information, consistently sold more merchandise than short ones.

Presentation is important. Bold type, at least seven or eight sizes larger than the text type (or up as subs would say) makes the headline stand out from the rest of the text. For instance, if the copy was set in 10pt, 2pt leaded, headings of 18pt or larger would provide sufficient contrast. Although it is a matter of individual style and taste, most headlines look better if set upper and lower case rather than in full capitals. A long headline of four or more words in capitals adds nothing to the effectiveness of the message. Do not underline or put capitals in an attempt to add emphasis: this will not have the desired effect and will look old-fashioned and clumsy.

Don't put a full stop at the end of a headline. Make sure that if a headline runs to more than one line that the first is not broken with a hyphen: that looks not only ghastly but thoroughly unprofessional. Either shorten the line so that there is no need to break the last word or rewrite the whole heading. Try not to exceed three-line headings for newspaper-style publications (three-deck in journalese) although a four-deck heading in a large size, say 42pt or more, would not look out of place in a tabloid format.

Nowadays, computer typesetting allows great flexibility in choice of headline styles and sizes, and there is no limit to the creative possibilities that can be achieved. The time taken on the writing and presentation of headlines is well worthwhile and deserves as much care and attention as the story itself. Subheadings, or crossheads, are just as important as their bigger brothers and demand just as much care in their wording and presentation.

SUBHEADINGS

Subheadings (also called crossheadings) can be centred or ranged

28 Point

DESIGN AS APPLI
ed to printed matter
is the meaningful ar

32 Point

DESIGN AS APP
lied to printed
matter is the mea

36 Point

DESIGN AS A
pplied to print
ed matter is the

Figure 7.4 *Helvetica medium in sizes suitable for headlines*

left and are a good way to break up long stretches of type. Pages look better with subheads and they can be handy for filling space, for instance when you have difficulty in equalising column depths. Too many subheads will look messy, particularly if the page is no larger than A4.

Subheads should consist of one or two words of not more than seven or eight characters each; they should never go into a second line. Do not have them in the same type style as the text. They

DESIGN AS APPLIED TO PRINTED MATTER IS THE
meaningful arrangement of the elements in a page or
other visual area. The arrangement serves as an invis
ible scaffolding or framework on which to display mean

DESIGN AS APPLIED
to printed matter is the
meaningful arrangeme

**DESIGN AS APPLIED TO PRINTED MATTER IS
the meaningful arrangement of the elements in
a page or other visual area. The arrangement
serves as an invisible scaffolding or framework**

DESIGN AS APPLIE
d to printed matter is
the meaningful arra

Figure 7.5 *Contrasts in type sizes and styles in Helvetica medium
and bold*

work best if they are in bold type or in italics. Sometimes they look
well in a second colour: it will not add to the cost if they are
printed in one of the colours already being used. Like headlines,
subheads do not require full stops at the end, but there is no objection to question or exclamation marks.

Stuck for an idea? Take a single, but significant, word out of the
text and put it as a crosshead. A few of them judiciously placed can
make a dull page look interesting and alive.

Extra emphasis can be given to a passage by inserting side-headings in the margins. Insert these at layout stage and do not attempt to write them in when the body copy for the text is written. Style and layout design will dictate how many there should be and where they should be positioned.

Never overlook the wording and presentation of headings. Time and trouble spent getting them right will always pay off: improved communication will inevitably result.

SLOGANS FOR BRAND RECALL

A memorable slogan is the mainstay of successful advertising campaigns: but it is not always the panacea that agency and client expect it to be. Often it is the slogan that is remembered, not the product, and with slim relationship to sales. Even so, slogans like 'Guinness Is Good For You', 'Go To Work On An Egg', 'Drinka Pinta Milka Day' and the wartime security slogan 'Be Like Dad, Keep Mum' worked brilliantly.

Research showed that wherever people went, they thought that Guinness actually *did* do them good (the slogan was dropped in 1963 as it was a claim that could not be adequately substantiated); the Egg Marketing Board ran its slogan for decades and it became advertising folklore. Despite objections by purists, the National Milk Publicity Council's slogan almost 50 years ago soon found its way to respectability, eventually gaining entries in dictionaries.

The snappy slogan, like a news headline, can bring lasting recall and has a significant influence on the target audience. But extra sales are hard to prove.

The best slogans are those with words of one syllable, as the first two examples illustrate. Another critical factor is choice of typeface: it should follow that used in advertising and in all printwork for the company's products. If colours are used, they should also follow those in promotions and corporate literature.

Lettering style, whether in bold or italics, should be consistent – from signs on vans and lorries to display cards and posters. And the slogan can go on releases as well, providing it is not too obtrusive. It should never overshadow the headline, and should be positioned well away from the story itself.

Above all, slogans must be simple and clear. Once they become over-wordy and clumsy, they will not be remembered and it would be better to use other forms of publicity. The slogan that produces instant recall is the one that is short and to the point, that is repeated and repeated, that makes you laugh, the one that is emotionally charged. That is the one to aim for.

Figure 7.6 *Broad use of the easy brand: easyJet (top), easyEverything; also in easy.com and easyvalue.com (bottom)*

ELEMENTS OF CORPORATE IDENTITY

Recognisable corporate identity depends on the design and execution of the communications process in all its aspects. That means a consistent type style and colours for everything from vehicles, website, printwork of all kinds from letterheads, memos, visiting cards to the annual report and publicity material, to press and TV advertising, to packaging, to the sign outside office or factory – easyJet is a good example of how a strong brand identity can lead quickly to marketing success.

Building an effective and memorable corporate identity of a company and its brands is largely the responsibility of the advertising agency, but at the design stage and for subsequent publicity, the PR practitioner has a critical role to play.

AT A GLANCE

- Make headings short, punchy and pithy.
- Present tense and active verbs work best.
- Go for single-syllable words whenever possible.
- Introduce humour but don't overdo it.
- Avoid slow, boring 'label' headings.
- The most powerful words are 'free' and 'new'.
- Bold type in larger size provides contrast with text.
- Use upper and lower case, not capitals.
- Subheads of one or two words are effective.
- Consistency with product branding maintains corporate identity.

8

Dealing with figures and abbreviations

FIGURING OUT THE NUMBERS

The way you treat numbers is as important as the way you treat words. A mixture of numeral styles can confuse the reader and make the production look amateurish. A set style for numbers should be a priority for everything produced whether for print, presentation, release or correspondence.

Style manuals set out a number of guidelines and provide plenty of examples. Individual publications adapt these and expand on them to suit their own needs and audiences. While rules of this nature are open to interpretation, they provide a starting point and this section draws attention to some of the important points for house style.

Basic considerations

The first rule is not to start a sentence with a figure. Spell it out instead. The reason for this is that the style is followed almost universally in newspapers and magazines and in most professionally produced publications. It is something we have all become used to and any diversion immediately stands out and looks 'wrong'. But it would be clumsy to spell out a multi-digit number; either write out *The year 1997* or else recast the sentence completely. However, there are occasions when it is difficult to avoid a figure at the beginning and when this happens, say in an annual report or in giving statistical data, then there may be no alternative but to start with a figure.

The second rule – and this is for numbers *within* a sentence – is to spell out numbers up to and including ten; above that write figures. But if there are sequences of numbers, some of which may be higher than ten, use figures throughout for the sake of consistency and clarity. Write out *hundredth* but after that put *101st* and so on. For decimals, use a full stop on the line as in 1.5, and do not attempt to centralise it as if writing a decimal by hand. (In other languages a decimal comma is used.) There is no point in putting a single zero after the decimal point unless it is called for in tabular matter, but a nought should go before the point as in *0.75*. Numerals should be used for page references, currencies and for groups of statistics.

Symbols, abbreviations and punctuation

Next: avoid using the % sign in text; spell out *per cent* as two words, but use *percentage* of course. The symbol should be kept for tables and charts and for text where figures predominate. Fractions should be hyphenated (*two-thirds*) and do not mix (or compare) fractions with decimals. When both a whole number and a fraction are spelt out, only hyphenate the fraction as in *one and three-quarters*. It is better to write (in formal text) *twentieth century* rather than *20th*. Note that *one in three* is singular but *two in five* are plural. Some newspapers will prefer to write *a mile and a half* instead of *one and a half miles*, but seldom, if ever, print *1½ miles*!

Avoid a combination of the *to/from* style (when comparing years, for instance) with hyphens as in *from 1997 to 1998*; put *from two to three*, or *from 12 to 13*, but not a mixture of the two styles. Reserve hyphens or dashes for numerals and never use them for spelt-out figures.

A *billion* at one time meant a million million but modern usage suggests that it means a *thousand million* – a definition accepted by most, if not at all, national newspapers. It is better to spell out a million and a billion, but if *m* and *bn* are used do not put a full point after the abbreviations unless they come at the end of a sentence. Full points should not follow units of weight and measurement (*cm, ft, kg*), and do not put hyphens in combinations like *half an inch* or *half a dozen*. With temperature put the degree symbol immediately before *C* or *F*. No punctuation is necessary in dates (*12 March 1997*). In compounds, put a hyphen in *half-hour* and *two-day*.

Nouns of measurement and quantity: singular or plural?

All nouns of measurement remain singular when used attributively: *a six-foot man, a five-litre can*. But plural feet or inches are used where an adjective follows, as in *he is six feet tall, she is five feet six inches*. Similarly, *stone* stays singular in plural expressions, as in *she weighs nine stone*. Unless used attributively, metric measurements always take the plural form as in *the tank has a capacity of 10 litres*.

Nouns of quantity – *score, dozen, hundred* – take the singular form if qualified by a preceding word: *two thousand will be sufficient*. But they will be plural when denoting indefinite amounts as in *the company publishes hundreds of publications*. Measurements of quantity and distance containing a plural noun can be taken as being singular and therefore take a singular verb: *twenty pounds/miles is too expensive/far*.

When we use the singular word *majority*, we write 'the majority of people *are*'. That's because it is *people* being talked about, so they take the plural. But if it's the majority itself that's being discussed then it needs a singular verb: the majority is smaller. (Note that *vast majority* has become an overused cliché.)

It is worth noting that the word 'number' takes a plural verb when it refers to a quantity or group as in a *number of people were…* but when it means a figure it takes the singular: *two hundred pounds is the number I quoted*. So much for figures.

ABBREVIATIONS: THE LONG AND THE SHORT OF IT

Now let's look at abbreviations and how to deal with them. First, the abbreviation everyone uses without hesitation: *OK*. What do the letters stand for? Unless you have seen it in my 'Last Words' column in the IPR magazine *Profile* or made a study of the subject, the chances are that you don't know – and that is the trouble with using abbreviations: readers may not know what a given set of initials stand for and that means communication not working.

OK, here are some answers. Take your pick: originating from the nineteenth century, it could come from Old Kinderhook, the upstate New York birthplace of eighth American president Van Buren who used the initials as an election slogan; or perhaps a contraction of American slang *Orl Korrect*, or of Orrins-Kendall crackers, according to Bill Bryson in *Mother Tongue*. Even though the origin may be obscure, we all know what the letters mean.

Few abbreviations are as familiar and instantly understandable as OK. Abbreviations are often used without hesitation, but are meaningless to the reader, simply because the writer is used to them and they have become part of the company's jargon. Get them wrong and your message fails. So what are the rules for dealing with them?

Avoid overuse

The first point, to quote a well-known saying, is familiarity breeds contempt. If you overuse abbreviated sets of initials they quickly tire the eye. Unless the initials are sufficiently familiar to be part of the language (BBC, CBI, TUC) the name should be spelt out in full before using abbreviations. Otherwise, spell it out in full after the initials at first reference. It would be equally tiring to see a repetition of the full name when a contraction would be more suitable and convenient. There would be little point in explaining the initials BMW, because besides being a well-known brand, there is usually no *need* for the reader to know what they mean.

Do not continue to use the same set of initials. For example, in references to the BBC use 'the Corporation' or possibly for informal speech or tabloid publication, 'the Beeb'. Again, for the CBI, it could be called after the first reference 'the employers' organisation' or just 'the organisation'. In other cases, use a shortened form such as institute/association/federation/body or, in the case of firms, company/consultancy/firm/group/shop/store, or name by product or service type. But keep clear of slang words like *outfit/shop* for public relations or advertising firms.

Be careful of ambiguities

Watch out for ambiguities like PC, which could mean personal computer, Police Constable or Privy Counsellor. You may be *in* PR, but you are not *a* PR. You see an *ad* but not an *advert*, you join a *demo* and you get *flu* not *the* (and no apostrophe). Ensure that descriptions are accurate. A common mistake is for BSI to be written out as the British Standards *Institute* instead of Institution; it was the Public Record Office, not Records, before it became the National Archives. Writers wonder how to write PLC (Public Limited Company). It is up to the company: it can be shown in caps, or lower case or a mixture of the two, although it seems that the all-capitals style, either in roman or italics, is the one generally favoured.

Capitals and full stops

Most house styles require all abbreviations to be set in capitals, but some organisations are read as acronyms and take lower case (Aslef for instance), while others are set upper and lower case for the sake of clarity (BSc, Dr). In general, full stops are not needed in abbreviations of company names, titles and civil honours, academic qualifications, and the courtesy titles of Mr/Mrs/Ms.

No full point follows numerical abbreviations (1st/2nd), units of length, weight or time (cm/ft/cwt/lb/kg/min/sec); am/pm; days of the week (Mon/Tues); months (Aug/Dec); or in points of the compass (NE/SW) unless used separately (N.S.E.W.). They are seldom necessary in acronyms (laser) and if there is no way of avoiding etc (never &c) don't put a point after it.

Make sure your text or office-produced documents have all abbreviations typed or set in a consistent way without (or with) full points as may be dictated by house style. Get out of the habit of using eg, ie, pa – they are what might be termed 'lazyisms'. For *etc* write a short listing of what the items are; for eg/ie just put a comma, for pa spell out per annum or annually or every/each year. Note that *eg* is not the same as *ie*: *eg* means 'for example', while ie means 'that is'.

Ampersands and definite articles

The ampersand is a useful and convenient abbreviation for *and*, but it should be restricted to company names (Marks & Spencer) and never used as an alternative to *and* in text. A check with the telephone directory will confirm whether or not a company name contains an ampersand.

The omission of the definite article has caused heated debate: the Queen's English Society has blamed this on advertisers, headline writers and bad teaching. But it is not something to be too bothered about unless *the* is there to describe a specific thing or event. It would be tedious to describe Joe Bloggs as *the* managing director of XYZ company. Drop it and you make the copy run faster. Name plus title in lower case is all you need.

The is certainly not needed when talking about branded products: you would say, in a release or article, Ford motor cars, not the Ford motor cars, in a general context, but the Ford when referring to a specific model, say in comparison with other vehicles.

When a title such as *The Times*, or the CIPR for that matter, is used attributively, you can drop the *the* as in *Times* reporters investigated…, CIPR policy decisions were made…. There is no objection to using *the* with less and more (the less/the more you have); but note nonetheless (not none the less) is preferable to not any *the* less.

You need *the* when referring to the particular, the specific. Keep it for titles of books, plays and films when it is part of the recognised title and when mentioning a person by title as in the Prime Minister, Tony Blair, not the American way Prime Minister Blair.

If a shortened word is pronounced, do not put a definite article before it (the CIPR but not the M&S). Hence the rule: *the* goes with abbreviated organisations but not the company names. You wouldn't write the ICI would you? Be careful in exchanging phone for telephone, photo for photograph, as both contractions are more comfortable when used informally and in speech.

Use facsimile, telephone in full for printed address details, fax/phone as a verb ('I will fax/phone you'). In formal contexts write telephone.

A full guide to abbreviations (but only those covering the larger commercial organisations) will be found in *The Oxford Style Manual*; advice on setting abbreviations for printed material is given in another section of the manual. Most dictionaries will indicate what abbreviated titles, honours and qualifications stand for. And, by the way, OK is preferred to *okay* or *ok*.

AT A GLANCE

- Don't start a sentence with a figure if you can help it.
- Spell out numbers up to and including ten within a sentence.
- Avoid the % sign in text; spell out per cent as two words.
- When comparing years use either *from/to* or hyphenate; don't mix.
- 'Number' takes the plural when referring to a group.
- For sets of initials spell out the full name at first reference or put it in brackets.
- No stops in abbreviated company names or titles.
- The definite article (the) is not needed for branded products.
- Consult the *Oxford Guide to Style* for guidance on abbreviations.

9

Keep it short, simple – and plain

Some of the strictures of purists who insist upon rigid adherence to rules of grammar are little more than mythology and have no place in everyday usage. Those who believe that it is always wrong to split an infinitive, end a sentence with a proposition, or start with a conjunction are in a linguistic straitjacket and unable to communicate as well as they might.

Likewise, unnecessarily long words, complex sentences and lengthy paragraphs confuse the reader. Double negatives, needless jargon, faulty or misplaced punctuation, and constant repetition of words and ideas can all lead to nonsensical, hard-to-follow text. And that means that the reader quickly loses interest in the face of endless waffle.

Plain English, written in a simple and straightforward way, is the recipe for clarity of expression. More than that, it is the basis of good style. Earlier chapters have discussed some of the ingredients for securing and keeping the reader reading, and, without trespassing on that territory, this chapter looks at writing with economy of language, a crucial factor in getting your message understood.

AIM FOR BREVITY

Brevity is the essence, particularly for the media. Complicated constructions and lengthy, unwieldy sentences not only bore the reader, they provide an instant barrier to effective communications. More important still, brevity spells time saved for the reader. Copy must be clear, concise and unambiguous. Whether the piece is for publication in a newspaper or periodical or for a brochure or leaflet, it should be written so that it grips the reader from start to finish. What are the best ways of achieving this?

First, use short words rather than long, and plain language instead of complex terminology. Try to keep sentences down to 25 to 30 words, fewer if you can. Use full stops liberally: they are the writer's best friend. Aim for not more than three sentences per paragraph for releases and news-style publications. But variety is the spice: an occasional longer paragraph gives colour and balance to a piece. And the one-liner can be effective – it jerks the reader to attention.

Sentences can of course be much longer than this; indeed, those of up to 60 or so words are acceptable for technical or legal contexts where detailed explanation is required. If a sentence is starting to 'look' too long, and tops the 60 mark, break it up with stops, or insert quotations if appropriate. With feature articles and corporate brochures you can be more generous with words. But even then, be aware that the longer the sentence the more likely the reader will tire and skip the copy you have tried so hard to get right in terms of style and fact.

As you write, get into the habit of asking yourself 'Is there a shorter word that means the same thing? Is there a better word? Are any words sheer verbiage and should be cut out? Is every word doing a job and telling you something?' In short, write tight to write well.

PLAIN WORDS

Your search for plain words and the removal of unnecessary ones will be aided by using *The Oxford Guide to Plain English* by Martin Cutts. There are, he says, three main techniques for dealing with 'dross' to allow your information to 'shine more clearly': strike out useless words and leave only those that tell you something; prune

Press Release (page 1 of 2)

Contact: John Lister
Phone: 01663 744409/07963 859058
Fax: 01663 747038
Website: www.plainenglish.co.uk
Date: 23 March 2004

For immediate release

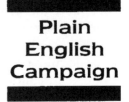

Plain English Campaign

At the end of the day... we're fed up with clichés

Plain English supporters around the world have voted "At the end of the day" as the most irritating phrase in the language.

Second place in the vote was shared by "At this moment in time" and the constant use of "like" as if it were a form of punctuation. "With all due respect" came fourth.

The Campaign surveyed its 5000 supporters in more than 70 countries as part of the build-up to its 25th anniversary. The independent pressure group was launched on 26 July 1979.

Spokesman John Lister said over-used phrases were a barrier to communication. "When readers or listeners come across these tired expressions, they start tuning out and completely miss the message — assuming there is one! Using these terms in daily business is about professional as wearing a novelty tie or having a wacky ringtone on your phone.

"George Orwell's advice from 1946 is still worth following: 'Never use a metaphor, simile, or other figure of speech which you are used to seeing in print.'"

ends

Background: Plain English Campaign is an independent pressure group formed in 1979 to fight gobbledygook and unclear public information. It funds itself through commercial activities including editing and training. The campaigning work includes annual awards for good use of plain English, and the infamous 'Golden Bull' booby prizes. The Campaign's Crystal Mark seal of approval, which is based on rigorous testing on the public, now appears on more than 9500 documents.

Note to editors:

A full list of the terms receiving more than one nomination follows on the second page of this release.

PO Box 3, New Mills, High Peak, SK22 4QP, England
Director: Chrissie Maher OBE, MA, DUNIV (Open)   Phone: 01663 744409   Fax: 01663 747038
E-mail: info@plainenglish.co.uk   Web site: www.plainenglish.co.uk
Plain English Campaign Limited Registered Office: 20 Union Road, New Mills, High Peak, SK22 3ES
Registered in England and Wales number 2564513   VAT registration number 548-7289-90

Figure 9.1 *Release from The Plain English Campaign on overused clichés. Its A-Z Guide on alternative words and CD are available on the Campaign's website*

the dead wood, grafting on the vigorous; rewrite completely. Cutts gives many examples of the overlong word or phrase, the useless word, and the officialese that defies understanding; as well as advice on how to rewrite lengthy and tedious text. When making cuts it is essential not to alter the sense in any way and to follow the basic rules of grammar.

With a little thought it is easy: see how 10 words in the following sentence can be lost without altering the meaning:

> XYZ company *had as its main objective the need* (wanted) to increase output by at least 10 per cent *in* this *current financial* year.

Here, the words in italics can be deleted without changing the meaning. The single word 'wanted' takes the place of seven needless ones. Verbiage like this throughout a piece of several hundred words would turn off the reader after only a few paragraphs. Expressions that can easily be shortened include: the question as to whether, (use whether); there is no doubt that (put no doubt or doubtless); in spite of the fact that (replace with though); owing to the fact that (write since or because).

Cutts includes helpful lists of plain and short words and phrases. For example, he advises facts/details not particulars; help not facilitate; idea not concept; buy not purchase; start/begin, not commence. Do not let long-winded phrases get the better of you: for instance, write although or despite instead of 'despite the fact that'. Sir Ernest Gowers in *The Complete Plain Words* demonstrates that simple prepositions can often replace wordy phrases: if for 'in case of' and to for 'with a view to'.

From my file of unnecessarily complicated words and phrases (preferences in italics): concerning, *about/on*; currently, *now*; donation, *gift*; in addition to/as well as, *besides/also*; conclude, *end/decide/stop/deduce*; duplicate, *repeat*; endeavour, *try*; fluctuation, *change*; general (adj), *broad*; give rise to, *cause*; in the course of, *during*; heterogeneous, *mixed*; intercede, *plead*; journey, *trip*; not less than, *at least*; language, *tongue*; master (v), *grasp*; principal, *main*; persons, *people*; remuneration, *fee/pay*; stipulate, *state*; subsequent to, *after*; tendency, *trend*; understand (v), *see*; virtually, *almost*; with reference to, *about/regarding*; warehouse, *store*.

Look for the shorter, simpler – the plain word: check for alternatives in the *Penguin Dictionary of English Synonyms*, *Roget's Thesaurus* and similar reference books.

LOCAL GOVERNMENT COMMUNICATION

Local government with its many different publics from house-holders to businesses, from contractors to social services, faces communications problems arising from a range of departments with widely differing staffing arrangements. A council's messages, anything from Council Tax demands to rubbish collection, must be widely understood and acted upon by the numerous publics. To achieve effective communication across such a broad audience, words and phrases must be written and presented in a simple, straightforward way. Take the North Lincolnshire Council for example: its guide on plain English and house style is a concise and effective aid for its officers and staff.

The North Lincolnshire Council's *Style Guide*, written and devised by Barry Fleetwood, the council's public relations and communications manager, emphasises the need for short words, avoiding the abstract and concentrating on the specific, using the active not the passive voice, and writing in the first person (I/we rather than 'the council'). It is emphasised that good writing depends on facts not waffle, without repetition, coupled with correct punctuation and delivered in plain and simple English.

Guidance on reports and documents, and results for using the council's name, are included. Any county council or local authority, or indeed any organisation wanting a set of basic rules on style and usage, can get an online copy from barry.fleetwood@ northlincs.gov.uk.

Another style guide comes from Derby City Council. Its useful *Plain English Guide* includes a directory of short words for long, a list of meaningless and patronising phrases, plus helpful grammatical and punctuation points. There's a four-page list of abbreviations and acronyms for spelling out at first reference.

Of special interest to local government communicators are examples of how copy can be improved by using simple language. Latin words and expressions are out, as well as long-winded and obscure wording in correspondence and documents. Even so, this guide insists on a capital initial letter for council and has yet to ban the verb 'to be', a signal of the passive voice, although implicit in some examples. An email version of the Derby guide is available on request from Julia.Buckland@derby.gov.uk.

It is now possible to test and measure your ability to write plain English if you have access to Microsoft Word (which most

Figure 9.2 *The North Lincolnshire Council's style guide, now in its third edition. Written and devised by Barry Fleetwood, the council's PRO and communications manager*

computer operators have). Once the user has finished spell-checking, Word can display information about the reading level of the document based on the number of syllables per word and words per sentence in three ways.

It rates reading ease on a 100-point scale; the higher the score, the easier the text is understood (aim for a score of at least 70). Second, the Flesch-Kincaid test ranks text on a US grade-school level, suggesting a minimum acceptable score of 7–8. Third, the most useful score is for passive sentences, the prime barrier to clear, concise language essential for effective communication. Here, writers should aim for a nil percentage score for press releases.

Once the figure starts to climb above 0 per cent for news items and articles, swap round to the active voice with the subject or 'doer' immediately before the verb ('Bob wrote the report', not 'the report was written by Bob'). For publicity booklets, brochures and reports, try to achieve a score of below 10–15 per cent.

The program counts words, paragraphs and sentences, and gives averages for sentences per paragraph, words per sentence and characters per word. Aim for sentences of 25 to 30 words with not more than three per paragraph.

To activate readability, go to 'tools', then 'options', spelling and grammar and to the 'show readbility statistics' box. For hard copy, scan into a document. Check out your last annual report, brochure or press release publication for passive voice, and use the program for your next printed message or even broadcast script.

WATCH OUT FOR TAUTOLOGY

If you use another word or words meaning the same thing in a single sentence or phrase, that's tautology: *free gift, new innovation* or that well-used cliché *at this moment in time* are typical. Repetition is seldom, if ever, desirable unless it is used deliberately for dramatic effect, perhaps for a speech or article. If you say you are going to *eat lunch* that is tautologous because what else would you do but eat it?

If you say someone *died* of a *fatal* dose, wrote a *pair* of *twins, full* and *total* exposure, or if you put 'he had nothing *further* to add' you are repeating yourself. Tautology abounds: *early beginnings, added bonus, inside of, meet together, mutual co-operation, over again, past history, repeat again, revert back, unite together, whether or not* easily reach type and tongue.

Don't risk repetition: it will never get past the good newspaper sub-editor.

LOOK FOR ACTIVE VERBS; AVOID CONTRACTIONS

The verb drives the text forward. First, look for single syllable verbs: *go*, not proceed; *send*, not transmit; *show*, not demonstrate. You *pitch* rather than compete, *know* rather than comprehend, *let* not permit. To *think* is better than to believe, to *ask* is better than to enquire. And so on. As mentioned earlier in the section on plain English tests, choose active-voice verbs by putting the 'doer' – the person or thing doing the action – in front of the verb. It is much better to write 'XYZ consultancy wants new clients' instead of 'new clients are wanted by XYZ consultancy'.

Try to avoid using too many adverbs as qualifiers. They are an indulgence, often a sign that noun and verb are not working properly, *Times* journalists are told. Much the same can be said for adjectives; avoid those that are flowery and expansive: *rather, very, little* (unless referring to size), *pretty* for example – especially in news stories. Never use them in releases, unless they are part of a quote, and even then it is better to cut them out if you can.

When you need to save words and shorten copy, do not fall into the trap of using contractions of modal or auxiliary verbs like will/shall/would; and so write you'll/you'd, or you're/you've, I'm. This is fine for speech and informal writing but not for formal contexts; it looks sloppy and chatty, but it can be admissible when you want to adopt a friendly, warm tone of voice. (Note that *n't* is an acceptable contraction of *not* for all but very formal usage.)

AVOID FOREIGN WORDS OR PHRASES – AND LATIN

Another barrier to understanding is using foreign words or phrases when an English one will do just as well. While it is true that many verbal imports are often just the words or phrases you want because there is no exact English equivalent, do not write above the head of the reader, who might think you are showing off.

Don't go Latin unless you have to: put among others not inter alia; yearly or annually not *per annum*; about, not *circa*; regarding, not *vis-à-vis*. Other Latin words to be avoided where English equivalents are available include ad hoc (for this purpose), a priori (from cause to effect), bona fide(s) (good faith), caveat emptor (let the buyer beware), et al (and others), ex officio (by virtue of official position), ex gratia (voluntary contribution), mea culpa (my fault) and quid pro quo (something given in return or compensation for something). In use, these words would not be italicised. As a general rule, don't go Latin and be safe! And be on your guard against pomposity: write before not 'prior to'; ultimately not 'at the end of the day'; but or however rather than 'having said that'.

Foreign words should not appear in releases. Put them in house journals and speeches, provided you think they will be understood. One or two will usually be enough. Once a word has become Anglicised (as in *role*) it is not italicised and loses its accent(s).

LOAN WORDS NEEDING CARE

Loan words and phrases include, from France, the italicised *bon mot* (clever saying), *déjà vu* (with accents, tediously similar), *de trop* (not wanted) and *tour de force* (feat of strength or skill). From Germany come the lesser known but useful *Sturm und Drang* (storm and stress), *Zeitgeist* (spirit of the times); Anglicised words include achtung, angst, blitzkrieg (or just blitz), diktat, to join kindergarten, rucksack and waltz.

Italy brings us ciao (hello, goodbye), conversazione, espresso, in camera, incommunicado, prima donna – all well known, but not *alter ego* (intimate friend) to the same extent. Greece lends hoi polloi (the masses), Russia perestroika (reconstruction, reform) and glasnost (openness), and Spain the slangy vamoose, pronto, olé and the more formal adios, fandango, grandee, armada, machismo and quixotic.

Every writer's vocabulary should make room for these Jewish words, none of which have a direct English equivalent: chutzpah (shameless audacity), mazeltov (good luck), nosh (food, to enjoy food), schmaltz (chicken fat, sugary sentimentalism), shalom (peace be unto you), shlemiel (fool, inept person).

DOUBLE NEGATIVES

Guard against double or multiple negatives with too many 'unwords' like unnecessary or unless; or putting more than one *avoid* or *cease* or phrases such as *less than* and *not more than* in one sentence. Don't use constructions like *hardly* or *almost* followed by *without*, or there were no trees *neither* instead of *either*. If you do, the meaning can become obscure and the reader has to struggle with negatives (or too many positives for that matter) in order to understand what you mean.

BEWARE 'MYTHS'

According to Cutts in *The Plain English Guide*, some of the so-called 'rules' of grammar religiously followed by purists and scholars are little more than myths. It is these myths that are a further barrier to clarity of communication. They are the territory of the pedant and do not have a place in everyday writing and speech. The top-of-the-list myth says you should never split an infinitive. While most commentators agree that it is better to avoid a split, by putting an adverb or another word between *to* and the infinitive verb as in *to boldly go*, 'no absolute taboo' should be placed on it (*Fowler's Modern English Usage*). Cutts himself says: 'If you can't bring yourself to split an infinitive, at least allow others to do so.' There is nothing to stop you splitting an infinitive but be aware that it will irritate some people.

Another myth is the long-held theory that sentences must never end with a preposition. Cutts says a few 'fossils' still believe this, but agrees that some sentences do need to be recast, not because they break any rule but because they 'sound ugly'. It all depends on the degree of formality the writer wants to achieve: it would be pedantic to write or say '*To* whom am I talking?' when 'Who am I talking *to*?' would be more natural. If the preposition looks stranded and unrelated to the word to which it belongs (or *belongs to*!) then rewrite the sentence and put it where it sounds natural. The more formal the piece, the earlier the preposition goes in the sentence. But do not move it back just because you think you should follow the schoolroom rule.

A third myth is that sentences must never begin with *and* or *but*. Authors throughout history have ignored this so-called ban: Cutts notes that Jane Austen begins almost every page with *but*, and *OED* gives several examples of sentences in English literature beginning with *and*. In fact, sentences starting this way tend to have a sparkle absent in others, and are an effective way of adding emphasis to a point already made.

TIPS FOR WRITING TIGHT

Writing tight in a plain, easy-to-read style is hard work and demands ruthless pruning. Try to keep cross-references to a minimum; divide complicated copy into vertical lists rather than having a succession of semi-colons or commas; don't bury key words or phases in slabs of text unrelieved by headings; don't confuse the lay-reader with jargon or technical terms and don't use slang words in any formal sense.

Cut unnecessary words and choose various verbs. *To be* and *to have* are often the only ones you need to achieve crispness. Make the punctuation work for you by dividing the copy into short manageable sections with liberal use of full stops. Create interest by asking questions – a technique more commonly found in articles and feature material than in news items – and include quotations if appropriate. Keep your sentences short, and have plenty of paragraph breaks. In a report or internal document organise points under headings.

Be careful not to duplicate words and phrases in the same paragraph. Repeating technical words may be unavoidable, but nothing is more off-putting than reading the same word over and over again. Look for alternatives in *The Oxford Thesaurus*, *Roget's Thesaurus*, the *Penguin Dictionary of Synonyms* or *The Wordsworth Dictionary of Synonyms & Antonyms*. Sometimes you can find the word you want in a good dictionary.

THERE IS STILL MUCH TO DO...

Don't think that once you've finished the piece that is the end of it.

The work should not get anywhere near your OUT tray until you have edited and polished it over and over again and convinced yourself there is no way it can be improved. The whole piece might need rewriting. (There's more about this in Chapter 12.)

Sometimes you will be rushed and get no chance to recast a piece. But don't despair – if you are quick you will undoubtedly have time for a bit of editing. Unless you are working on a news release or are up against a tight deadline, there is usually time for another draft. And don't think, 'Oh well there is still time to look at it again at proof stage.' That is fatal and can lead to mistakes, particularly for rush jobs.

Out with redundancies

Don't allow redundancies (unnecessary words in italics): *advance* planning, *brand* new, *concrete* proposals, divide *up*, *join* together, filled *up*, follow *after*, *general* public, *penetrate* into, limited *only* to, petrol *filling* station, *total* extinction, *revert* back, *watchful* eye. Many more are in *Essential English for Journalists, Editors and Writers* (Pimlico Random House).

Cut wasted words

Cut out those wasted words: *actually, basically, hopefully, really, kind of/sort of* and that favourite ploy of speakers starting a new thought with Well...' Phrases like *lodged an objection, in many cases,* and *tendered his resignation* can be replaced with *appealed, often* and *resigned*: in each case one word is doing the job of three. And there's 'then' after everything, or 'to be honest', almost as bad as the favourite terminator 'ah right'. Plenty more wasted words are in James Aitchison's *Cassell's Guide to Written English* (Cassell).

Be aware of confusables – words that look and sound alike but have different meanings (Appendix 2).

Revise and revise again

Even when close to deadline give your copy one more read. Take a break and come back to it: there will always be a fact to check again, a word to lose, a better, shorter one to find. Every minute you spend on revision will be rewarded by brighter, brisker copy. And I bet you will have saved at least one mistake!

Swapping paragraphs, changing words, even rewriting whole passages, are easy. Writing takes time and effort: here are 10 rules for making it better:

1. In headings, use the present tense and an active verb.
2. Check the facts; put them in a logical order and rewrite non-sequiturs.
3. Edit to cut, not add. Put in plenty of paragraph breaks.
4. Confirm that there are no ambiguities.
5. Replace long words with shorter ones; avoid repetition, redundancies.
6. Correct grammar but don't be pedantic.
7. Delete clichés and jargon.
8. Watch for legal pitfalls, particularly libellous statements.
9. Check that there is no vulgarity.
10. And ensure that spelling and style are consistent throughout.

You may not have a chance to see your copy again before it appears in print: check, check and check again. Only when you have satisfied yourself that all the above rules have been met, do you hit the PRINT button.

AT A GLANCE

- Be brief. Long, clumsy sentences only bore the reader.
- Cut out dross, verbiage, no matter what you write.
- Use short, simple words. Plain English communicates best.
- Don't repeat yourself. That's tautology.
- Choose active verbs, put the 'doer' first.
- Avoid Latin words and expressions.
- Kill redundant and wasted words.
- Write tight, prune ruthlessly.
- Revise as you go along. And again at the end.

10

Writing for the press

There are special requirements for preparing written material for publication in newspapers, consumer magazines and trade journals, and also for broadcast in news outlets. The news release – whether emailed, faxed or issued as a video news release (VNR) – is still the basic form of communication between an organisation and its audience, and there are various rules and conventions that should be followed to ensure the material gets published and does not end up in the bin. In this chapter I uncover important points concerning the writing and issuing of news releases, and then turn to commissioned articles.

NEWS RELEASES: BASIC REQUIREMENTS

When you send out a release you want it to be published. Remember that national and regional newspapers, consumer magazines and trade journals, all receive hundreds or perhaps thousands of news stories every day all vying with press releases for every inch of space. Broadcasting media – BBC and ITV programmes and the many national and local radio stations – also have huge demands on their airtimes for news items and, like the press, need information presented in a succinct way.

OFFICE OF FAIR TRADING

20/03   3 March 2003

˙FAIRER CONTRACTS FROM NIAGARA THERAPY
OFT secures fairer terms from bed supplier

Niagara Therapy (UK Ltd) has agreed to change its contracts to give consumers a fairer deal, following action from the OFT.

Niagara Therapy manufactures and distributes therapeutic beds, chairs, and massage equipment. Its products are aimed at older people and sufferers of arthritis, rheumatism, sports injuries and other painful medical conditions. The OFT considered that some of the terms of Niagara Therapy's contract with consumers were unfair and took action under the Unfair Terms in Consumer Contracts Regulations 1999.

Niagara Therapy sells its products mainly through visits to consumers' homes. The OFT challenged contract terms that potentially allowed Niagara to disclaim responsibility for oral statements made by sales representatives. These terms have been now deleted from contracts.

The OFT also had concerns about terms that:

- required consumers to pay in full on delivery thereby excluding the consumer's right to retain part payment until goods were satisfactorily installed. This term has been changed to state that

News Release ▲▲ News Release ▲▲ News Release

Fleetbank House, 2-6 Salisbury Square, London EC4Y 8JX. Press Office direct lines: (020) 7211 8900/8901/8899/8898

Figure 10.1 *First page of a well-written release reproduced by permission of the OFT. The story runs on to a second page, and a third carries contact details*

What the press don't want

The release that is wrongly targeted or lacks news value is worse than useless. If you send a release for a new kind of shelving or for a breakfast beverage to a national daily, there is no chance that either will be used: you have wasted time, not to mention postage and printing costs. The only hope for the shelving story is a paragraph in a DIY magazine; for the drink, a paragraph in a catering paper. And even that's doubtful if there are similar products on the market.

Targeting and news value are critical factors. So is timing. Popular nationals will look for a 'human' storyline with the accent on people rather than things. Broadsheets need items that stretch the intellect, specialist papers the subjects they normally cover. Anything else will be binned. Journalists receive hundreds, possibly thousands, of releases daily but few will be printed. Even those getting as far as the news desk will be rewritten or used as background material.

Never telephone or email editors or their staff to find out if they are going to use your story. Even worse would be to ask why not. Did they want more information? Asking that tops the horrors. If journalists want to follow up a story, they won't be long contacting you. That's the time to start adding to the facts you have given, or suggesting someone to interview.

Your news will be in competition with information from many other sources, not least stories coming in from staff journalists, freelancers and news agencies. The essential points are that releases must be worthy of publication and able to attract the journalist's attention. Here are the main points to watch.

Headings

The release should be clearly identifiable as a communication for publication or broadcast, and should carry a heading such as 'News Release', 'Press Release', 'Press Notice', 'Press Information', 'Information from XYZ' or just 'News from XYZ'. If sent out by a consultancy, it must be made clear that it is issued on behalf of the client company or organisation.

Such headings should be in capitals or upper and lower case of not less than 18pt so as to stand out from the mass of other material on sub-editors' desks. Print the heading in the corporate colour, typeface and style of the issuing organisation.

Essential information

Put the full name and address of the issuing organisation, with telephone, fax numbers and email/website address (if there is one) in a prominent position. Type the date of issue. Give a contact name for further information, together with his/her telephone/fax numbers if different from the main switchboard numbers. Give also the contact's email address.

Always include an out-of-hours telephone number since many journalists are still working when you have left the office. It is not necessarily good PR for the managing director or chairman to get your calls when you should be talking to the media in the first place!

Ogilvy's Public Relations Worldwide

AIR TRANSPORT INDUSTRY TO SAVE US$60M ON TYPE B MESSAGING

- SITA delivers 25% cost reduction on 200 key routes -

London – 14 July 2004 – SITA S.C has announced that its members in the air transport industry are to benefit from a 25 per cent reduction in Type B messaging costs across 200 key routes, effective from July 1st2004.

The SITA Type B messaging service is the world leader in air transport messaging that provides a common link to the world's major airlines, aerospace and government agencies. It is used by over 1,800 of the world's largest air transport and travel-related companies and provides a secure network link to transport applications, such as seat bookings and cargo tracking, and the network of agencies, such as air traffic control, Global Travel Distribution Systems and the airlines. Type B messaging costs are of increasing relevance to the air transport industry as the volume of messages required to serve the network is growing with an increase in the number of passengers boarded, and with an increasing number of applications migrated to an IP platform.

SITA estimates that the cost reductions passed on to its members will save them US$60 million over the next three years. As step one in a campaign to reduce costs through ongoing investment in its operations, SITA S.C was conscious that savings on the price of its Type B

Figure 10.2 *Part of a release from Ogilvy Public Relations Worldwide. Note the understated consultancy mention and neat dateline. Explanatory notes follow on a second page*

103

RCGP **News Release**

EMBARGOED UNTIL 0001 HOURS ON THURSDAY 15TH MAY 2003

PRIMARY CARE MANAGEMENT OF DRUG USERS: WHICH WAY FORWARD?

Drug users being treated in a new primary care programme have shown a 61 per cent reduction in criminal convictions and cautions in the year following treatment, new research in Sheffield has shown. The findings of this research and other key issues relating to primary care management of drug users will be the focus of the RCGP's eighth national conference in the management of drug users in primary care, to be held in Sheffield from May 15th - 16th 2003.

Chair of the Conference Organising Committee and Clinical Director of the Sheffield Primary Care Clinic for Drug Dependence Dr Jenny Keen said the huge drive to treat drug users in primary care was beginning to show results.

"It's really important that GPs keep up to date with the latest research, evidence, best practice and what people are doing in primary care settings. The extraordinary level of interest in this conference shows that family doctors are getting this message.

"Drug users have traditionally been a much neglected group within primary care – if it's difficult for drug users to access treatment, morbidity and mortality levels will be much higher, so it's really important for GPs to get involved at any level."

Dr Keen will present research outcomes from the Sheffield model of care showing clear reductions in heroin use and injecting behaviour among those treated.

In addition to the 61 per cent decrease in all criminal convictions there has been an even greater decrease in the most common drug related crimes: "We've seen a 70 per cent decrease in acquisitive crimes, such as burglary and shoplifting, in the year following treatment compared to the year before," Dr Keen said.

./2

Royal College Of General Practitioners

14 Princes Gate Hyde Park London SW7 1PU Tel: 020 7344 3135/6/7 Fax: 020 7823 8645

Figure 10.3 *Short sentences and paragraphs give punch to this release from the RCGP. Note the clear embargo details. The tiny 'th' in dates is not needed. It continues on second page with contact details*

Other topics for discussion and debate at the conference include psychological interventions in primary care, an update on buprenorphine prescribing, new directions in treating drug users and an update from Home Secretary David Blunkett on drugs, primary care and government policy.

Workshops will look at GPs with special interests in drug dependence, models of shared care, working with drug users who have alcohol problems, and how to get research in primary care off the ground.

The national conference attracts more than 300 delegates annually, including members of the primary care team, policy makers and academics who are involved in the development of primary care treatment of drug users.

Ends

Press Contact: Jacqueline Blissett – 020 7344 3135

NOTE TO EDITORS:

The 8th National Conference: Management of Drug Users in Primary Care will be held at the Hilton Hotel, Sheffield, from Thursday 15th – Friday 16th May 2003. Journalists wishing to attend should contact Jacqueline Blissett, 020 7344 3135, jblissett@rcgp.org.uk

Figure 10.3 *continued*

Titles

The title of the release should be typed (or word-processed) in bold capitals but not underlined. (Don't write a too-clever-by-half or facetious heading – it won't work!) It should say in as few words as possible what the release is about, and should not, if possible, run to more than one line. Use a present tense verb. If secondary subheadings or side-heads are needed, then these should be in upper and lower case, either in plain or bold type.

Some ideal examples of release titles are: GOVERNMENT ANNOUNCES NEW USER-FRIENDLY CROWN COPYRIGHT LICENCE FOR ELECTRONIC PUBLISHING SECTOR (Cabinet Office); BLUNKETT CUTS RED TAPE (Department for Education and Employment); WALKERS CRISPS KICK OFF SCOTTISH SPORTING HEROES PROMOTION (Walkers Snack Foods); NEW PREMISES HERALD A NEW IMAGE FOR BPIF (British Printing Industries Federation); VIRGIN PLUGS INTO THE ENERGY

British Printing Industries Federation

Press information

Farringdon Point, 29-35 Farringdon Road, London EC1M 3JF Tel (020) 7915 8368 Fax (020) 7915 8395

15 December 2003

BPIF Response to Pre-Budget Report

Cautious Welcome for Pre-Budget Report from BPIF

The Chancellor's bullish Pre-Budget Report was cautiously welcomed by the BPIF, as it contained sensible measures, of little surprise to the business fraternity, which have the potential to benefit printers. The benefits are reliant, of course, on whether the 2004 Budget retains the sensitivity to businesses set out in the report. Drawing on the themes of the 2003 Budget and the Treasury's recent reviews, the Pre-Budget Report covers initiatives to help more companies enjoy small and medium size enterprise status, improve access to finance and also take forward the government's skills strategy regarding training, eg:

1. Capital allowances: 40 per cent first year capital allowances extended to manufacturers with turnovers to £22.8 million. This will provide a cash flow benefit for smaller firms investing in plant and machinery. (As explained in the 2003 Budget the 100 per cent first year capital allowance for information and communication technology (ICT) will expire on 31st March 2004).

2. Access to growth capital for small businesses: a pilot round of small business investment companies (SBIC) will be launched, which have the potential to benefit printers because the SBICs will be encouraged to spread their funds across many companies who need relatively small amounts of funding and will increase the business mentoring available to SMEs. Enhancements to Venture Capital Trusts and Enterprise Investment Schemes are also to be made. The BPIF will continue to engage with the government on, for example, the question of how best to improve the Small Firms Loan Guarantee schemes.

3. Small and medium sized enterprise (SME) threshold: as announced earlier in the year the company law thresholds for SMEs will be increased to the maximum possible under

Figure 10.4   *The first page of a release from a national industry body, which sets out clearly the complex issues in response to a pre-Budget report*

MARKET (Virgin Energy); CONSUMER REALITY EXPOSES FINANCIAL SERVICES MYTHS (Deloitte Consulting).

Content

Be brief and factual and keep sentences short. Two sentences per paragraph is about right, and often just one sentence will be enough to get a point over. The opening paragraph should contain the essence of the story and display the news. Here you must answer who?/when?/where? questions in the same way that a reporter is required to do. For example, if a company chairman has made a statement, give his name and position, the date (if you say 'today' put the date in brackets afterwards so there can be no mistake), where the statement was made, and, if at a hotel, name it.

A trick here is to put the last two details in a second paragraph saying Mr So and So was speaking on (date) and (where) to save cluttering up the opening paragraph with detail that might easily obscure the point of the story. Never write 'recently' but always give the date.

Following paragraphs should expand on the story. Try not to let the copy run over to a second page. It will make the sub-editor's job much easier if you start with the main point, fill in the detail in the succeeding paragraphs and end with the least important point. Your news release can then be edited down with far less trouble.

Write in a factual style without flowery adjectives and superlatives or emotive words when you are describing products and services (*exciting* development). To repeat the point, don't put *recently* in a release if you can't be precise: say *last week/month* with the date in brackets. Avoid clichés, jargon words and comments as expressions of opinion. If you wish to make a comment about something, put it as a quote from someone in the organisation. Just stick to the facts and let them stand on their own without embellishment. It will be up to the journalist to put his or her interpretation on the story you are issuing.

If there is a lot of technical data to be included put this as an attachment. Similarly, you can attach a verbatim speech, providing reference to it is made in the covering release.

Layout and style

The copy must be typed double-spaced (though this is not

SOTHEBYS.COM

Press Release

Date: FOR IMMEDIATE RELEASE

Press Contacts:
Amanda Stücklin (tel: 020 7293 5169)
(email: amanda.stucklin@sothebys.com)
Helen Griffith (tel: 020 7 293 5168)
(email: helen.griffith@sothebys.com)

VINTAGE HEUER WATCHES IN SPECIAL ONLINE SALE ON SOTHEBYS.COM

A COMPREHENSIVE group of more than 60 classic Heuer watches from two distinguished private collections will be sold in a special online sale on SOTHEBYS.COM. The sale will run from September 30 until October 20, 2000. The collections have been consigned by Mr Jonathan Scatchard, who owns a jewellery and watch business in York and who has always been passionate about Heuer watches, and Mr Neil Duckworth, Managing Director of Tag Heuer U.K., who is selling his private collection.

Heuer watches are instantly recognisable for their distinctive, innovative and often unique designs. The company was founded in 1860 by Edouard Heuer and since that day has been one of the leaders in sports watch technology, focusing on assisting explorers, technicians and those in the sporting world to deal with the growing problem of accurate timing to within

Figure 10.5 *Sothebys has got its act together for this announcement. Note email contact details*

essential for online releases). The reason for this is to give the sub-editor plenty of space to make changes.

Put at least a couple of lines between the heading and the first paragraph. Put extra space between paragraphs.

Do not underline any of the copy. This is the universal mark used by printers for copy to be set in italics. Do not set any of the text in italics or bold in the forlorn hope that it will be seen as more important. If a title of a book, film or article is used within the text, put it in single quotes.

Type on one side of the paper (white, A4) and if there is a continuation sheet, type 'More' at the foot of the page. Do not break a

NEWS RELEASE

The Advertising Association
Abford House, 15 Wilton Road, London SW1V 1NJ
Telephone: 020 7828 2771   Fax: 020 7931 0376
e-mail: aa@adassoc.org.uk   web: http://www.adassoc.org.uk

Issued on Monday 21 June 2004

AA PUBLISHES *ADVERTISING STATISTICS YEARBOOK 2004*

Advertising expenditure in the United Kingdom rose by 2.4% to £17.2 billion in 2003 (before accounting for inflation) with the strongest growth taking place in the last quarter, according to the Advertising Association's *Advertising Statistics Yearbook 2004*, researched and compiled on its behalf by the World Advertising Research Center (WARC). This annual growth rate equates to an increase of 1.1% in real terms.

UK Advertising Expenditure 1993-2003

Year	Expenditure (current £m)	Annual % change	
		Current Prices	Constant prices
1993	10,136	10.9%	8.8%
1994	11,026	8.8%	6.0%
1996	12,080	9.6%	6.9%
1997	13,340	10.4%	8.5%
1998	14,415	8.1%	6.4%
1999	15,412	6.9%	5.5%
2000	16,988	10.2%	9.4%
2001	16,537	-2.7%	-3.8%
2002	16,817	1.7%	0.4%
2003	17,227	2.4%	1.1%

Note: Constant price data calculated using the Consumer Prices Index
Source: AA's *Advertising Statistics Yearbook 2004*, WARC.

Advertising expenditure has recovered steadily since the decline of 2001, but annual growth rates are still below those of the 1990s.

Figure 10.6 *Clear presentation of statistics in this release. The story continues with background notes for editors and further statistical data*

paragraph at the end of a page; if necessary take the whole para-graph over to the second page rather than leave a few words dangling (as a 'widow', the printer would say) at the top of the second page.

Leave a decent margin on each side, about 30mm (1¼ inch). Do not try to achieve justified type when both sides are aligned. It is a waste of your time!

Use double quotes for direct quotations (the actual words spoken); this is standard newspaper style. For reported speech follow the style in this extract from *The Times*: Eddie George [now known as Sir Edward George] *admitted* yesterday... he *suggested* there *were* some signs...

At the close of the copy, type END or ENDS in capitals. If there are special points to be made for the attention of the editor, such as explanations of technical terms or how to obtain follow-up infor-mation, put these against a side-heading 'Note to Editor'. If possible, give a word count. This is usually easy to ascertain with reference to the spellcheck facility provided by most software packages. The sub-editor can then easily calculate the amount of space the copy will occupy when it is typeset.

Embargoes

Journalists dislike embargoes – which is a request to withhold publication until a specific time and date. Avoid them if possible, as they are not binding on the media and are there to give the jour-nalist time for research or follow-up before a speech, or in advance of an announcement by a company or organisation. If you decide to issue a release under embargo, make this clear above the title of the release. A suitable form of words would be:

> **EMBARGO**: THIS INFORMATION IS ISSUED IN ADVANCE FOR YOUR CONVENIENCE. IT IS NOT FOR PUBLICATION, BROAD-CAST, OR USE ON CLUB TAPES BEFORE (TIME) ON (date).

Alternatively the embargo notice could simply state, 'Not for use before 00.00 hours (date)'. The wording of embargoes for releases giving advance information on winners of awards requires care to ensure that details do not leak out in advance of the presentation event. An example is the wording for the Charter Mark Awards 1996 issued by the Office of Public Service, the Cabinet Office:

EMBARGO: THIS MATERIAL IS PROVIDED SO THAT RECIPI-
ENTS MAY APPROACH THE NAMED CONTACTS IN ANY OF
THE 1996 AWARD WINNING ORGANISATIONS FOR INFORMA-
TION ABOUT THEIR WIN, PROVIDED THERE IS NO PUBLICA-
TION OR PUBLICITY IN ANY MEDIA, ELECTRONIC OR
WRITTEN, BEFORE 0001 HOURS GMT ON MONDAY 2
DECEMBER, 1996.

A simplified embargo notice with just the time and date can also be
used so long as the restriction is absolutely clear and unambiguous.

Issuing the release

Timing the release is fairly critical. If you are mailing it, don't
forget that the post can take at least a day, and a release to a trade
paper or magazine posted on a Friday night will not be seen until
the following Monday morning. It's better to send it by messenger
or to fax it, providing you are not sending photographs. Email is
popular nowadays, but be aware that journalists have to sift
through dozens, if not hundreds, of releases daily. A telephone call
to the news desk saying a release is coming and will be on their
screens (or has been sent) might help. Try it and, if it works, use it
regularly. But there is little to beat hard copy on paper.

Is it news?

There is no point in sending out a news release if it is not news.
You will only annoy the journalist if you do and your hard work
will be wasted. So has your release got news value? The short
answer is: does the news editor think it will interest the reader?
News is something not known before.

To quote Pat Bowman, former head of public relations for
Lloyds Bank:

> News value is relative; minor stories make news on a slow day. Only
> big news counts on a busy day. A boring product story may be valu-
> able news to a trade paper, but no publication with a general reader-
> ship would look at it. How it is written will make all the difference in
> perception of a story: if it is written in a lively, interesting way it is
> more likely to be seen as important; if it is expressed in a boring
> fashion, using tedious, hard-to-grasp, waffly words and phrases
> then it will be considered dull. Then the only future for it is the waste
> bin.

17 April 2003

AMATEURS: THE EXPERTS

**The Natural History Museum and English Nature seek expertise
of Britain's 100,000 amateur naturalists**

To help save some of Britain's most threatened species, professional scientists are calling on the UK's 100,000 amateur naturalists to share their expertise. The Natural History Museum and English Nature will run a series of projects across the UK as part of the new Amateurs: the Experts scheme, with the aim of encouraging amateur naturalists to help monitor and record Britain's wildlife.

'I've always been driven by a love of nature and a need to understand my local environment,' commented Anthony Keith Bridgett, Honorary Secretary for the Leek & District Fly Fishing Association, and participant in the scheme. 'As a fly-fisherman of 60 years, over the last 30 years I've seen a definite decline in river insects, which were once abundant. As fly-fishers spend so much time actually in the water, I think we're in the ideal position to investigate this trend,' he said.

Johannes Vogel, Head of the UK Biodiversity Programme at the Natural History Museum and project co-ordinator for Amateurs: the Experts agrees. 'Sharing knowledge and expertise is essential for us to maximise our efforts to conserve the UK's wildlife,' he says. 'There's a long history, reaching back several centuries, of amateurs playing a major role in researching and preserving Britain's species. But this is the first time such a wide range of British organisations have attempted to bring the full wealth of amateur and professional knowledge together.'

Amateurs: the Experts projects include:

- **Riverfly identification and survey workshops**
  Since 1997, workshops have been run by amateur naturalists at the John Spedan Lewis Trust for the Advancement of the Natural Sciences for fly-fishermen and river keepers to increase their understanding of the identification, monitoring and surveying of riverflies. A wider collaboration, including specialists from the Natural History Museum and the National Recording Scheme Officers, is now delivering regional workshops teaching anglers identification techniques and encouraging them to contribute data to the National Trichoptera (caddis flies or sedges) and

*Press Office The Natural History Museum Cromwell Road London SW7 5BD
Telephone 020 7942 5654 Facsimile 020 7942 5354*

D&P0945

Figure 10.7 *The first page of a well-produced release. The active voice would improve it: prefer 'call' to are 'calling'. The two-deck headline makes a meal of it*

Tabloids, says Bowman, are likely to be influenced by the entertainment and novelty value of a story, while the quality press will be more interested in stories that excite the intellect and imagination. Immediacy can also have an effect: it can outweigh importance in the assessment of news value, particularly for TV and radio. 'Don't try to bamboozle journalists into thinking that the story you are putting out is a good one when there is nothing new in it at all,' says Bowman. It could be an utter waste of time.

Robert Hornby's *The Press in Modern Society*, first published in 1965 but still relevant today, gives penetrating thoughts on news and news value. To summarise Hornby: what may appear as news in a provincial newspaper holding a dominant position in a city will bear little relationship in presentation to the same news splashed across the front page of a national daily. It is like comparing a seaside revue with a West End musical. So what are the basic elements of a news story? First, it must be something new. Other factors can be grouped under three headings – importance, human interest and topicality.

Importance can mean a well-known person connected with the story, perhaps a politician or public figure, especially if they have been in the news before.

Human interest is exemplified by something that is interesting to the many rather than the few. Anything pathetic, or that causes indignation, and the topics of prices, crime or abuse of privilege gets read. Other people's big financial gains, rags-to-riches stories, romances, children, animal welfare, good/bad luck items, the unexpected, the surprising and the unusual always attract attention. Most people prefer reading about people to things: many column inches of publicity can easily be lost if releases ignore the human angle.

Journalists' requirements are changing in line with the instant delivery of news on television and radio. In consequence, newspapers are increasingly filling their pages with background stories and feature articles on such subjects as lifestyles, health, entertainment, sport, home and garden. These subjects are all fertile ground for human interest stories.

Topicality means facts about a subject of intense current interest, with excitement, danger and rapid movement (like chases and police hunts); well-known faces must be photographed in easily recognised places and backgrounds to provide maximum impact and make for easy recognition. A great deal of the trivial derives its news value from such topicality, especially in the popular press.

Study newspaper style

Look at newspapers to see how journalists write: whether broadsheet or tabloid, extremes of style determine the way different newspapers approach a given story. The former will probably give far more detail, while the latter will tend to oversimplify, leaving little room for intelligent interpretation.

Write to catch the eye of the reader in the same way as the journalist does. One thing is certain: a 'new' story or one that has not been published before has got news value; and if it is exclusive it will have an even better chance of publication.

No puffs please

Releases must not become blatant advertising messages on behalf of the client company or other organisations. If you put out an advertisement under the guise of a news story it is sure to put the editor off and ruin your reputation as a public relations professional into the bargain.

These so-called 'puffs', which attempt to gain editorial space, should properly be paid-up advertisements. But a new product or service can of course be a news story for release to the specialist press covering the industry sector you are covering.

Releases to the specialist press

If you write a release containing technical matter there is no profit in using jargon meaningless to the average reader, or writing in a highbrow way to woo white-coated boffins.

Where releases to the national media are on scientific or financial subjects, write in simple, concise language that will be understood by a lay audience. The only place for the technicalities and jargon of the industry or business is the trade press. Few technical journalists are specialists and fully trained in the technologies they write about. If you provide copy that needs little editing your release is far less likely to be changed than if you give them gobbledygook, however well intentioned that may be.

HEIDELBERG

Speedmaster SM52-4 put under surveillance and then taken in

The Staffordshire Police printing inplant is to take delivery of a Speedmaster SM52-4 this month, replacing a two-colour Sakurai Oliver.

Acting production team leader Mel Mincher says: "Over the past two years we have seen the work mix change from a 50-50 split between forms and four-colour work to about 90% four-colour. Forms have been superseded by computers and e-mail. This investment reflects the change in demand."

The inplant already has a two-colour SM 52 which has worked well and which will be able to handle four-colour overspill in two passes.

A recent four-colour contract was for brochures on tackling crime against race and religion, work which was used nationwide by all police forces.

This reflects a change at the Staffordshire Police inplant. It plans to take on a larger amount of external work in future and the press will be a help with that.

Next year it is also hoping to add CtP as a complement. Its finishing facilities are currently up to date.

August 2004

Figure 10.8 *Release from Plus Point PR. Strong branding for press manufacturer Heidelberg. The snappy sentences and opening quote make this an ideal trade press story. Thoughtful headline*

What journalists want: a specialist view

Diana Thompson, managing director of Plus Point PR, a specialist consultancy for the graphic arts industry, has surveyed editors and freelance journalists to see how they wish to receive copy and pictures. It seems that there is a 50/50 split between those wanting releases by post and those by email. Faxes are out.

As far as photographs are concerned, she doesn't bother with hard copy prints any more. Says Thompson: 'Everyone wants digital CDs with press packs or emailed news shots these days. CDs provide the opportunity for higher resolution images, but for releases 300 dpi [dots per square inch] and 1Mb as a jpg file is safe for transmission and an acceptable quality for most trade papers.' Never send a picture in a Word file, she advises, simply because they take long downloading time and are often unusable.

For releases going by post, she notifies editors that there is a picture available. For her key target trade publications, she sends the digital photo directly to the editor with a copy to the production editor, indicating the story it is to accompany and often attaching a text file.

It is crucial, she says, that public relations people send copy and pictures in a way that is acceptable and helpful to the journalists. The worst thing they can do is to send a press release and pictures in several versions by post, fax and email all at once. 'That just duplicates work and can even result in a story being written twice. Imagine the time and waste that involves.'

Only good stories will reach news desks

Most releases go by email to newspapers and broadcasting outlets these days. Only a very few are sent by post: gone are the spikes and dustcart-sized bins for dud copy. This means that copytasters are faced with a thousand or more stories on their screens every day: only the ones that are newsworthy, or have some human or perhaps financial angle, will be read and passed to the news desk. If it is about a specialist subject, then send it to the correspondent dealing with it, say the one covering financial, health or media stories.

Releases that come from news agencies such as the Press Association (020 7963 7000), Reuters (020 7250 1122) and Bloomberg UK (020 7330 7500) have a good chance as they will have already been sifted and sorted first by agency subs.

It is important that releases have short headlines giving the main point of the story, preferably in the present tense with no fancy typography or gimmicks in a vain attempt to attract attention. The originating firm or organisation should be clearly shown with embargo details (if needed) and background information and contact details. Even more important is for mailing lists to be kept up to date: it is next to useless sending a release to a named correspondent who left a year ago.

Freelance journalists, on the other hand, usually work on home computers and dislike having their in-boxes clogged up with emailed press releases. Says freelance Michael Watts: 'At least for the moment I am not, in general, giving out my email address. I much prefer to have releases in the post.'

Remember: if the story is a good one, it will have a chance of publication. And on a slow news day, it has an even better one.

Words and phrases journalists hate

Journalists' pet hates include enormity (doesn't mean huge), the chattering classes, ironically (unless in the proper sense), luvvies, crippled/disabled or any kind of disability, punter, legendary, luxury, fulsome, 'creeping' Americanisms, blocks (verb), 'gender' words like career girl, signal or signalling (unless a transport story) and, needless to say, needless to say.

They also reject any needless or wasted word. Redundant words (in italics): appear *to be*, *brand* new, *close* proximity, crisis *situation*, *frown* on his face, few *in number*, include *among them*, merge/join *together*, *more* preferable/superior, if and *when*, *invited* guest, *new* tradition, penetrate *into*, *on the question of*, *passing* phase. The reader will find plenty more in *Essential English for Journalists* (Pimlico Random House) by that master of style, Harold Evans.

Journalists are always on the look-out for clichés, flowery adjectives and overused expressions. If something can be said or written with fewer words or in a shorter way, they will cut without hesitation.

Don't forget the internet

Most large companies and organisations now make their press releases available on the internet, and they can be printed out if required. Leading organisations in the communications field, such as the Institute of Public Relations, the Institute of Practitioners in Advertising, the Advertising Association and the national media organisations all have internet sites from which their press releases can be downloaded. Again, it is important that contact names and day/night telephone numbers are included, as well as background information.

If you are setting up a virtual press office (VPO) to provide a 24-hour service for journalists on the internet, ensure that access is simple and that contact details, including email addresses, are included. Allow for pictures and graphics to be downloaded, and update regularly.

Video news releases – for broadcasting stories

Broadcasters need stories too. Airtime takes a lot of filling on a slow news day. But your story will be in hot competition with items from the station's own reporters, news agencies and free-lancers. To be of interest to a TV show, there must be strong visual appeal. The video news release (VNR) is usually presented in two forms: a short tape of only a minute or two, tightly edited and ready for transmission, and another containing interviews and background.

If you go to a specialist company to produce a VNR, costs can range from £5,000 to £15,000 for UK transmission, much more for broadcast abroad. Another route is to upload your VNR to the station's website by tape or CD ROM. DIY videos or CDs have only a slender chance of success unless the story is a heart-stopping one. The production of a professional VNR is expensive and you may not always get the results you would like. Question the company carefully on its record of success before signing up.

The virtual press office speeds PR service

According to studies by Benchmark Research reported in *PR Week* in 2004, 88 per cent of journalists writing about a company visit the firm's website for information. Just over half of them feel that enquires are better handled by websites than by traditional press offices. (The full research paper may be downloaded for free from www.internetpresscentre.com/research.)

While it is true that most websites provide immediate access to press releases and statements, it takes time and effort on the part of the public relations staff to post it on the site, and this may not be all that well executed if deadlines are tight. Furthermore, the press enquiries section of the site is mostly restricted to little beyond the provision of releases, with no service for pictures, live audio soundbites and video interviews to give both immediacy and fuller information.

Very often the needs of the journalist are not provided for, with the 'press room' page of websites being regarded by management as something of a poor relation, even though it is often believed by the PR department to the be-all and end-all of its communications objectives. On the whole, the website press room will only be able to supply a 'scattergun' distribution, with no ability to target specific media and audiences, and with 74 per cent going straight to the screen trashbin.

The answer lies in the virtual press office (VPO) such as that provided by Glide Technologies. The service, under the name of the Internet Press Centre (IPC), is a software tool used to build a state-of-the-art VPO for a company's website. In short, the IPC allows the PR department to publish press information such as releases, photographs, interviews and so on through its online press office.

Says Glide Technologies managing director Sam Phillips: 'With this service, PR staff can build multimedia press communications giving them the opportunity to enhance their stories with sound, video and photographs. Once published on the site, any release can be automatically distributed to a targeted press list to named journalists if required.'

Once the information has been sent out, the PRO is then able to review the distribution list and see who had actually seen the story and everything that went with it. For anyone interested, Sam Phillips says the corporate entry level for setting up a VPO is typically around £17,000 to cover website design, configuration and consultancy to ensure the service meets the company's public relations needs. An ongoing support and licence charge applies once the VPO is in operation. For more details, log on to www. glidetechnologies.com which provides an online brochure giving what it calls an 'Online dashboard for PR' listing the main features.

The verbal content of anything put out on the VPO is, of course, the responsibility of the public relations professional.

Advice from the CIPR

In the helpful *PR Guide to Virtual Press Office* available to members on the CIPR website (www.cipr.co.uk), Pauline Christie, managing director of the Internet PR Company, says that it is important to provide a facility where journalists can register to receive automatically press releases as soon as they are posted on the VPO. All that is needed is name, email address and name of publication. At all costs, do not force journalists to register for access to your VPO. 'Journalists hate doing this, and when confronted with a registration screen, no matter how brief, may decide to look elsewhere for subject matter.'

The guide gives tips on building an image bank, virtual press packs and making the VPO a separate website with a simple link from the home page. It stresses that the content of the VPO must be fresh and up to date. It should contain all the information about your company or organisation that you don't want a journalist to get from somewhere else.

Releases for radio transmission

Radio is equally demanding, if not more so. It is better to mail, fax or email copy to radio stations rather than sending audio tapes, though if you have close personal contacts this helps to get your story on air. The specialist VNR company can also arrange for syndicated audio tapes to be distributed to national and regional radio stations.

Again, research your audience well and try to provide items that will fit timewise in your chosen slot. Don't send a 15-minute piece that would take up half the allotted time of a current affairs programme, or a news story of a minute for a slot of only a few seconds!

COMMISSIONED ARTICLES

If you are asked to write an article by a newspaper or magazine, or if you put up an idea for a feature, the content and prime thrust of the piece should be discussed with the editor well in advance. The brief subsequently agreed must be scrupulously followed. If you diverge from it then it is likely that the editor will ask for amendments, some of which may be substantial. Worse than that, changes may be made that you know nothing about until the article is printed – and then it is too late!

Write in the style of the publication and keep to the number of words requested. Nothing is more annoying for an editor if the article is well over the length specified and won't fit into the space allotted for it. If that happens, then your copy will be cut, and that may defeat your objectives. Similarly, if you commission someone else in the organisation to write the article, then be sure that the brief is followed, even if you have to exert some persuasion.

Don't forget to include illustrations. Most editors will require photographs, drawings, graphs or tables to support the points you are making or just to catch the reader's eye. Give the piece a title and put the author's name – the by-line – underneath. Make sure the article has shape: a beginning, a middle and an end. And if you type the number of words at the end, the editor will be a friend for life. But above all, keep to the deadline!

AT A GLANCE

- Make sure releases are properly targeted.
- Give full contact details, and show the date of issue.
- Be brief, factual; type double-spaced on white A4.
- Embargoed releases: ensure clear publication restrictions.
- Is it news? If not, you've wasted your time.
- Don't try to turn a 'puff' into news.
- Write the way journalists do. Keep to the point.
- Follow newspaper style for snappy stories.
- Don't forget to send releases to news agencies.
- Put your releases on your company's website; ensure easy access.
- It's essential to keep mailing lists up to date.
- 74 per cent of journalists trash wrongly targeted releases.
- Consider specialist services for VNRs and VPOs.
- Agree the content of feature articles in advance; keep to the agreed wordage.

11

Captions: how to handle them

Always provide captions for any photographs or illustrations accompanying news releases; these are used extensively in company annual reports and brochures. Care is essential in their preparation and handling: too often captions are left to the end, with the result that the caption lets down the illustration and the news story or article.

The important point about captions is that they lead the reader to the body copy. They provide an instant point of interest and will often turn a magazine 'page flipper' into a reader. Much thought should go into how a caption is written and presented, for if it misleads or contains errors, the communication can be irreparably spoilt.

PHOTO CAPTIONS WITH RELEASES

The caption to a photograph or illustration either accompanying a news release or sent separately as a caption story, is as important as the picture itself. If it fails to describe the person, product or service, all the effort and cost involved can be wasted. It can turn into a public relations disaster waiting to happen: once the photograph with its caption has left your hands there is little you can do to put matters right if you have misnamed someone or misspelt their name. If you are issuing a picture as an attachment to an emailed release, make it clear who or what the subject is.

Only when the picture is published do you realise that you have made a mistake – you go hot all over – but by then the damage is done. Although you may know who the people are in a picture, others may not, and will rely on you to tell them!

Caption content and style

Captions should be brief, certainly not exceeding 15 to 20 words, and reveal the content of the photo. Put a heading, typed double spaced, and give the name of the issuing organisation, company or consultancy with date, contact name, address and telephone/fax numbers. Refer to the source organisation, service or product.

If the photo shows a person or group of people, put job titles and names from left to right. When a well-known personality is featured, write the caption round the VIP, not someone else, even if you feel you ought to mention the chairman first. Photographic prints are expensive – so take care that the caption does justice to the story.

Captions for the press

Always use a stiff-backed envelope when sending out photographs or illustrations. Do not write on the back of prints as Biro or pencil marks can show through and make the picture useless for reproduction. Captions should be attached with strips of Sellotape. Never glue or paste them to the backs of photographs; just stick them on lightly so they protrude from the bottom of the print and can be read in conjunction with the picture.

Copyright issues

When you send out photographs to the press, always be aware of the copyright issue. News editors and picture desks will assume that photographs received from public relations people, especially when they accompany a release, will be free of copyright restrictions.

Photographs should be rubber-stamped on the back with a statement of the copyright position; ideally, similar wording should appear on the caption itself. Never issue a photograph or illustration unless you are sure who owns the copyright. (The owner of the copyright is the author or creator – members of the Institute of Public Relations can obtain advice on legal points such as this by logging on to the member-only area of IPR website, www.ipr.org.uk, which provides much useful information.)

CAPTIONS IN PUBLICATIONS

Clear, concise captioning is the hallmark of a well-produced, stylish publication. In many cases, particularly with annual reports, shareholders get no further than the pictures. One way of getting the reader to take notice of the text is to have an arresting photograph with the caption leading on to a particular point.

Distinguishing captions from text

Set off captions from the text by using smaller type, different typeface, or by setting in italics or bold if the text is in plain or roman type. You can position captions in the margin, away from the bulk of the text. Sometimes it is possible to reverse out the caption on a photograph if there is a sufficiently dark area. There is a danger of the caption being unreadable if it is reversed out of a light-toned part of the picture.

An effective way to make captions stand out from the text is to print them in a second colour, preferably using one of the colours chosen for corporate house style. But take care that the colour is a strong one: if it is a pastel shade then the wording will be lost on white paper! If you set two- or three-word headings as intros to captions then you give added visual impact.

Always describe the picture or drawing, unless it is purely for decoration. State essential details, but not what the eye can see for itself. If it is an action shot say what is happening. Even if you think it is obvious, it might not be so to the reader. It is infuriating, for instance, to see an interesting photograph featuring a new product and management team, and not know what it illustrates or who the people are. Don't forget that a wrongly named person could mean a furious client, possibly a reprint, or even – horror of horrors – a libel action.

Draw-down quotes

The draw-down quote is a useful device for livening up a text-full page devoid of what is called 'colour weight' – ie with a total lack of light and shade provided by illustrations or headings. The editor takes a few words from a quote within the copy – usually a pithy or significant comment – and puts it in bold type positioned prominently on the page, perhaps between columns in the middle of the page, or at the top. This layout idea, which amounts to a caption or subheading to the text, also acts as a handy space-filler. But its prime use is to give sparkle to a drab page.

Lure the reader to the text

The caption should arrest attention and lure the reader to the text unless the photograph or illustration is there just to brighten up the page and not meant to tell a story in itself. Write crisply; you don't want just a 'label' making a bland, boring statement.

The caption might be read and understood while the text may not: the reader may not get as far as that! Make sure it contains a verb, preferably in the present tense, and if possible some news value. Journalists often get stories from the captions in annual reports, and from house journals and brochures.

Captions for charts

The chart caption should describe the essential finding or purpose and lead the reader to the relevant part of the text. With graphs and tables ensure that legends and headings are clear and unambiguous. Make sure that graph axes are explained and show the appropriate units.

Captioning groups of photographs

When you have several photographs or illustrations to caption, arrange the captions together in a block and number them. If there are several photographs of people, or a photograph of a group of individuals, it is convenient to have an outline line drawing showing people's positions, with a numbered key for identification.

Take time and trouble in the wording and presentation of captions. Increased readership and improved communication will inevitably result.

AT A GLANCE

- The caption can be as important as the story.
- Keep brief: confine it to 15–20 words.
- Be aware of the copyright issue.
- Distinguish captions from text by size and typeface style.
- Use draw-down quotes to fill space.
- Avoid verbless 'label' captions.
- Explain graph axes and show units.
- Include a numbered key with group photographs.

12

What editing is all about

The success of any newspaper, magazine, or current affairs broadcast depends on the skills of the editorial team from editor to junior reporter. But it is the subeditor, or sub for short, who gets the copy ready for printing or transmission. The sub's job is to ensure that news stories, articles and scripts coming in from reporters, foreign correspondents and freelancers are written to style, make sense, are newsworthy, and above all are not only interesting but gripping to reader or listener, something that makes them read on or keep listening, no matter what.

What, in fact, *do* they do? To answer that you have to realise that editors are usually one step ahead of the daily (or weekly, perhaps monthly) task of producing the newspaper, magazine or programme. Their job is largely to decide what appears and how it will be presented, to set the policy, the tone, in relation to the audience.

The task of getting the words right is handled by the subeditors, copy tasters and finally the chief subeditor, who decides how long an item should be and how it should be treated, with perhaps a referral to the editor if there is a problem. Is it newsworthy? Is it of sufficient interest to be given a page, a column or two, a 30-second soundbite or a two-minute interview on the *Today* programme?

Individual newspapers and other media outlets organise their editorial offices in many different ways. There is no set system: it all depends on whether it is print or broadcast, trade or technical, or consumer magazine. The objectives are the same, to make the written and spoken word fit for publication or transmission.

Let us now examine what the desk editorial team look for in every story or feature that reaches them by post, email, fax and telephone. Any readers wishing to delve deeper into the points raised in the following sections should refer to the relevant chapters in this book.

NEWS STORIES

All copy coming in from whatever source is subject to editing. That is that kernel rule that applies throughout journalism and publishing. No story, no article, no script ever escapes the eye of the subeditor, news editor, even the editor him- or herself. And no release will ever be 'used', as the jargon goes, without being subjected to severe editing or, more likely, a full rewrite. The only exceptions are the local freesheet desperate for free copy to fill the space round advertisements and small-circulation trade papers which also need to fill their pages with stories that are just, and only just, good enough for publication. So what do these subeditors and news teams look for in your carefully crafted copy?

Is it newsworthy?

This is the first hurdle for any news story in daily and evening newspapers. It must first get past the copy taster, the person who decides whether the piece has news value. Is it something that is not generally known? Is there a human angle? A financial success or failure? Is it, in fact, newsworthy? If your piece doesn't pass this test there's only one place for it: the trash can on the screen or the bin on the floor.

In the same way, if a news programme or paper receives stories that do not seem credible, or as journalists say don't 'stand up', 'have legs' (and will run and run) or are just plain boring, they will quickly be discarded. In trade papers, it may be the assistant editor, news editor or perhaps the editor who decides. The result is the same: if it isn't news out it goes.

Accuracy

After news value, the editors and subeditors must decide if the story is credible, and consider whether it is factually correct. Accuracy is naturally the responsibility of the reporter, the writer, or whoever originates the story, article or script, but it is the sub who is always on the look-out for something amiss, that doesn't add up. Is the spelling of names correct: is it Clarke with an 'e' or not? Is the spelling of company names right? Are there any trade names that should be capitalised? If there are statistics or figures quoted, are they mathematically correct or are they doubtful in some respect?

The intro

Is the essence of the story in the opening paragraph(s)? Does the rest of it follow in a logical sequence, with following facts in descending order of importance? Can it be sharpened up to catch the reader's attention?

Grammar

Are the tenses right? Does verb agree with subject? Is there a verb missing; is it the right one? Are there any double negatives, and if so, do they make sense? Should it be who or whom, which or that? Are there too many adjectives, particularly flowery ones, or unnecessary adverbs? Has the writer used active 'doing' verbs and avoided the passive voice? Is it written in plain English? Is the text easy to understand? Have the basic rules of grammar been followed throughout?

Style

Has the writer stuck to the style rules of the publication? Are there needless capitals? Are there American -ize verb endings instead of the more usual -ise used in Britain? Is there over-hyphenation? Are the sentences and paragraphs too long? Should there be more par breaks? Has the writer followed the rules for numbers and dates?

Redundancies

The sub will be on constant watch for the wasted word, the one that can be deleted without any loss of sense or meaning. Are there any sentences or parts of them that can be deleted, shortened or rewritten to get rid of wording that adds little or nothing? Is there a single word that can replace a phrase? Is there inelegant repetition?

Non-sequiturs

Does one statement, word or phrase following another make sense? Is the sentence relevant to the preceding one? Does one paragraph follow on logically from the one before? Are there any ambiguities? Does the story itself make sense?

Punctuation

Are there too many commas in one sentence? Are there semicolons when full stops would be better? Has the writer a sense of rhythm, and given the piece balance by providing a mix of short and longer sentences? Are there exclamation marks to be deleted? Is the position of punctuation in direct quotes right?

Clichés and tautology

Are there clichés to be written out? Any repetition to be eliminated? Are there overused and stale words and expressions to be replaced? Is there a better word or way of putting something?

Jargon

Are there unfamiliar or foreign words that might not be understood? Are there any statements that will make sense only to specialist audiences? Are there abbreviations likely to be meaningless to the average audience?

A job to do

As you will have seen, the subeditors and the editorial team have a job on their hands once they get your copy. And remember that newspapers and broadcasting outlets will have hundreds, possibly thousands, of stories to go through every day. Your story is just one of them, and it must be as newsworthy as it is interesting, as meaningful and as well-written as it can possibly be for it to have any chance of publication or transmission.

FEATURE ARTICLES

Journalists working on feature articles are not under the same pressure as those on the news desks. Nevertheless, the features editorial team on either a newspaper or magazine will be asking themselves much the same questions as their news colleagues, but with some significant differences. Sentences and paragraphs can run longer, there will be photographs and illustrations to be accommodated and captioned so that pages will not turn out to be long slabs of grey type. The editors will make sure that the page is livened up by headings, crossheads, standfirsts (short wording above article titles), boxed paragraphs and draw-down quotes.

The feature article will give creative opportunities for alliterations and play on words in headlines to provide both humour and freshness. These editorial tricks are not generally used in news pages apart perhaps from the tabloids once termed 'red tops'. In order to encourage the reader to go right to the end of an article and not give it a quick flip, the sub will try to make the article interesting by making it lively, relevant, arresting and, at the very least, worthwhile and useful.

RADIO AND TV BROADCASTS

You will certainly be a fortunate public relations practitioner if you can get your client's products mentioned on air, particularly by the BBC, which has a veto on references to named goods and services. Other broadcasters also have restrictions on product mentions and you must be prepared to have them deleted.

Much the same applies to financial services and products which may be of interest to business programmes on both radio and TV. But you may be lucky if there is company news that is of sufficient interest for transmission to a range of viewers and listeners.

Many of the principles outlined above will be followed by the editorial teams involved with radio and TV broadcasts, with one exception: the words spoken on both radio and TV must be clearly enunciated so that they can be understood widely. If the script when read out is unintelligible to listener and viewer then there is no point in broadcasting it. This means that scripts must be free of words that are difficult to speak, for instance whilst and amongst instead of while and among (*whilst/amongst* are largely banned nowadays). Other sibilants, words pronounced with a 'hissing' noise, should be used with caution.

The first test for a script

Let Pat Bowman, former head of public relations at Lloyds Bank, once a frequent broadcaster and now presenter of an audio magazine for the blind, add his experience. He says that the first test for any broadcast script is to read it aloud, no matter who will eventually speak it. 'That will quickly show up any awkward words or phrases that need to be adjusted. Better still, tape the script yourself and play it back: that can be very illuminating. Most important of all, keep the structure simple, avoiding complexities like too many dependent clauses and, incidentally, allowing the speaker to breathe.'

If you are writing a script for yourself, you will need to be aware of the principles of pronunciation. Assume you are using Received Pronunciation (see Chapter 16) and know whether the stress goes on the first syllable (*a*dult) or on the second (dis*tri*bute). Ignore also the 'myths' of never ending a sentence with a preposition or starting a sentence with and or but. A *to* or *in* at the end of a sentence is far more acceptable in speech than in writing: it doesn't seem to matter at all.

Make the piece short and accurate

Another comment comes from Ken Brazier, a former BBC broadcaster with first-hand experience as a foreign correspondent in the Middle East and later as editor of the Overseas News Service. He says the way to get the best out of your script so that it appeals to the listener is to make the piece short, clear and of course accurate and meaningful, just as you would for the press. 'Before starting to write, think the piece through from beginning to end, sort the facts into logical order so that they link easily from one to another. As a rough guide aim at one major fact or point for each sentence.' Even if space is short, he says, it can be useful to repeat an essential fact such as a location or subject description: 'If the listener misses a point he can't refer back in the way he can with the written word.'

ON-SCREEN EDITING

With so many stories and other copy coming in via emails and the internet, the subeditor must be skilled in on-screen editing. Public relations practitioners too must develop these skills, for they will be presented with on-screen copy from press officers, and from people in sales and marketing, customer service and financial departments. Some of this copy may be suitable and not require editing, while other material may have to be subbed, some of it heavily, and perhaps rewritten for a printed document or press release. On-screen editing may be the only way to turn a hopeless cliché-strewn, turgid article into a publishable piece.

The best way is to make a copy, paste it into a new document and work on that. There are software programs to make on-screen editing easier: check with your IT department.

TECHNICAL EDITING

Many of the attributes and skills of the features sub are also needed for editing technical publications, from trade magazines and brochures to sales leaflets and instruction manuals. The difference is that some knowledge of the industry or trade is needed so that accuracy is preserved. Most journalists pick up the tricks of the trade, know who the personalities are and how the particular business works fairly quickly.

There is no reason why a PR person with an enquiring mind and a way with words cannot do the same and become an almost overnight 'expert', able to pump out a release or article for the house newspaper just as well as a specialist journalist can. But remember that, unlike with newspapers and consumer magazines, the audience will know more about the subject than you do.

Special care will be needed when describing technical procedures, particularly in spelling unfamiliar terms; it is always worthwhile to spend time with the expert who can explain functions and how they work before you get anywhere near the keyboard. Then you can show the specialist a draft and get the OK. Take great care in the checking process: the more people who see the copy in advance, the better, and the less chance of something going wrong. Put plenty of leeway in the production schedule to allow for last-minute changes.

If the item is for publication in, say, the house magazine, mark up the copy clearly so that the operator has a clear run. And when the proofs come in, make sure a set goes to the specialists and technical staff for approval. The same goes for pamphlets, brochures and instruction manuals.

EDITING OTHER TYPES OF DOCUMENT

No particular skills apart from those covered in this chapter are needed for editing documents like minutes of meetings or contact reports. Such paperwork should be totally factual, free of opinion unless it is contained in reported speech. Minutes and reports should be confined to matters agreed at a meeting, not a long-winded who-said-what account of the discussion. See Chapter 13.

EDIT YOURSELF

This chapter closes with the firm message that it is essential that you edit your copy as you go along. Since most of us type with word processor or computer, this is no problem: it is easy to switch round one word for another, change the position of sentences and paragraphs, or rewrite complete sections. It is no use thinking that you've finished that release or article after slogging away for an hour or more on it. That is just the beginning: you must look at your work in the same way a news subeditor would, deleting unwanted words, cutting the dross and sharpening up the copy. And then it's just a matter of starting all over again.

AT A GLANCE

- All copy for publication is subject to editing.
- The first hurdle for releases is: is it newsworthy?
- Ensure copy is accurate and grammatically sound.
- No clichés, jargon or repetition.
- Provide illustrations and include quotes in feature articles.
- The sub livens up slabs of type with headings and boxes.
- BBC producers usually ban brand names and products.
- On-screen editing requires special skills and computer software.
- Technical work ideally requires some specialist knowledge.
- Edit yourself as you go along.

13

Skills and styles for the office

Good, consistent style is just as important for correspondence, forms of address, wording for invitations and correct use of courtesy titles, as it is for publications and other printed matter. Good style is good manners, and that means answering – or at least acknowledging – letters no later than two or three days following receipt, and returning telephone calls where possible the same day.

Presentation and layout are also key factors in getting your message across. Every letter, report, paper or printed invitation that goes out must reflect the style and corporate image of your organisation. If it is not up to standard or specification, then your public relations effort could well be wasted. If there is no set house style, then now is the time to establish rules for everyone in the office to follow.

SUGGESTED STYLE FOR CORRESPONDENCE

Most firms and organisations have style rules for letters, envelopes and other office stationery such as invoices, order forms, fax messages and internal memos. A properly addressed and signed-off letter is the first point. Here are some of the basics.

Layout

File reference and date should be ranged left and aligned with an element of the letterhead design. Do not put full stops, commas or other punctuation in addresses typed at the top of the letter. The following specimen layout style is commonplace:

Mr John Smith
123 Any Road
Anytown
Kent AN5 1ZZ

When addresses are set in a line, say in the body of a letter, then commas are used to separate the components as in Mr John Smith, 123 Any Road, Anytown, Kent AN5 1ZZ.

Courtesy titles

Titles at tops of letters and salutations are normally Mr/Mrs/Miss/Ms. When answering the telephone do not just say 'Hello' or even the modern but overused and insincere response 'This is Mandy, how can I help you?' Give just your surname or add your first name if you want. Do not give yourself a courtesy title and say 'This is *Mr* Smith speaking.'

Despite some past objections to the use of Ms, there is little sign of its decline. It has the advantage of a simplified style, but there is a trend nowadays for all courtesy titles to be replaced by first name and surname only.

Men are mostly given the title Mr in correspondence, but Esquire, Esq for short, is almost dead. Banks, insurance companies, accountants and other professional bodies retain it for fear of upsetting clients. Once Esquire denoted social standing, but by the middle of the 20th century it ceased to possess any sense of rank. Nowadays, it is hardly ever seen in the communications business.

The styles of Mr/Mrs/Miss/Ms are clean and uncluttered. But they are fast disappearing in everyday correspondence.

Honours and qualifications

Where style calls for the inclusion of designations such as civil honours and qualifications, these should follow the established abbreviations, ie, MBE, BA, BSc. No stops go between characters or after separate designations.

Dates

Separate the day of the week from the month, as recommended by *Fowler's*: 1 January 2001, not the American style January 1, 2001. The comma needed to avoid collision with the year looks messy. The th/st/rd/nd style for dates has mostly been dropped in business correspondence and printwork, along with deep paragraph indents and punctuation in addresses and salutations. Nevertheless, the style persists, principally in the professions and where there is no PR person to give the right advice. Avoid *nd/st/rd/th* after the day numeral.

When referring to times of day, type these with no space between the figures and *am/pm* as in 9am, 9.30am. Do not put noughts after the figure: for instance 9.00am would look cluttered and pedantic. The signee's name should be ranged left with the person's title typed underneath when needed. Do not underline the name or title, or put either in capitals. Use a fountain pen to sign letters. If you do, it is a sign that you have taken the trouble to make your signature stylish and not just dashed off. Get into the habit of using a proper pen: keep your ballpoint or felt-tip for memos and note-taking.

Copies

Where copies of the letter are sent outside the organisation, the addressee's name should appear beneath the signature, ranged left as in:

Copy to: Mr John Smith, XYZ Company

Details on people receiving blind copies, where the name(s) is not disclosed to the addressee, should ideally appear in a different position. Attach a compliment slip to the copy, with a note for that personal touch.

Letterheads

These should be printed in the same typeface, colour and style as all other in-house stationery. Postal address, telephone, facsimile and email address and, if appropriate, the website address should all be shown in a prominent position. Public relations department headings should carry, where appropriate, out-of-hours telephone and mobile numbers of senior executives, although many firms will prefer to show this information separately rather than have it printed with the heading.

OTHER STATIONERY

Style for invoices, statements, order forms, fax messages, envelopes and other printed stationery should all follow the house style with logo (if there is one), and typefaces and colour identical to those used for letterheads. Infinite variations in size are possible with computer-controlled typesetting systems. Your printer and designer will advise on how these can be employed to the best advantage from both a design and cost point of view.

STYLE FOR EMAILS

Informality is the key to successful emailing. But it can be taken too far, and messages written with poor punctuation and ghastly grammar can be forwarded to a client or your boss – with disastrous results. Stick to the usual rules but relax the style a little. Leave the CU4lunch message to friends and family. Chapter 18 has more on this subject.

HAVE CLEAR, CLEAN LAYOUT

If the layout of reports and documents has been well designed, then the message and information contained is more likely to be communicated and acted upon. The basic requirement for an effective layout is a legible typeface, following house style, and preferably the same as the one used for letterheads and other printed stationery. If the typeface, style and creative approach are used for everything, and uniform headings and subheadings are adopted, then all paperwork is immediately identified with the organisation. If it can follow the style for printwork as well, so much the better.

A distinctive 'look' to your correspondence and reports will be achieved if style is standardised: width of margins, number of words per page, page size, uniform space between the lines (leading), type and weight of paper. Put a little extra space between paragraphs, but do not try to squeeze too many lines into one page. Do not use italics or bold type within the body copy in an attempt to give added emphasis.

WRITING A PRÉCIS

A systematic approach is needed. To produce a précis, first read the report or article through to see what it is all about. Set down the important points with a target length, so you will not give too much or too little information. (Don't mark the actual document – you might want to make a photocopy and anyway the owner will not thank you for defacing it.) Do a rough draft, preferably on your PC, incorporating the main facts. Compare it with the original and fill in the gaps.

Check to make sure you haven't exceeded your target wordage. Aim for between a quarter and a third of the length of the original. Read through the draft carefully to see that the matter flows freely and is grammatically correct. Check for any departures from house style.

If you include quotations, they should be short. Quotes should be in reported speech, using the past tense in the third person: 'The committee/he *agreed* to do such and such' or the future past 'the committee/he *would* do…'. Don't use the present (*is/are*) or simple future (*will/shall*) tenses. Treat quotes in the same way as journalists write reported speech. Give it a heading, with your initials and date at the end.

WRITING REPORTS AND MINUTES

A report can run from a short memo to any number of closely typed pages in a bound volume, perhaps an annual or interim report to shareholders. Minutes, too, vary in length and style, from a contact report to notes of a meeting.

Essentials of a report

A report must contain the important facts and, ideally, end with a conclusion and recommendations. Open with a title page, moving on to a list of contents, including illustrations or charts, acknowledgements and a short abstract. The body of the report should give the key points from research or investigations, quotations where appropriate and again be written in the third person. Conclude with appendices, if any.

Keep to significant points and comments; otherwise the reader will skip the detail and jump to the conclusions and recommendations. That is what journalists do: only if there is something that appears to be particularly interesting or might need additional information will they go back to the full text.

Start with a draft, then flesh it out with the detail, but only that which is strictly essential to the purpose and objective of the report. Make sure that there is a title and that the author(s) is/are shown on the cover and/or title page. Put the body of the text into numbered sections. Produce the report on a word processor or PC and use bold type for headings.

Restrict minutes to decisions

Minutes should be written and circulated within a week of the meeting, earlier if possible. They should be concise and restricted to decisions unless there is good reason to go into details. They should not be long dialogues of who said what. Use reported speech in the third person, and past and future past tenses. For example, in reporting a committee decision, you would write 'It *was* agreed that the company *would* pay a dividend' and not 'It *is* agreed that the company *will* pay a dividend'.

Set down the items in the order of the agenda. Distinguish between superior and inferior headings by underlining or using capitals, or by using bold or larger type sizes. Restrict italics to points of emphasis, though it is better to do without them if you can. Include an 'Action' column as a reminder for those who have agreed to do something.

Put the list of attendees, date of meeting and date of issue at the top and finish with date of next meeting. And get the chairman trained in returning your draft promptly. If you fail to achieve a quorum, just produce notes of the meeting, making it clear that it was not quorate. These notes can subsequently be put to the next meeting and taken as minutes.

FORMS OF ADDRESS

Public relations people often have to decide how to begin and end a letter to royalty, and how to address government ministers, peers, MPs and civic dignitaries. Bad form – or at least insensitivity to tradition – can mean that your invitation to give a keynote speech or perform an opening ceremony will lead to a frosty reply. Care in addressing everyone with whom you are in contact, not just VIPs, is essential.

The British system of titles, forms of address and precedence is one of the most complicated in the western world. Nevertheless, most – if not all – answers are to be found in *Debrett's Correct Form*, which covers every conceivable situation in correspondence and in sending invitations to social and business functions. A few examples may be helpful to the reader, but for full guidance refer to *Debrett's*.

Writing to firms

When writing to firms, avoid 'Dear Sir/Madam'. When you do not have a name – it is usually easy to find it in telephone or trade directories – address your letter to the position, ie to the chairman, managing director or secretary. When writing to the press, write Dear Editor if you do not know his or her name. But it is always worth taking the trouble to write personally if you can, although a name on the envelope and letter will seldom ensure a reply or even an acceptance!

Royalty

When writing to the Sovereign, all communications should be addressed to The Private Secretary to The Queen, to the office holder rather than by name, unless you know the person. For other members of the Royal Family, write to the Equerry, Private

Secretary or Lady in Waiting as appropriate, the letter beginning Dear Sir or Dear Madam, again to the holder of the office rather than by name. In direct communications, start with Dear Sir or Dear Madam, with 'Your Royal Highness' substituted for 'you' and 'Your Royal Highness's' for 'your' in the body of the letter.

Peerage

When writing to the peerage, put (for example) 'My Lord Duke' in the formal form and 'Dear Duke' in the informal, or the 'Duke of —' if the acquaintanceship is slight. Verbal address is 'Your Grace' (formal), 'Duke' (social). Special styles are accorded to the wives and children of peers.

Baronets

With baronets, letters begin 'Dear Sir John' (for example) with Bt added on the envelope. A similar style applies for knighthoods where the title is held for life, but the surname should be added if you do not know the person well. Should you meet a baronet or knight in the street or at a function, he should be addressed as Sir John, never 'Sir' on its own. The wife of a baronet or knight is known as 'Lady' followed by the surname.

Government ministers

Ministers of cabinet rank and some other junior ministers are members of the Privy Council and have the prefix The Rt Hon before their names, with the letters PC after all honours and decorations awarded by the Crown. Privy Counsellors (the preferred spelling) are drawn from many other areas of public life, so watch out! Addressing letters to Government ministers is straightforward: Dear Sir (or Madam) for the formal style, Mrs or Miss for the informal with the option of Dear Minister when writing by his/her appointment.

Members of Parliament

Unless MPs are Privy Counsellors, they have just MP after their name plus any civil or military honours. They are addressed Mr/Mrs/Miss in the usual way. Members of the House of

Commons do not have MP after their name once they lose their seat. Always check with the current edition of *Vacher's Parliamentary Companion, PMS Parliamentary Companion* or other reference source when writing to MPs and members of the House of Lords. These publications also include details of ministers and senior civil servants in Departments of State, and the names of officials in other Government departments and agencies.

Civic dignitaries

There are widely differing styles for civic dignitaries, depending on the particular town or city. The Lord Mayors of London and York are unique in that they are styled 'The Right Honourable' while the remainder are generally titled 'The Right Worshipful'. They are addressed at the beginning of a letter 'Mr Lord Mayor' and the envelope should bear the wording 'The Right Honourable the Lord Mayor of —'. Mayors of cities and towns are addressed 'Mr Mayor' and the envelope should carry the words 'The Right Worshipful the Mayor of (City of—/(Royal Borough of)' or 'The Worshipful the Mayor of —'. Letters should be signed off 'Yours faithfully' (or 'Yours sincerely' if a social occasion).

Debrett's should be consulted for checking titles of church dignitaries, officers in the armed forces, ambassadors, and for deciding precedence for table plans and guest lists.

INVITATIONS TO FUNCTIONS

Printed invitation cards should be sent for most functions, although in many cases – say for press conferences and for informal or social events – a well-presented letter, or even an email if time is short, will suffice. Gold-edged cards are best and use of a script typeface is particularly suitable for formal occasions. The card must state the name (or office) of the person making the invitation, the nature of the function, where it will be held, the date and time and the dress. It should also state if decorations should be worn. The card must provide enough space for the name of the invitee, and an RSVP name and address, plus telephone number if appropriate. If possible, provide a prepaid reply card. The invitee's name should be handwritten in black ink. Those who do not bother to reply should not be invited again.

REPLIES TO INVITATIONS

Replies should be sent out on the organisation's usual printed letterheads and ideally be written in the formal style, stating either acceptance of the invitation or regret at being unable to accept. State the reason for non-acceptance, examples being 'owing to a previous engagement/absence abroad/out of town that day'. Whether accepting or declining, the name(s) of the invitee(s) should be given, together with details of the function. If replying by telephone, send a written follow-up.

ACKNOWLEDGING CORRESPONDENCE

Good style means good manners. And good manners is good PR. Nothing is worse than not replying to a letter offering or giving you something. It is usually possible to send a reply within a day or two. If you are too busy to post a typed letter, then a hand-written one will do just as well, even if you have to handwrite the envelope yourself.

An acknowledgement card is also helpful and should be sent as a matter of routine for all correspondence where a detailed and immediate response is not possible. This might simply state '(name of person of company/organisation) thanks you for your communication of (date) which is receiving attention'. It takes only a minute or two of your time to get off a reply of some sort: a tele-phone call, email or faxed note will often do the trick.

Replying to emails promptly is a courtesy not to be forgotten. It is not so important in inter-office memos, but essential for other messages – particularly those to clients and customers, if only a simple OK. Ensure that someone monitors your mailbox regularly for outstanding correspondence.

SETTING OUT DOCUMENTS

The layout for reports, documents, agendas and minutes calls for a consistent and well-ordered style. A printed heading should give the name, address and telephone/fax numbers of the organisation on all documents. Date and reference numbers to aid identification should be included. Insert extra space between items and leave generous margins (at least 25 mm on the right-hand margin, more on the left). Call in a professional designer to give you a template for typists to follow. That way everybody will produce documents to a consistent style, an essential requirement for developing a recognisable corporate image.

WRITING A CV

Style for presentation of a curriculum vitae (CV) is important and could affect an applicant's chances of securing employment. It should be clear and concise, consistent in style, accurate, without spelling errors or wrong punctuation, use plain English and should concentrate on skills and achievements. Ideally a CV should be typed on two sheets of plain white A4 paper, with plenty of space so that the words and headings are not jammed up tight. Always address the CV to a named person, never Dear Sir or Dear Madam. It only takes a minute or two to find the right name. Do not use coloured paper or ink and pay particular attention to the way it is laid out. It could mean all the difference to getting the job or not.

A CV should provide the following information: name, address, date of birth, marital status, nationality, education and qualifications, career history and the names of two referees.

There are numerous books on preparing a CV, *The Jobsearch Manual* by Linda Apsey being particularly suitable for younger people starting out on their careers. *Super Jobsearch* by Peter K Studner is appropriate for those seeking management positions. (Both are published by Management Books 2000.)

There is a new method, the Talking-CV!, of putting your personal details in text, voice and picture on a CD ROM which can then be sent to potential employers and headhunters, and also uploaded to the internet. See Chapter 18.

AT A GLANCE

- Establish a corporate style for everything.
- Omit courtesy titles (Mr/Mrs/Miss/Ms) on the telephone: just give your name.
- 'Esquire' is hardly ever used these days; mostly by banks and financial services companies.
- Agree style for dates, times, and correspondence format to be followed by all staff.
- Develop a clear, clean layout for reports and documents.
- Restrict minutes to decisions: long dialogues are not needed.
- Refer to *Debrett's* for guidance on forms of address.
- Use printed cards for formal invitations.
- Acknowledge all correspondence; respond the same day if possible.
- Update your CV regularly; keep it to two pages of A4.

14

Traps, snares and pitfalls

Appropriate choice of words is of paramount importance for imparting the sense and tone of any message. But for that message to be properly understood, and for it to be clear and unambiguous, not only must spellings be correct but the writer must avoid slang in formal texts, guard against overusing fashionable but sloppy phrases, and know whether words are hyphenated or not, or spelt as one word. This chapter examines some of these traps, which can lead to mistakes or even howlers that make your hair stand on end when you see them in print.

SPELLING POINTS

Difficulty often arises with advis*or* or advis*er*: the preferred spelling is *-er*; *-or* is pretentious, even old-fashioned. A useful rule is that unless preceded by a 't' or 'ss' verb (or less frequently noun) endings are usually *-er*. In order to avoid a spelling hiccup (not *hiccough* nowadays) you have to be on guard for mistakes like *prac-*

tioners – or literals and typos as printers like to call them. There is no 'd' in allege, it is contractual, not -ural, flotation not floatation, hurrah/hurray not hoorah/ay unless you are talking about a Hooray Henry; idiosyncrasy not –acy; minuscule not -iscule; nerve racking, not -wracking. It is a gentlemen's agreement, not -man's.

Confusion often occurs between *passed* and *past*. The past tense and past participle of the verb to pass is passed as in it passed from you to me, whereas *past* as an adjective describes things or events that have occurred (past times); it can also be a preposition as in first past the post and a noun (memories of the past).

For words of more than one syllable ending in *-ed* or *-ing* and with the stress on the last syllable, the final consonant is doubled as in permit/permitted. But where the last syllable is unstressed, as in target and focus, the final consonant is not doubled: thus any argument on how to spell focused/focusing and targeted/targeting is instantly resolved. In the same category go other favourite words in the PR vocabulary such as benefited/ing, budgeted/ing. Another way of telling whether you are right or wrong is to pronounce such words with a stressed double final consonant and so get foc*uss*ed and targ*ett*ed. Or say to yourself mark*ett*ing, with a double 't' and the emphasis on the second syllable; it is obviously wrong and you will instantly recall the rule. (Get into the habit of looking out for a double 's' or 't' in these words – you won't have to wait long!)

With suffixes of words ending in a single 'l', the last consonant is usually doubled whether or not the final syllable is stressed as in labelled/travelled, but not appealed/paralleled.

Spellings of similar sounding or pairs of words frequently cause trouble. Take these examples: canvas (for painting pictures) but canvass (to solicit votes); dependant (relative) but dependent (upon). How many times have you seen these words misused and misspelt? Then there is the draughtsman (of a specification) but someone who drafts a document, the official who makes a formal inquiry, but a person who questions and makes an enquiry. Further has quite a different meaning from farther: the former suggests something additional to say or do, the latter increased distance.

Install becomes installation but instalment (sometimes with a double 'l'), all three having a totally different meaning from instil. A common mistake is to mix up licence (noun) with license (verb): how many times do you want to tell a shopkeeper to correct licenced to licensed? (In America, it is the other way round and 'practice' is both noun and verb.)

How often have you asked someone whether the first 'e' should be dropped in judgement? The rule here is that when a suffix beginning with a consonant (*-ful, -ling, -ly, -ment, -ness, -some*) is added to a word with a silent 'e', the -e is retained – but not always (exceptions include argument, fledgling). Judgement usually loses the first 'e' in legal works. In American spelling, the 'e' is dropped before a suffix beginning with a consonant as in abridgment, judgment. Another rule worth noting is when adding *in-* and *un-* to the beginning of a word; there is only one 'n' unless the word itself begins with an 'n' as in inseparable, unending, innumerable, unnecessary.

Other confusing spellings are principle (basis of reasoning) and principal (main); stationary (still) and stationery (paper stocks) – a way to remember this is 'e' for envelope. Note that the start of the last syllable in supersede and consensus is often misspelt with a 'c'. Keep a colander for straining and a calendar for giving the date; reserve program and disk for computer terminology, and resist the temptation to put an 'e' in whisky (whiskey is for the American and Irish, but never Scotch whisky – the Scots wouldn't hear of it!).

More examples are in Appendix 2.

BE CAREFUL WITH FOREIGN WORDS

Take special care with foreign words. They are easily absorbed into English, but can just as easily be wrongly spelt. Even in newspapers we see fruits *du* mer instead of *de*, hors d'oeuvres (not plural) for *hors d'oeuvre*, crime passional for crime *passionnel* and bête noir for bête *noire*. Keep foreign dictionaries handy, particularly those covering English–French and English–German and vice versa for checking phrases like *couleur locale*, since computer spellchecks are not much help for other languages.

Errors can occur simply because you have seen the same words wrongly spelt before. It is easy to *think* you have got it right, but it's easy to miss, for example, the first u in *de rigueur*. Familiarity breeds contempt.

While occasional foreign words can liven up dull copy, keep them out of releases. When used in print, the reader will quickly tire of them, particularly if the expressions are unfamiliar. Keep to Anglicised words, otherwise you might be seen as showing off. *The Oxford Dictionary for Writers and Editors* and *The Oxford Style Manual* will confirm spellings of commonly used foreign words and phrases, and will show, by italics, those that are not yet accepted in everyday English.

USE YOUR DICTIONARY

It is difficult to remember different spellings for similar-sounding words, but being aware of the similarities and possible spelling errors encourages the writer to reach for the dictionary.

Before leaving the subject of spellings, one sure tip is always remember to use the computer's spellcheck for everything – releases, articles, reports and letters; not only will it pick up errors that might otherwise not be noticed, it will often provide a word count by recording the number of questionable words. This is extremely useful information for both the writer and editor, saving the tiresome task of counting up copy word by word to estimate the length when set in type. More examples are in Appendix 2.

-ISE OR -IZE VERB ENDINGS?

Both spellings are common in the UK, while the *-ize* ending is usual in North America. Readers in America may notice that -ise has been used throughout this book since this style is now generally favoured in the UK. There are some words which must always end with *-ise*. Words which must always end with *-ise* include advertise, appraise, apprise, arise, chastise, comprise, disguise, excise, exercise, franchise, improvise, incise, merchandise, premise, promise, praise, raise, supervise, televise. Few will object to *-ise* spellings throughout, although the use of *capsize/sterilize/ familiarize* will seldom be criticised.

In the UK until a few years ago *-ize* endings were commonly seen in *The Times* and elsewhere, but as both the Oxford University Press and the Cambridge University Press switched to *-ise*, so newspapers tended to follow suit and thus another style trend was born. Even so, -*ize* appears to be as firmly embedded in America as ever. However much you may hate nouns becoming verbs, you have to realise that services are *privatised*, but most of us will object to being *hospitalised* or having plans *prioritised*.

ONE WORD OR TWO?

Many words once happily hyphenated, and some two-word phrases, soon found themselves living together, joined without remorse. Thus we have seen railwayman/paybed/turnout enter everyday usage as examples of lost hyphenation. Many still persist in using alright ('Gross, coarse, crass and to be avoided', says Kingsley Amis in *The King's English*) instead of the preferred all right.

The American tendency to write underway as one word has few followers here. But who is to say that it is no different from *anyway*. Then there is the frequent confusion between forever (perpetually) and for ever (for always), as in 'He is forever complaining' against 'He will be in the same firm for ever.' Amis again: 'I'm forever blowing bubbles to be outlawed altogether.' Few will condone the modern trend for anymore or anytime which cry out for their original two-word forms.

Many hyphenated words eventually end up as one for the simple reason that the style is modern and favoured by the popular press. We are used to them and no longer worry whether they are hyphenated or not. However, it is advisable to check with the usual reference sources such as the *Oxford English Dictionary* for recommended style for individual word-sets.

PUZZLES AND POSERS

When you accede to something you give assent to an opinion or policy; do not use it to mean grant, allow, agree. Rather than write accordingly, put so or therefore; adverbs like hopefully, admittedly, happily are usually unnecessary. It is better to write you plan or intend to do something than hope to do it, which suggests doubt that it will ever be done. Rather than adjust something, *change* it; you appraise it when you judge its value, not apprise which means inform.

Among is often confused with between. When writing about more than two things or people, among is usually needed. But when considered individually, between is preferred. Contrast 'food was shared among six people' with 'cordial relations between the UK, France and Germany'.

Avoid hackneyed words like factor which can usually be omitted without loss of sense. You can dispense with it easily, for example, 'in an important *factor* in the company's success' by recasting and writing simply 'important in the company's success'. Feature (as a noun) is another word that adds nothing and can easily be dropped. Meaningful has lost all meaning and is another candidate for excision. Also cut these out: one of the most, respective/respectively, currently, the foreseeable future, the fact is... and other words that contribute little except waffle.

Don't be old-fashioned and write amongst and whilst when among and while will do just as well. You should *try to* do something, not *try and* do it. Instead of writing *practically* all the time put almost, nearly, or all but. The world is populated by people, not persons; but that is not to say that there is no place for person. The noun person is normally only used in the singular as in 'he was a person of character'. Avoid using persons when people would be more appropriate.

Be careful not to add a qualifier to ungradable words like unique or perfect. You cannot have degrees of uniqueness or perfection: either something is unique or perfect or it is not. Other words like this are peculiar, sole, single, spontaneous.

LOOKALIKES NEED CARE

Is it big or large? While they are synonymous, you can't always swap one for the other. There's a big salary rise, not a large one; but you can drive a big or a large car. Differences are subtle: big is the colloquial and more familiar adjective. Amount of/number of goes better with large (a large amount of column inches, there was big publicity). Use whichever *sounds* right. Much the same applies to small/little.

Lookalike words with different meanings include simple/simplistic. The latter implies oversimplified, unrealistically straightforward; avoid when simple in 'easy' contexts will suffice.

Biennial is once every two years, biannual twice a year; continual means frequently happening, continuous is non-stop.

To mitigate is to create conditions for reducing the severity of something, to militate against something is to have a significant effect against it. Affect is to have an influence on, effect to accomplish something. Discreet means circumspect, showing good judgement; discrete means unattached, unrelated. Practical is suitable for use, practicable able to be done.

CHESTNUT TIME

Now that chestnut: is it less or fewer? The quick answer is that if the noun is countable, it's fewer; otherwise choose less. Fewer tables and chairs, less hope, less anger. Less/little goes better with size and quantity than few/fewer: thus for time, distance, money, reading, writing it's less than 10 minutes before we leave for home, there's less than 1,000 words to write, and less than £50 for doing it. Fewer or less people or miles? Since people take the plural verb, it's fewer than 20 per cent of the workforce who leave so early. And it's fine to write less than 25 miles away since it's a measure of distance, not individual miles.

Keep 'nots' out of attention-seeking standfirsts, those short intros to feature articles, as they can confuse the reader. There's no place for 'not for nothing'. Negative constructions should always be avoided: too many 'nots' and 'un' words joined with 'not' (for example 'not unwanted') can be brain-twisters. And as I've said earlier in this chapter, you can't be too careful when using a computerised spellchecker: there's really no better way to check spellings than to use a good dictionary.

THEY'RE NOT RIGHT, THEY'RE NOT WRONG

Watch out for get/got. While there is nothing actually wrong with them, they appear informal and should be avoided. Use obtain or possess instead, or consider rewriting. Also take care with to lay, to lie: the verb to lay takes an object while *to lie* does not (I *lay* my body on the floor as I *lie* resting). But you never have a *lay down* which makes a noun of it!

Like is another pitfall. Used parenthetically, to qualify a following or preceding statement, as in '*like* I was going to tell you something' is a vulgarism of the first order, Fowler says. But resistance to its use as a conjunction and as a substitute for *as if* or *as though* is crumbling.

Keep clear of *nice*. Fowler says: 'It should be confined in print to dialogue... ladies have charmed it out of all its individuality and converted it into a mere diffuser of vague and mild agreeableness.' It is better to forget *nice* and choose a synonym for it, unless you are in America and use the catchphrase 'Have a *nice* day.'

Arguments abound on whether to write (or say) compared to or compared with. The first is to liken one thing to another as in 'critics compared him to Olivier,' while the second points to differences or resemblances between two things as in 'comparing the speaker's notes *with* what has been written'. Use *different from* in writing, keep *different to* for speech.

Another poser is the placing of 'only' in a sentence. Put it as close as possible to the word or words it qualifies: when it strays too far away, it can be obscure or remove the element of exclusivity. If, for example, you say you had *only* two drinks, that is better than saying you *only* had two drinks.

Avoid imprecisions such as lots of, many or things when figures or definitions can be given. Keep *an* for words beginning with a silent 'h' (an heir, an honour, an honorarium); otherwise it is a hotel, a harbour, a hero, a hope. Introduce a list of items with such as or for example, not eg.

Note that *anybody* and *anyone* are singular (anybody is able to visit the museum), as are every, everybody, everyone (every dentist *has* information on care of teeth; everybody is able to discuss his or her problems with a lawyer). *Each* is singular (each contributor should check his or her paper), and so is nobody or no one (no one is certain).

VOGUE WORDS AND PHRASES

Numerous words are not only overused or become clichés but suggest the writer has not bothered to think of anything better. Top of the list must be 'or whatever' when it means in effect 'including many other things'. Don't say it and certainly never write it.

Then there are the clichés of having said that, at the end of the day, in-depth, ongoing and ongoing situation, geared to, in terms of, I'll get back to you, name of the game, no problem, take on board, track record; and words like feedback, concept, consensus, lifestyle, viable, syndrome, validate, interface, scenario. Some, if not all, of these words are current coinage in the communications business and it is virtually impossible to avoid them. Try to find synonyms.

GETTING IN THE MOOD

If you fail to distinguish between auxiliary (modal) verbs, and between relative pronouns, verbal inelegances and even mistakes arise. While sometimes interchangeable without loss of sense, look out for pitfalls. Here are a few examples.

Modal verbs shall/will, should/could, can/could, may/might possess different shades of meaning, expressed as moods or modes of action. Also within this category are *must* and *ought*. Unlike ordinary verbs, modals do not have *-s* or *-ed* added in present and past tenses; there can be no shalls, mighting or oughted apart from being *willed* to do something.

The general rule is that *shall* and *should* go with first person singular and plural; *will* and *would* the others. Thus, *should* accompanies *I* and *we*; and *would goes* with *he, she, it* and *they*. Both express simple future tense; *will* showing intention or determination, especially a promise to do something. You are more likely to be taken seriously if you say 'I *will* be in the office on Sunday.' '*Shall* be' somewhat dilutes the intention.

Care is needed in choosing *should* or *would* for there is a subtle but important difference between them. *Should* has moral force behind it, whereas *would* acquires mild conditionality. *Should* expresses three future possibilities: conditional, probable, and a less likely outcome as in, respectively, 'I *should* be grateful if you *would* answer my letter'; 'she *should* avoid the angry client'; 'should you see him, remind him about the meeting.' *Could*, like *should/would*, indicates a conditional or future possibility, while *could/can*, used interrogatively, suggests seeking permission.

Difficulty often occurs in using *may/might*. Permission is expressed through *may* as in '*may I*', but both imply simple possibility in 'the client *may/might* come' and are indistinguishable. In some contexts *might* hints at uncertainty and suggests less optimism than *may* as in 'they might use the release' against 'they may be able to edit it'. Thus, *may/might* are often interchangeable where the truth of an event is unknown, but if there is no longer uncertainty, use *might*.

James Aitchison in his *Cassell's Guide to Written English* neatly expresses *ought* and *must* as 'duty, obligation and necessity'; *ought*, he observes, suggests likelihood of fulfilment, while *must* indicates strict or absolute necessity.

Another trap can arise in writing *which* and *that*. These pronouns are normally used with non-human nouns, otherwise write *who* or *whom*. While *which/that* can often be interchanged or even omitted without loss of sense, distinctions exist, particularly when sub-clauses beginning *which* are enclosed in commas. It is rare to punctuate *that* clauses in the same way. *That* defines, *which* informs.

It is a sound rule (says Sir Ernest Gowers in *The Complete Plain Words*) that *that* should be dispensed with whenever this can be done 'without loss of clarity or dignity'. Consult *The Oxford Guide to English Usage* or *Fowler* for examples of current *which/that* usage.

GENTEELISMS

Substitution of a normal, natural word for another that is considered by some as less familiar, less vulgar, less improper or less apt is defined by Fowler as a genteelism. For instance, *assist* for help, *ale* for beer, *endeavour* for try, *odour* for smell are all genteelisms, along with ladies for women and gentlemen for men. A word that is simple and unpretentious is to be preferred to one that has a high-sounding, euphemistic ring to it. Words that were once listed as genteelisms (chiropodist for corn-cutter for example) have long since gained acceptance for everyday usage, and are no longer indicators of social class.

Here is a short but easily extendible list of other genteelisms for you to be aware of and preferably avoid: euphemisms such as *conceal* for hide, *corpulent* for fat, *ere* for before, *demise* or *passed away* for died, *dentures* for false teeth, *donation* for gift, *lounge* for sitting-room, *perspire* for sweat, *retire* for go to bed, *reside at* for live at, *sufficient* for enough, *take umbrage* for take offence, *toilet* for lavatory. And so on.

KEEP CLEAR OF SLANG

Unless part of a direct quotation, say in a speech delivered at an event other than at an AGM, avoid slang words in formal writing. But you need to appreciate that today's slang is tomorrow's idiom. Slang words for 'publicise', drawn from the *Wordsworth Thesaurus of Slang*, include the following: promote, hype, plug, push, pitch, splash, spot, boost, build up, puff, ballyhoo, beat the drum for, tub-thump, hard/soft sell. If you are a publicity seeker, you are a hot dogger, publicity hound, showoff. Slang for 'publicity' includes hoopla, flack, flackery, big noise, ink, get ink.

While state of the art and cutting edge began as slang, these phrases have now found a place in the everyday language of communicators. Doubtless, many other spoken slang words will eventually find a final resting place in formal writing.

KEEP MISSION STATEMENTS SHORT AND SIMPLE

Mission statements can be a waste of time; those wordy, self-congratulatory, pretentious platitudes tend to be meaningless waffle. No one wants to know about your firm's passion, your destiny, even your vision for the future. Too many beliefs, aims, objectives fail to convince. It is almost like saying what life is for. A mission statement, if you insist on having one, should be a description of what your company is and does in just a short paragraph.

It can be useful for background notes in a press release, provided it doesn't start talking about your commitment to excellence, your integrity, how enthusiastic your staff are. Look at is as your 'reason to be', a statement in plain language that will ring true with all your audiences, from employees to customers, from suppliers to opinion formers.

TOP 10 TIPS FOR WRITERS

1. **Brevity.** Restrict sentences to 25 to 30 words, three per paragraph maximum.
2. **Repetition.** Never repeat a word in a single passage. Look for synonyms.
3. **Clichés.** Kill stale, overused words and phrases. Consult a thesaurus.
4. **Jargon.** Cut out mumbo-jumbo. Will the reader understand?
5. **Facts, Facts.** Give facts, not waffle or comment, unless it's a quote.
6. **Qualifiers.** Write with verbs and nouns, not adjectives and adverbs.
7. **Accuracy.** Ensure the accuracy of everything. Watch for non sequiturs.
8. **Punctuation.** The full stop is your best friend. Use it liberally.
9. **Readability.** Make sure your copy is easy to read; does it look boring?
10. **Consistency.** Keep style consistent throughout.

AT A GLANCE

- Watch out for 'difficult' spellings.
- Keep two-way dictionaries handy for checking foreign words.
- Use your computer's spellcheck for everything you write.
- Keep verb endings consistent: -ise is mostly preferred in the UK.
- Most hyphenated words soon end up as one.
- Look out for differences and distinctions in lookalike words.
- Some words and phrases are not right, but not wrong.
- Avoid vogue phrases: they soon become clichés.
- Distinguish between modal (auxiliary) verbs.
- Avoid euphemistic 'genteelisms' where possible.
- Make mission statements simple, short, meaningful.

15

Americanisms – the differences

English is the dominant language in more than 30 countries: it is estimated that almost 400 million people across the world speak our mother tongue as a first language, the largest concentration being in the United States where there are some 226 million English speakers against the UK's 56 million. Around two-thirds of the world's population speak English as a second language.

English as a global language has important implications for the public relations practitioner. The indigenous differences between native speakers of American English and British English are significant. Global English, the way the language is spoken and written, is the voice of a national community: a mixture of accents, dialects, catchphrases and slogans coupled with grammatical and vocabulary variations.

Fewer than one in seven North Americans are able to read all the way through a newspaper article in another language. The part that language plays in the communications process is crucial, and the differences in style and usage between American English and British English must be recognised by all public relations professionals irrespective of their industry sector and the jobs they do.

ESSENTIAL DIFFERENCES

American English differs from British English in vocabulary, spelling and inflection, grammar and construction, and punctuation. Familiar terms here are unknown in the United States and vice versa. Some Americans advise that releases, articles and other printwork going there should be in US style. Others say that it is better to write the way we do here and let editors change the copy to suit. That can be done for press releases and other word-processed documents but will not do for printed communications such as reports and brochures addressed to American audiences. And there are occasions when both styles are needed. Which to use for websites with global audiences?

Releases and websites

American PR executive Susan Stevens, who once worked here for National Grid as the company's director of corporate affairs, says that because news release messages are usually different in the two countries, separate versions are issued and language is not an issue. Where a single version goes out, it uses the language of the land where the release is being issued, regardless of where the news originates. American news issued in the UK would therefore be in British English.

This is particularly true for a financial news release, where key terms like 'turnover' should be translated into the local language before issuing, so as to avoid confusion. (See under 'vocabulary and usage', later in this chapter.) For National Grid's website, both are used – American English for the US pages, British English for the UK. International websites should offer the user a choice of language, but that can be costly.

So the advice is when mailing or posting a release on your website for an international audience, keep it in British English and let journalists in other countries make the changes. If it's an internal employee communication or a publication, get someone steeped in US style to write it. Never let language get in the way of the message. Says Stevens: 'We found that even as our corporate writers became more proficient in the language of the other country, it was still best to have someone from the home country review the text to catch the nuances and subtleties that would otherwise be missed.' Just as it could take years of fluency in a foreign language to be proficient with its idioms and slang, so it could take years to learn American or Queen's English like a native, she added.

PR terminology

Where there's a communications director here, it's a vice-president there. In the United States you go to a clipping service; a video morgue; the local editor. Titles, as here, are changing fast: vice-president or manager replaces communications director/manager here. Over there the title public relations officer is hardly known.

Vocabulary and usage

Here lie the main variations. To emphasise the main ones to US employees on being told about a merger, Susan Stevens says the National Grid simply printed a booklet *May I pinch your seat?* A few examples of US versus UK English: ground floor here is *first floor* there; drawing pin/*thumbtack*; kennel/*doghouse*; receptionist/ *desk clerk*; skip/*dumpster*; Joe Bloggs/*John Doe*. Here's a built-in recipe for a meeting disaster: if you write to *table* something, in the UK it means to discuss it, while in the United States it means to put it aside for later. It's turnover here, revenue there.

We write *and*, not additionally; *district*, not neighbourhood; *oblige*, not obligate. In Britain a parking lot is a car park, a hood is a bonnet, a truck is a lorry, a freight train is a goods train, a stove is a cooker. You go on the sidewalk in New York City, but in London you are on the pavement. There you buy gasoline, here petrol (gas stations offer both gasoline and diesel). The subway in a US city is the Underground in London. You go for a week's vacation if you work there; here it is a holiday. In America, you say first name not Christian name (a term that is also now removed from most style manuals here), inquire not enquire, billboard not poster, clipping not press cutting.

Americans normally give verbs *-ize* endings where we mostly use the *-ise* style. They prefer license/practice for both noun and verb, while here the 's' is for the verb only; the nouns defense/offense/pretense take a 'c' here and not an 's' as in the United States. Commas and full stops fall within quotation marks in press releases in US style, regardless of whether they are part of the quoted material. For any other communication, say a letter or brochure, punctuation marks go within the quotations, but only if they are part of the original quote. Americans use the terms parentheses for round brackets, and brackets for square brackets.

Co-operation is seldom hyphenated there, often here; while full stops are often inserted in abbreviations there, but hardly ever seen here nowadays. A stroke is a slash over there; it's v. for versus here, vs. there. Here, your phone is engaged, for Uncle Sam it's busy. To a Yank, 'turnover' means the rate at which employees leave the company. To them 'natural wastage' means attrition. *To deliver on a promise* means to keep it. A hike is not only a walk, it can also be an increase.

Verbs inflect differently: *gotten* for got is commonplace (although not always considered to be good grammar), and so is *dove* for dived. Plural verbs and pronouns seldom go with words like audience, group. Do not write *meet with* nowadays, an old import from America, or say *outside of*.

Spelling

American English puts -er where we have -re, as in center, meter (measurement) but not always: theater and theatre are allowed there, and both forms permit acre and mediocre. Here, where verbs ending in double 'l' (dialling/travelling) in American English there is one 'l'. But there are exceptions: the verbs distil and enrol have double 'l' in the States. A cheque here is a check there, a tyre is a tire. There a word is spelled, here it is spelt; there's no 's' in towards in US style. Consult an up-to-date dictionary and usage guide if attempting to write and spell the American way – or better still consult an American.

Idioms and expressions

Some British and American idioms are similar in their phrasing whereas others are quite different. We say at a loose end, there it's at loose *ends*; not by a long chalk becomes not by a long *shot*. We write 'as sure as eggs is eggs', there they say 'you can put it in the bank' or 'it's a slam dunk' (a baseball expression).

More recently we have heard in Susie Dent's *Language Report* of a smoke-easy where smokers go in order to escape the anti-smoking laws; a stained glass ceiling, an adaptation of the familiar phrase describing the barrier to promotion of professional women;

a job spill, a situation in which job-related work encroaches on one's leisure time; a fake bake, the process of getting a sunless tan (also as a verb). If ever you wonder what POTUS means you will now know it stands for the President of the United States.

Many so-called Americanisms such as fall for autumn, candy for sweets, elevator for lift, will doubtless soon find their way into British English in the same way as truck, commuter and teenager have crossed the Atlantic with alacrity. The process is being reciprocated as more UK firms acquire US companies, and as UK expats introduce Americans to the British way of speaking.

The habit of using British words and phrases is apparently growing apace over there. The late Mr H W Fowler would no doubt be pleased and surprised, but perhaps dismayed if only he knew.

However, the two languages are still distinctly different, something PR people working with their American counterparts or with the media must not forget. Says Sue Stevens: 'If you are in a meeting or on a phone call and don't understand what the person is saying, be sure to ask what they mean. Otherwise, at best there can be confusion, at worst the spreading of misinformation.' And for the public relations practitioner trying to get a foothold in the States this could spell disaster and a quick flight home.

UNDERSTANDING THE MEDIA DIFFERENCES

Like their British counterparts, US journalists are busy, constantly looking for exclusives, and have little time for PROs who don't understand their individual needs and deadlines. American journalists often consider the public relations executive as an acceptable source, and will attribute quotes to him or her by name, rather than use the 'spokesperson' tag when they can't quote the chief executive.

The media markets are quite different. Here, we are dominated by a number of major national newspapers. The US market, by virtue of its sheer size, has few newspapers with truly national reach, although most wire services cover nationwide news and the number of national cable television stations and internet outlets has grown.

Anyone working over there will soon learn that the main targets of US publicists are the major regional news markets of print, television and radio and even the local media outlets, as well as the trade press.

While Sunday editions of major newspapers have different editors from the daily paper of the same name, they fall under the same corporate umbrella and often share reporters, so it is less likely that the same story can be placed in both the weekday and Sunday editions. Unlike here, you can usually get a photo editor on the phone.

The US media are generally more optimistic than here: they let go of a negative story when there is nothing new to report, and the writing style is more straightforward, with less dependence on intros and standfirsts. Their attitude towards exclusives is quite different, and can spell trouble for a naïve PRO in Britain. Here, virtually every major news story is leaked to the media, and competing media then run it the next day.

Certainly, exclusives and 'leaks' are used in the United States, particularly in politics, but they run the risk of alienating other journalists who have long memories and will withhold coverage in return. In fact, if you give an exclusive to one media outlet, other media in the same market may refuse to run the story a day later. Exclusives must be justified to the other journalists whose interest you need.

The above section is based on advice given to a UK press officer by Susan Stevens when she returned to the States after a spell in the UK with the National Grid.

Useful references

Examples of the main differences between British English and American English will be found in the *Oxford Guide to Style, Garner's Modern American Usage* (OUP) and in early editions of *Fowler's Modern English Usage*. Many of the examples in this chapter were drawn from *The Right Word at the Right Time*, published by the Reader's Digest Association but now out of print. If you see a copy in a second-hand bookshop, grab it. There's also a handy two-way pocket glossary *American English/English American* (Abson Books).

AT A GLANCE

- Appreciate and recognise the differences between American and British English.
- Use British English for one-version websites.
- For dual version sites, consider American English for US pages, British for UK.
- Keep releases in British English; let subs there make the changes.
- Public relations terms and titles differ.
- Check dictionaries for variations in definitions, spellings, grammar.
- American usually prefer -ize verb endings to -ise.
- There are wide variations in idiom and expressions.
- Be aware of the different ways American journalists treat exclusives.

16

The spoken word: pronunciation matters

The way words are spoken is just as important as the way they are written. Well-enunciated speech, pronounced according to established guidelines, can help platform performance, aid communication between an organisation and its audience and make a significant contribution to the public relations effort.

Corporate image is not just the logo and visual impact of literature – the typeface, colours and house style. Much also depends on word of mouth and the mental picture of the speaker that is built up by tone of voice. And that picture is the one which can make all the difference between success and failure at a client presentation, a shareholders' meeting, a conference speech, or even a job interview.

No one wants to hear slipshod, careless speech like 'See yer layer', dropped or wrongly stressed vowels and syllables, missed consonants, a high-speed mumbo-jumbo of words shortened to the extent that they become almost unintelligible. Here are some basic points of pronunciation and a selection of verbal mishaps that are so easily made, but seldom corrected.

RECEIVED PRONUNCIATION

Among the many varieties of English, Received Pronunciation (RP) is the standard most dictionaries follow. This is said to be 'the least regional being originally that used by educated speakers in Southern England' (*OED*), and *The Oxford Guide to English Usage* takes it as 'the neutral national standard, just as it is in its use in broadcasting or in the teaching of English as a foreign language'. The new edition of *Fowler's Modern English Usage* makes specific recommendations based on RP and the pronunciations given are largely those of *The Concise Oxford Dictionary* (*COD*). It is from these, and other sources such as the BBC guide *The Spoken Word*, that examples have been taken for pronunciation where uncertainty exists.

It is useful to differentiate between pronunciation and accent. As Kingsley Amis points out in *The King's English*, 'everyone's *accent* [his italics] is a general thing that depends roughly on a speaker's place of birth, upbringing, education and subsequent environment whereas *pronunciation* is a question of how individual words are spoken'. It can thus be deduced that pronunciation of a given word can be considered 'correct' while another may be 'incorrect'. RP provides a useful but limited yardstick by which pronunciation may be judged correct or not.

One of the most argued points is the placing of stress. If you know where it falls, the pronunciation of vowels can be determined. Look for the stress accent ´ (like the French acute) after the stressed syllable or vowel sound which is shown in almost every word in the *COD* and in most popular dictionaries, even the well-thumbed pocket editions to be found in most office drawers. The stressed syllable (or vowel) is italicised in the following examples.

RP speakers will put the stress first in *ad*ult, *ap*plicable, *contro*versy, *com*munal, *bro*chure, *in*tegral, *for*midable, *ki*lometre, *mischie*vous, *pat*ent (*pay*-tent), *pref*erable, *pri*marily, *rep*utable, *tem*porarily; but second in ba*nal*, con*tri*bute, de*mon*strable, dis*pute*, dis*tri*bute, re*search*, trans*fer*able. *In*teresting loses the second syllable to become *intr*'sting, *com*parable to *compr*'ble. Stress on the third syllable occurs with appar*a*tus (as in *hate*), compos*i*te (as in *opposite*), inter*n*ecine (as in *knee*).

Make sure there is not an intrusive 'r' in *drawing room* (not draw-ring), *an idea* of (not idea-r-of). Avoid the American habit of stressing -ar in *n*ecessarily (not necess*a*rily) and *t*emporarily (not tempor*a*rily). Remember that *cog* in recognise and don't let it become *reccernise*, the short 'i' in privacy and don't it become *eye*, and that the final 't' is silent is restaurant. Sound the 'u' in popular, don't say *pop'lar*.

While 'h' is silent in *hour*, it is aspirated in *hotel* and so therefore takes the 'a' indefinite article (except in *The Times*, for example, which still insists on *an* hotel). While it is wrong to use 'n' for 'ng' in *length/strength* and so get *lenth/strenth*, the sound *lenkth/strenkth* is acceptable.

A long 'o' goes before 'll' in *poll* (vote) and before 'lt' in *revolt*, but there is a short 'o' in *resolve/dissolve/solve/golf* as in *doll*. *Either* as in *eye* or in *seize* – both are acceptable (the Queen is said to prefer *eye*). *Envelope* starts -en as in end (-on is disliked by RP speakers). *Data* has a long first 'a'.

In formal speech, say before an audience, avoid dropping the 'r' if it is closely followed by another 'r' as in *deteriorate* to get deteriate: similarly, *February* can slip to Febuary, *temporary* to tempary (but temp'rary OK), *honorary* to honary (hon'rary is preferred), *itinerary* to itinery, *library* to libr'y, *probably* to prob'ly. Avoid dropping the fourth syllable in *particularly* to get particuly but the elision of the middle syllables of adjectives of four syllables ending in -ary makes the words easier to pronounce as in milit'ry, necess'ry.

Watch out for syllable elisions in *chocolate, police, mathematics* to get the sloppy choc'lte, p'lice, math'matics. Don't let *fifth* become fith, *months* drop to 'munce', *camera* to 'camra'; make *lure* rhyme with *pure* not 'poor'. Articulate *railway*: don't let it become 'ro-way'. Don't let *conflicts* sound like 'conflix'. And don't lose the 'e' in *create* and let it sound like crate. Take care with the 'u' sound in some words: it should be *uh* in *uncle, multi, adult* not owcle, mowlti, adowlt.

GET THE WORDS RIGHT TOO

In speech, the rules that apply in written work can be eased a little, otherwise you could sound stilted and unnatural. Where there are uncertainties, like ending sentences with prepositions and split infinitives, forget about offending anyone. Don't worry too much about whether it is different *from* or *to*; but where *only* goes in a sentence can make a big difference to the meaning.

Never make grammatical errors like *there*'s two cars in the garage, every one of the delegates *were* present, the object of her articles *are* to inform, between you and *I* and so on, or colloquialisms like he was *sat* there. Follow the advice in earlier pages on style and construction. If you do that, you won't be far wrong when you are on your feet.

For more about speechwriting and delivery, see Chapter 17.

When speaking quickly, pronouns and auxiliary verbs easily disappear. Avoid *gonna/wanna, kinda, doncher* (don't you), *innit, wannit* (isn't it/wasn't it), *'spec/spose'* (I expect/suppose). Careful speakers will retain the 't' in *facts, acts, ducts, pacts*; otherwise the listener hears fax/axe/ducks/packs. But it is silent in *often* as in *soften*. And don't forget the final 't' in *that*: it is often lost to become *tha is* for example.

American pronunciation differs markedly from the British. Some examples from *The Oxford Guide to English Usage*: the 'r' is sounded by American speakers wherever it is written, after vowels finally and before consonants, as well as before vowels, like *burn, car, form*. The sound of *you* (as in *u, ew* spellings) after s, t, d, n, is replaced by the sound of *oo* as in resume (*resoom*), Tuesday (*Toosday*), due (*doo*), new (*noo*).

Americans pronounce asthma (*ass*-ma in RP) as *az*-ma; detour (*dee*-tour not *day*-tour in RP) as *de*-tour; *gala* (*a* as in *calm* in RP) as *gale*. They will say *trow*ma as in *cow* whereas RP speakers will say *trau*ma (*au* as in *cause*).

Some forms of pronunciation are to be especially avoided. Among these are *Arctic* (do not drop the first 'c'); *et cetera* (not *eksetera*); don't let *garage* (with stress on the first syllable) sound like *garridge*; do not drop the first 'n' in *government* or the whole second syllable; do not say *pee* for pence in formal speech; avoid making *people* sound like *peeple*; ensure *plastic* rhymes with *fantastic*; *sovereignty* is pronounced *sov'*renty, not sounding like sov-*rain*-ty; a *suit* is now pronounced with an *-oo* sound although the *you* sound is still frequently heard. *Secretary* is pronounced *sek*-re-try not *sek*-e-terry or even worse *sukk*-a-terry). *January* should sound like *Jan*-yoor-y, not Jan-yoo-ery (except in America).

You take your pet to the *vet*-er-in-ary practice, not vet'nary. You buy jewel'rey not *jool-ler-y*. You look at a *pic*-ture not a *pitcher* and you make a *fort*-une, not a *forchoon*. And it is all a matter of pron*u*nciation, not pronounciation!

There are probably more regional forms of speech in the United Kingdom than anywhere else in the world, and it is in no sense suggested here that everyone should follow RP; adjustments have to be made as circumstances demand in various parts of the country. Just as much depends on *how* you say something as *what* you say. RP provides a useful guide.

AT A GLANCE

- The key to effective verbal communication lies in good diction.
- No one wants to hear slipshod, careless speech.
- Received Pronunciation (RP) is a useful yardstick for 'correct' language.
- Placement of stress identifies RP speakers.
- In fast talking, pronouns and modal verbs are easily lost.
- Enunciate words precisely; don't drop consonants.
- Don't allow words to become slurred.
- Avoiding grammatical errors is equally important in speech.

17

Principles of presentation

Sooner or later everyone has to speak in public. PR practitioners are no exception: as organisers, they soon find themselves on stage; even the youngest recruits will be presenting to clients and customers before they know it. And there is always the staff meeting with a room-full of blank faces waiting for that important announcement, perhaps the seminar, the conference or after-dinner speech.

The ability to express yourself clearly with confidence and style is a key business skill. And the better you are, the more likely you are to land a better job or even reach the conference circuit, with attendant financial rewards.

Public speakers are made, not born. Even fast talkers with the 'gift of the gab' are not necessarily going to be good on their feet. If you can develop the skills of presentation, use body language effectively and deliver with force and aplomb, you are on the way to becoming a star on stage.

We have all suffered from after-dinner speakers too nervous to say anything but platitudes, lecturers fidgeting and waving their hands around like a windmill, technical boffins reading word-for-word from a prepared script, grim-faced production executives looking and sounding petrified, glaring at the audience, and the chairman who hisses into the mike 'Can you hear me at the back?'. Avoid anything like this and at least you will have made a start.

Even if the speaker performs well, success or failure will depend on the organiser. If the mikes don't work, if the slides are upside down or if the session overruns, that is what is remembered; if the press handouts are inadequate, if anything major goes wrong, there's the possibility of lost business and, horror of horrors, a 'See me in the morning' message on your desk.

So, what makes a good speaker and organiser?

FIRST STEPS FOR SPEAKERS

When you are invited to give a speech, there are several things you must know: the audience, title, length, timing, visual aids facilities, how the discussion will be handled, and the publicity plans. If you are advising executives on public speaking, or an event organiser, these are all crucial factors. Let's look at them.

Know your audience – and the facilities

First, find out all you can about the audience: who they are, what they do, where they come from, their average age. Establish likely attendance, whether there will be media coverage. If you are the organiser, make sure that the event is widely reported unless there are special reasons for it to be off the record. Find out if the delegates will be sympathetic or critical, the prime questions they will ask, the one you will *have* to answer.

Be prepared to involve the audience: arrange for someone to put up another flip chart and work between the two. Ascertain the name of the chairperson and who the other speakers will be, especially those just before you. And while you are at it, check the technical facilities, lighting, stage set and platform plan. Get to know the production crew. Ensure every seat allows an uninterrupted view of the stage. Check the lighting – and find out where the switches are. And make sure the doors don't squeak; take an oil can with you!

Title

Is the title you have been given right or do you want to suggest something else? Unless the talk has to follow a certain theme, you can probably agree a change with the organiser. If so, ensure that it is provocative, not a 'label' devoid of punch and verve. Keep it as short as possible. Many years ago a leading advertising agency creative director called his pleas to production executives 'Why can't I get what I want?' That title worked extremely well and was quoted for years afterwards. Make sure you have a say in the 'blurb' about the subject of your speech; provide a colour photograph of yourself.

Length and timing

Agree to speak for no longer than half an hour, with a further 10 to 15 minutes for questions. Forty minutes would be the absolute maximum, otherwise the audience starts to get fidgety. For specialist seminars 20 to 30 minutes plus a short discussion period would suit most people. The shorter it is, the better the chance of your holding the audience's attention.

The worst time for any speaker is the session immediately following lunch. Avoid it whatever you do. Simply refuse that slot: it is when the audience is the least receptive to any serious, in-depth presentation. The organiser will appreciate your dilemma. The best time is a morning session, but not at the very beginning because there will always be latecomers. If you are stuck with it and there is nothing else you can do, use the 'wake-'em up' tricks of a noisy tape, a snappy video or an an eye-catching slide or stage prop.

The same timing principles apply to smaller meetings and seminars. In-house sessions don't present such a problem: staff don't dare to nod off! No matter what kind of event, you cannot expect much response at question time if you are the last afternoon speaker. Keynote speakers usually take one of the first morning slots.

Visual aids

Slides generated by a computer program such as PowerPoint, overhead transparencies (OHPs), videos, DVDs and audio tapes all help to pep up a presentation. Don't show horizontal and vertical slides one after the other; keep to one format and include plenty of photographs or drawings. Ensure that images fill the slides and overheads as much as possible. Keep text to bullet-points and don't exceed 25 words – use fewer if possible.

Make sure you have a broadband connection so that you can quickly log on to the company website to show some particular feature of its work, personnel or premises. Consult with your IT department to see if the web pages could be projected on to a large screen rather than relying on a desk-top computer.

If there are a number of statistics, keep the slides simple with a minimum of figures. For AGMs in particular, don't have more than five or six figure-slides; any more will have nil recall. Use bold type so that text and figures can be easily read; put bar charts in strong, contrasting colours. Keep to house style throughout and repeat the company logo on everything. PowerPoint computer-generated slides from Microsoft allow maximum creative possibilities. Provide delegates with all the statistical data as a handout – but only afterwards.

Questions

Be ready for the awkward question that comes from the back. If you can't answer it straight off, there's always the 'See me afterwards' ploy. But don't use it more than once if you can help it. You can always ask 'What do you mean by that?', which can silence the questioner for good. Or you can change the question to one you can deal with. Or, as a last resort, you can refer to a book or publication, even the handout material. Run through the questions you are likely to get beforehand and have your answers ready.

Publicity

Find out the plans for publicising your speech. Important points will lead to headlines, but be on your guard against leaks. (A deliberate leak can often help to spark interest.) The organiser will give you a deadline for a summary and for the completed paper with visual aids requirements.

The summary, which should contain the salient points in not more than around 150 words, will be used for the conference or seminar programme and also for advance press releases. Provide photocopies of the slides with the text of the speech, which can be made available to the press during and after the event. Consider VNRs (video news releases) to give broadcasters footage of important segments. Ensure all information in the publicity material is accurate and does you and your subject justice. Consider putting your speech on your website afterwards with access to charts and statistics.

GETTING READY FOR THE SPEECH

You have decided on what you, your client and/or your boss want to say and have supplied a summary to the organiser. You've decided on the title, you know how long the speech will be and you have a pretty good idea of what visual aids you are going to need. Now comes the crunch. It's writing time.

Preparation

The longer you can spend on preparation the better. Unfortunately, there is not always much chance for detailed research: start to gather notes, put basic ideas together. Don't forget the internet: it could provide much additional information – but check sources. If you are writing about a familiar subject, say a company development, service or product, the information will be to hand. But if you are dealing with a fresh topic, perhaps an after-dinner speech, then it's not so easy. You'll have to devote time to digging out interesting, yet relevant, things to say.

Look for facts and figures that will in themselves tell a story. But try to restrict yourself to statistics that have direct relevance to the subject. Unless they are essential background or are needed to substantiate a financial or technical subject, don't let statistics predominate. Don't try to be funny and start off with a joke. It could fall flat. Or someone will have heard it already! But take heart from the audience that *pretends* to laugh.

Structure

Like a report or feature article, your speech should have a beginning (an introduction), a middle (the body of the talk) and an end (a conclusion). The introduction should include something about yourself, who you are, what you do, followed by a quote or attention-grabbing fact, what the talk will be about and your main message.

Build on this for the main part of the talk, with the significant points and ideas you want to put over. For the conclusion, summarise the main points and finish on a high note with a recommendation for action of some sort. If there is no action as a result of what you have said, there was not much point in saying it.

Writing the script

For your speech to impart the desired message, for it to be well received and remembered, polished writing skills are essential. Go back to the earlier chapters 5 and 8–10 in particular, for help in getting the words and style right. Now for the rest.

Brevity

Ensure that no unnecessary words creep in. This demands extreme self-discipline, but the tighter the copy the better. The script should be more like a press release than, say, a long, fully reasoned article in a learned journal. Keep to plain English (see Chapter 9) and avoid clichés and jargon (Chapter 5), also avoid pleonasms (two concepts or words containing an element of redundancy, eg frozen ice, past history).

Be factual

Use the 'you' factor. Keep to facts or else you are likely to bore the audience stiff. Concentrate on new developments, services, the advantages and benefits of what you are going to talk about. If you have a comment or personal view to express, then use the personal pronoun 'I' and not the royal 'we'. But don't overdo the 'I', otherwise you will be seen as egotistical. Sprinkle your talk liberally with 'you'; if the ratio of 'you' to 'I' is not 10 to 1 in favour of 'you', rewrite your speech.

Repeat important points

Avoid repeating a word or words in close proximity to one another. It is, however, sometimes helpful to recall a point to give it extra emphasis. The audience will understand this.

Keep to the rules of grammar

Nothing will irritate your audience more than sloppy English. But don't worry about those myths of split infinitives and ending sentences with prepositions – in fact your speech could well sound a lot better, more natural, if you are not in the straitjacket of school-room strictures. Don't succumb to pedantry.

Avoid foreign words and phrases. Don't try to impress with your knowledge of foreign languages or you could be seen as showing off. Stick to plain English: avoid *ad hoc, quid quo pro, raison d'être, nom de plume,* for example.

Be controversial

Controversy sparks interest but be careful with sharp criticism. If you must find fault with somebody or something, make sure you present your arguments succinctly and back them up with solid evidence. In any case you could have lawyers at your door!

Keep anecdotes pithy

Beware of humour, which might not be appreciated by all your audience. If you have a joke up your sleeve which might offend one person in the audience, don't tell it. Rarely is anyone other than a professional comedian good at being funny on stage!

Be active and positive

Keep to subjects you care deeply about. Use the active, 'doing' tense, not the passive: choose verbs like go, tell, make, show. Once you allow as/were/have been/being in your presentation, you're stuck in the slow lane. Use single-syllable verbs when you can: they give punch and push. Don't write 'keep you abreast of' instead put 'Tell you' (see Chapter 9).

Kill double-talk

Tautology – saying the same thing again in another way (free gift, new innovation) – offends. It's the enemy of tight, crisp delivery.

No slang, bad language

Never use bad language no matter how informal the presentation. Be careful with slang: too many geeks, spiels, luvvies, gizmos or techno-nerds lower the tone. Don't use abbreviations, acronyms or technical jargon that might not be understood. Catch the mood of the delegates and don't talk down to them.

Draft and redraft

Never think that the first attempt at putting the speech into final text will do. Your effort will need several drafts by the time you have cut the verbiage, deleted useless words, and cut out confusing double-negatives and meaningless abbreviations. Type it double-spaced, not in capitals. And don't forget to run it through your spellcheck, not once but twice or once again for luck. And when you do, be careful you don't introduce more errors: they can easily happen.

Getting ready

Unless you plan to memorise your speech (which rarely works), put the salient points on cards with key words and phrases clearly marked. Have the typescript at your side (in loose sheets paper-clipped together, not stapled) in case of panics. Prompt cards should be numbered and of a convenient size; postcard-size is ideal.

Text should be in fairly large type, so that it can be easily read in dark conditions. Just a few bullet-points, not all the words, otherwise you will be tempted to read them out. Visual aids should be in the right order and be sure to rehearse and re-rehearse with the production team beforehand, ending with a full run-through. Ensure the lectern is at an appropriate height; if not, ask for adjustments. Don't tap tap the mike when you are about to start – all that should have been taken care of.

WHEN YOU'RE ON STAGE

You've patted your pocket to make sure you have your script or notes ready. When you go to the platform or make your way to the lectern from the speakers' table, here are a few tips.

Making the speech

Don't read it out word for word, turning the pages over one by one. That's boring. Put passion in your speech. Use those prompt cards and back up with visual aids or other props like books or objects relevant to your talk. Don't bellow into the mike. Keep your hands and arms still unless you want to point to a chart, and then preferably use an electronic pointer. Fix points in the audience and make eye contact in several places.

Always stand up when you address an audience, even at question time. The only exception is a break-out discussion session, when informality is usual. Your goal as a communicator is for people to understand and absorb your message. Pauses contribute substantially to the power of your delivery.

Silence before a particular point adds depth. Take a lesson from the way you write: punctuate the spoken word with pauses – long for a full stop, short for a comma.

If you have a standing mike, always keep it between you and the audience: if, for instance, you are looking towards the left, move slightly to the right so that the mike is directly between you and them. Otherwise, your voice might drift away. If, on the other hand, you have been given a clip-on mike, it won't matter where you are, but remember to take it off when you leave the stage.

Appearance counts

Look happy, confident and, most important, look good. Use body language: a wooden, stiff speaker will put off an audience before a word is said. Don't adjust your hairdo, and keep as still as you can with your eyes on the audience. Don't fold your arms, don't fiddle with coins, don't grimace. Deliver your presentation as if your whole world depends on it.

Dealing with fear

Everyone suffers to a greater or lesser extent from fear when speaking in public; however much effort you've made in getting the words right, the visuals spot on, it's of no avail if you're frozen stiff with stage fright. Take every opportunity to be on your feet. Offer to take part in the next client presentation or staff meeting: it will give you first-class practice for the real thing in a packed conference hall. Don't drink alcohol before a speech or presentation; this slows reaction at the very point when you need to be on your toes and alert.

Take some tips from Roy Topp, public speaking coach. He advises:

> Breathe deeply and slowly. This controls the heart rate. Also, strange as it may seem, roll the soles of your feet from heel to toe, on the floor under the table. No one will notice and although it sounds improbable, it certainly helps. Look round the room. Concentrate on the broad picture.
>
> Move slowly and do not let anyone rush you. When you stand up or move across the floor to approach the lectern, move easily and at leisure. This will not stop you being nervous, but it will control that anxiety and give the impression that you are in full control.
>
> Do not flap your hands. Keep them out of your pockets. Let them rest by your side. Keep your fingers off the lectern unless you are making a point; don't wave your arms about. Take your speech at a reasonable pace. Count slowly to three when pausing. Do not rush it. Pause, and look at your audience occasionally (you are in control). Do not talk over laughter or applause. You have earned it.
>
> Do not be too hasty to dash away. Remember, if you have a clip mike on your dress or lapel, remove it first, otherwise you might literally bring the house down!

Further help on dealing with stress and on many other aspects of speech-making will be found in Sarah Dickinson's *Effective Presentation* (Orion Business Books) and a book of the same title by Ros Jay and Anthony Jay (Pearson Education).

In conclusion

Sum up the important points of your presentation – not more than 10, as above that they'll be forgotten. Make a recommendation, or a series of them, for action to make something happen. End on a high note. Thank the audience for their attention.

At question time

Note down each question and listen to all of it. Thank the person asking it. Repeat it for the benefit of those who may not have heard it. If you get a difficult question, you can possibly refer it to an another person in the audience. And there's always that get-out 'See me later' or 'I don't have the facts with me right now' – time to find a satisfactory answer after the session.

POINTS FOR ORGANISERS

The programme

A well-designed, printed programme is essential. It should give the title of every session, the speaker, with a photograph, the chairman and a brief summary of the subject, as well as the fee, registration details and information about the organisation running the event.

It should be widely distributed to the target audiences and the press, and be accompanied by a supporting letter from the organiser. This is the main 'selling' medium for the event and it should not be skimped. The print run should allow for at least two mailings. Design should follow style for the company and the logo should appear prominently. Put the programme on the company website.

Conference papers

It is important that copies of conference papers are available not only to the press but also to delegates. However, ensure that delegates are only able to obtain copies after the speech; otherwise, they will be turning over the pages one by one and not listening or watching the screen, or – worse still – might skip the session altogether! Conference papers can be made available afterwards as a printed book – and add to the revenue.

Publicity

Press releases

Restrict press releases to reporters and other editorial staff. Copies of speeches, background information, the programme and other administrative material should be available in the press office. Follow-up releases, giving important recommendations and findings, should be issued. Don't forget to provide plenty of telephones and facilities for sending and receiving emails with a broadband connection.

The press conference

If you are responsible for press conferences and briefings, take a low-profile stance and let those responsible for making announcements take the stage. Your job is to introduce the speakers, see to the administrative details and make sure the journalists have the information they need. The principles outlined in this chapter apply to press conferences and briefings in the same way as to any other presentation.

AT A GLANCE...

- The organiser's role is crucial for a slick, professional event.
- First priorities are to decide on the objectives and theme, visual aids and timings.
- Employ a professional conference organiser, designer and production company for best results.
- Look for opportunities for financing an event through sponsorship and exhibitions.
- Decide on whether to open the meeting to the press and to publish the proceedings.
- Estimate print costs for the programme, tickets and the delegate list.
- Allow for costs of celebrity chairman or after-dinner speaker and speakers' fees, and travelling and accommodation expenses.
- Then work out the registration fee.
- Choice of venue is the most crucial decision for organisers: should it be a hotel, conference centre, perhaps even abroad? Look for unusual venues, especially those relevant to the subject.
- Delegates will remember the event for what went wrong, not what was good about it.
- Build in plenty of time for rehearsals when booking the venue.
- Establish clearly at the time of booking the period of notice if cancellation is necessary.
- Ensure that all written material is in the company style: visual aids should carry the company logo and follow house colours, the badging and programme; the stage set should be well designed and stylish. Consult your designer at all times.

18

The words for IT

The Computer Industry Almanac estimates that about 934 million people were online worldwide by the end of 2004, a figure expected to reach 1.63 billion by 2009. In the UK alone some 33.1 million adults were using the internet in 2004; by 2005 usage here will have jumped by perhaps 20 per cent.

No one knows. What we do know is that information technology (or IT) has transformed the way we work, the way we write, the way we deal with clients/customers, the way we communicate with media, and how we reach our target audiences.

Accuracy and consistency of language is essential. That much is obvious: but presentation is equally important. Whatever the message, its style must reflect a corporate image, whether for an internet website, an email message or an electronic communication system.

An internet presence is a public relations tool second to none. The job of public relations is to ensure that the website is clear, understood and used by each of an organisation's publics. There can be meaningless jargon, the logo might be missing, or if there is one it's in the wrong colour, there's bland design, sloppy English, poor navigation from the home page, emails with poor spelling, or missing punctuation.

All these things – or any one of them – can ruin the best of campaigns. Enthusiasm to complete the site and get it on the web can transcend everything else; reputation suffers and the PR effort is wasted. There's a hall of horrors. So what are the crucial points? Here's a round-up.

STYLE MATTERS

Variations abound because of the number of new words in day-to-day diction. Inconsistencies occur everywhere from humble email to in-depth website: wrong use of capitals is typical. Look at some examples:

- *Internet.* While some dictionaries say that Internet should have a capital 'I', most newspapers use lower case, and that is the style throughout this book. The small 'i' is, in the author's opinion, cleaner and less cluttered, especially if there are a number of references to it. Be consistent in all printed work, as well as in press releases, printwork and stationery.

   The lower-case style is also preferred by many public relations practitioners for the shortened version *net*; context usually avoids confusion with other meanings. The term *intranet* always has a small 'i'.
- *World Wide Web.* Again, in public relations *worldwide web* and *web* are often preferred, and this is the style for this book.
- *Online.* No hyphen, one word.
- *Dotcom*, as in a dotcom company. One word; don't insert a full point.
- *Email.* A hyphen is used for 'e' prefixes, *e-commerce, e-PR, e-tailing*, etc, to avoid confusion with words starting with a vowel. However, email is increasingly common and is the style used in this book.
- *CDROM.* In public relations the preferred style is caps *with a hyphen*, though the hyphen is not used in this book. Again, you should be consistent and extend the style to derivatives such as CDR, CDRW (CD recordable/rewritable).

Style for 'old' technology
Use *facsimile*, not the informal *fax*, for address details in letterheads

and other stationery, but use *fax/phone* as a verb ('I will *fax/phone* you').

Abbreviations generally

As a general rule, keep the caps (no points) for the numerous sets of initials that form jargon for the internet: for example FAQs (Frequently Asked Questions), FTP (File Transfer Protocol), HTML (HyperText Markup Language), HTTP (HyperText Transfer Protocol), ISDN (Integrated Services Digital Network) and URL (Uniform Resource Locator, often called the web address or domain name).

Other words

Unless an abbreviated name, use lower case throughout, with an initial capital for proper names such as Gopher (menu-based server, derived from *go for*), Mega/ Gigabytes (MB/GB for short), Netscape, Outlook Express and so on.

GETTING THE MOST OUT OF EMAILS

Emails provide a fast and efficient means of communication. As a marketing tool email is brilliant: no matter how many messages you send out at one time, the cost is the same – just one call to your service provider. And if it is included in your website, the potential marketing benefits and opportunities increase substantially. We all use email. But there are dangers lurking 'twixt keyboard, screen and printer that could spoil or diffuse your message. Here are some of them.

No room for 'Weblish'

Since email is informal, punctuation, grammar and spelling suffer. A message to a colleague with no capitals and lacking apostrophes, commas and colons, with missing or wrong characters and with sloppy construction, could easily go to a client. You wrote 'Weblish', the language of the couldn't-care-less. And that could be disastrous for the client/agency partnership.

While emails can be breezy and friendly, there's no excuse for downright bad English. Never write an email in all lower case;

think what the client might think if his favourite product fails to get a capital letter! Equally poor is the email with words fully capitalised: that in terms of 'netiquette' is shouting.

Keep to proper paragraphing, follow the basic rules of grammar, and retain the apostrophes (because they aid sense and clarity), brackets and minor punctuation marks like commas, semicolons and hyphens when you would normally include them.

When addressing someone, it is – for some at least – old-fashioned to put 'Dear so and so'. Don't worry about courtesy titles Mr/Mrs/Miss/Ms, just open with Hi, Hello or similar.

For inter-office memos, you can relax: use short-cuts like BFN (bye for now), BRB (be right back), BTW (by the way), FYI (for your information), GTL (gone to lunch), thx (thanks), IMHO (in my humble opinion), and 4 for four/for if really pushed. There are lots more to help you to speed up office life in www.chatdictionary.com – but keep them there.

The occasional 'smiley' can be useful for in-house memos and informal communications. Some of the popular ones are: :-) happy ● ;-) wink ● :-(sad ● ;-(chin up ● ( ) hugging ● :-x I'll say nothing ● x-) I see nothing.

See www.netlingo.com for more smileys and emoticons.

Keep clear of trouble

Get your company's policy on emails and internet usage in writing to avoid misunderstandings. If there are no established rules, ask for guidance. If you follow company practice for personal telephone calls, you won't be far wrong.

WRITING AND DESIGNING WEBSITES

Basic principles

Websites demand short copy. Give an overview to start with on the home or introductory pages, then the detail. You must first know how the site is going to fit together, the level at which the copy will feature – on the home page, on the primary section page or buried in a niche content area?

According to June Dawson of a leading website design company, the writer must be clear about the target audience.

Producing appropriate links that take the reader to the longer copy requires a clear understanding of what will attract attention. She comments:

> You may find that you require two writers, one for news stories with punchy, factual, short pithy copywriting skills and the other capable of producing compelling, but longer copy. This is key because the two – like magazine journalists – each need to adopt a different approach.
>
> Generally, short news stories are key: people are busy, time is money, so deliver the important points quickly and efficiently or they will move on and not come back.

When you start to think about a website, familiarise yourself with the technicalities so that you can talk to the designer on equal terms. Much help will be found in *Creating web pages for dummies* by Bud E Smith and Arthur Bebak (Wiley, 2002) and *Creating killer web sites* by David Seigels (Hayden Books, 1997) .

Steve Sawyer, web consultant at Computer Software Group (CSG) Integra Division, says that what is needed is a readable, usable site through which the visitor can interact with the organisation. 'A clearly labelled, navigational structure which lets the readers know where they are in the site at all times is essential.' It should be remembered, he says, that users will have computers with differing software. It is therefore important to preserve the 'look' of the site by specifying web-friendly font types such as Verdana, Arial or Helvetica (sans-serif fonts), or Georgia, Times New Roman or Times (serif typefaces). He warns that if specialist or non-standard fonts are used, which may form part of house style, they must be 'embedded' or only used in graphics, ensuring that the text will not be reformatted with unknown results.

What makes a good site

The internet has, as we all know, the http:// prefix to every website (there is no need here to go into the complexities of what these initials stand for). Users navigate by typing web addresses directly into their browser or by clicking links on a page. Links via text or images enable navigation around a site and between websites. The way in which pages and links are written and designed significantly affects the usefulness of a site and the information available.

It is the designer who spells success or disaster for every website. Freelance Barry Skeates says a good site is the one that quickly and easily communicates information to its target audience. That could be achieved with a printed brochure, newsletter, sales aid, or catalogue; but the website could be all of these things – and more – at lower cost and with a wider penetration. But it will only work if users are encouraged to navigate through it.

It is the designer's and writer's job to make sure this happens. Colour, graphics, creative use of typefaces and animation can all help to make written statements stand out above others. But don't overdo it: too many colours look a mess and can detract from the copy. Words should be kept to a minimum with lively, short headings and liberal use of bullet points.

Building a website

Once you have chosen and registered a domain name – through your ISP (Internet Service Provider) for example – you will have your own Uniform Resource Locator (URL). This is your website's connection to the internet and the worldwide network of computers. Start with a site plan for navigating from the entry point, the home page. Then create a site map to provide links to other pages.

PR strategy

Most companies these days have a presence on the internet. Advice will be needed on the style of the site in much the same way as it would for a corporate brochure or house magazine. Moreover, internet strategy must fit in with the organisation's overall business plan. Making the website work for the user in the most effective and profitable way should be the prime objective. PR objectives must, therefore, be settled at the outset.

You must decide how much information should be freely available, how much should be restricted through a password and, if appropriate, how to handle payments. And you must agree policy on the provision of media information – press releases, biographies, and details about the company structure, history, staffing and contacts.

Working with the designer

Your IT specialist must not be allowed to take charge of the design.

Look for a graphics designer with broad experience of setting up websites for a range of companies and products, plus a knowledge of print typography.

Ensure that the site is compatible with current browsers and with current sound and video software. Take account of any material subject to copyright and make sure that your logo and house style are followed throughout. Pay special attention to the home page: if it's a yawn, the user will give up and go elsewhere. Be wary of the design that looks pretty-pretty at first sight, but with a content so complicated that it is slow to load. That could be frustrating and a good reason to click off. And it is important to take account of accessibility: this applies particularly to users with poor eyesight.

The central object is to provide information – but not too much in one go – and with no spelling or grammatical errors. It must be updated regularly. Above all, the site must look good, sound good and read well.

Building Products Home Page

Figure 18.1 *Pilkington Inside, winner of the Web/Intranet category in the 2004 CiB Awards. Acknowledgements: Pilkington plc, David Roycroft, site designer*

Getting the pages right

The home page will set the tone. It must explain the site in a few words, preferably in bullet-point form, If there are house colours, use them; put the company logo on all pages.

Every page needs a title, and a link back to the home page. Headlines must be lively, short and pithy. Look for active, 'doing' verbs and put them in the present tense. Don't overdo the text, concentrate on graphics to tell a story in themselves; use snappy, two/three-word headings, give detail in short paragraphs of not more than two sentences. Susan Wright, a freelance technology journalist, says: 'Devise a menu that stays with you throughout the site so that you don't have to keep on going back to the home page. Make the type easy to read and reasonably big and don't drown the page in words.'

Keep all pages consistent in appearance: if there is a colour scheme, follow it religiously. Style sheets are available for typography, colours and for formatting different elements of the page, including background sounds, videos and graphics images.

Essentials of site typography

Website typefaces and styles are as much the 'voice' of your company as those for printwork and press advertisements. Correct choice of typestyle is crucial to the link between word and message.

There is no point in, say, an engineering company using a delicate, slender typeface when a strong, bold one would be more appropriate. There are hundreds of typefaces available from software suppliers: only your designer will know which one would work best.

Keep to the typefaces you normally use for brochures, house journals and stationery. However, since type can be manipulated electronically, departure from house style is likely. See that the designer's zeal doesn't spoil visual impact and the company's image. For this very reason, where possible give your usual designer the task of creating the website.

Aim for simplicity of layout and ease of navigation. Make the pages lively and appealing: out with the bland page, lacking strong colours. But don't use combinations that tire the eye: words reversed white out of black or red, and green on yellow are hard to read. It is better to have more pages and less text; increased links make the site easier to use. Text looks best black on

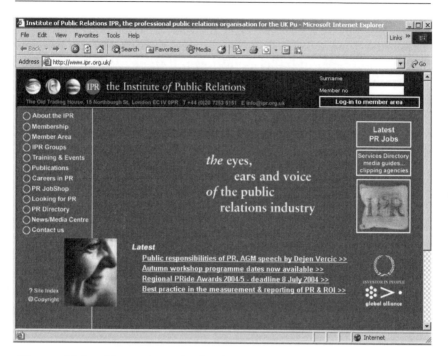

Figure 18.2 *Class winner in the Communicators in Business Awards 2003: the internationally acclaimed IPR website, produced by the Institute of Public Relations*

white, with colours for headings. Don't set the type too small; think of the viewer with poor eyesight. But make it attractive, snappy and full of facts. Don't let it look dated: look up the new sites for ideas.

Basic rules for typesetting

Set your copy ragged right where the text is aligned to the left. If it is justified, or flush on both sides, irregular letter- and word-spacing will result. Do not break words if just two or three characters would go over to the next line (see also Chapter 6). Never use hyphens for dashes; computer keyboards distinguish between the two marks (see Chapter 3).

Avoid over-hyphenation: rewrite or space out. Never specify paragraph indents; insert extra space instead. Most other general rules for typesetting as set out in *The Oxford Style Manual* should be followed for websites.

The reader is looking at a screen, not a printed page; text is easier to assimilate in bite-sized chunks. Aim for brief sentences of not more than 20 words, and no more than two sentences to a paragraph. Go for short line lengths of 30 or so characters compared with the more usual 65–70 characters.

Susan Wright, who has viewed thousands of sites, says that there's nothing worse than lines that stretch right across the page. Put the text two or more columns if necessary – anything would be better than a line of 8pt or smaller lettering going from one side of the screen to the other. Type size should be no smaller than 12pt for ease of readability. Don't forget that the eye tires after prolonged exposure to the computer screen, just as it does when watching TV continuously.

Use clear language

The language should be clear, plain and to the point. Put important conclusions and summaries at the beginning, so as to attract attention from the start. Avoid slang, but don't be afraid of humour. Make sure everything you say is believable. Keep the need to maintain brand loyalty uppermost. Keep strictly to the logo shape and colour: any departure will be immediately noticeable.

Adding pages and graphics

Put in new pages regularly: users will go for good if you don't update. Your designer will advise you on all aspects of adding pages and graphics; but if you want to have a go yourself, full information will be found in *Creating Web Pages for Dummies*. In a couple of clicks you'll have the site up and running. That's exaggerating, but you know what I mean.

Avoid that jargon

Don't use buzz words; they may not communicate the message in the way you intend. Out with the jargon; don't baffle your online users with words and phrases that are meaningless to the vast majority. Only use general expressions, not the vocabulary of the specialist. As has already been stated in Chapter 5, jargon could spoil your carefully designed site simply because it fails to communicate.

Don't put a string of initials together and expect the user to know immediately what they stand for; some, however, will be known and understood by most if not all users, like CD-RW (CD rewriter). Not everyone will know what ISDN (integrated services digital network) means. When referring to sets of initials, explain them at least once, preferably at first reference.,

Publicity

Your website is an unsurpassed communication tool. A well-designed, fact-full, look-good website can be a dream come true. But it will only be so if your customers – current and potential – know about it and use it. While a search engine should lead a stranger directly to your site, aim for easy and quick access. Print the address on business cards, office stationery, press releases, all printwork including brochures, leaflets and the house magazine, and show it on TV advertisements, posters, direct-mailers and shop displays. Give it out on radio ads. Put it on the firm's CD ROM, if there is one, on presentation slides, on company videos. Everywhere.

Count the number of site visitors regularly, and when they reach a record, say so. Mention it in interviews for the press and broadcasting media, at conferences and at seminars. Brief your staff when it is updated, and make sure the receptionist can go online and show it off to visitors!

LANGUAGE FOR THE TELEPHONE

Consider the way in which your telephone system is used, or perhaps abused. The operator is often the first point of contact. One bad experience can leave a lasting impression: business can be lost to a competitor simply because of ineptitude on the part of the receptionist.

If the operator is rude, offhand or at worst clueless about the firm and who does what, the organisation could suffer irreparable damage. Imagine a visitor having to compete with a gaggle of gossipers at the reception desk! Sloppy telephone technique and indifferent treatment of visitors can ruin corporate image faster than anything else.

Dealing with calls

Calls should be answered in no more than five or six rings, then automatically routed to an answering device if the line is busy. Better still if the call is answered in two or three rings, but unlikely. If the caller is holding on, the operator, or automatic answering service, should return every 30 seconds or so to check that the person hasn't been forgotten.

Modern systems take you through a list of touchtone options like 'If you know the extension you want, press it now.' This is a daft instruction because there can be few callers who know the number of the extension they want: much better to give numbered departmental options. Even so, these need to be kept to a minimum. Nothing can be more frustrating than having to listen to a long list to reach the extension you want. Worse still if it is a journalist seeking the press office for information on an important story.

Answering techniques

Operators should answer cheerfully, but without overdoing it and give the name of the organisation or its initials if well known. Don't say 'Hello', or 'Mr so and so', just give your name. Don't allow staff to say something like 'This is Tracey, how can I help?' That's overused and insincere.

Voicemail messages should be brief, warm and welcoming, not bark at you like an angry dog. Check messages regularly and return calls the same day. If you are answering for a colleague, note down messages and take the number even if you think you know it – the call might be coming from somewhere else.

Provide a monitor at reception for website and email access; let visitors use it. Circulate press releases, news bulletins, house journals and reports to the receptionists, so that they are aware of new products and services. Don't let other people make your calls and tell you the person is waiting on the line. It's not only a waste of time, it's discourteous.

MAKE YOUR CV TALK

Chapter 13 touched on some of the points to consider when writing and producing your CV on paper. Now there's a new way: on CD ROM through a special country-wide service. It's called Talking CV! – a software package providing a CD with your history in text and with your voice and picture beside it. You go to an assessment centre (there are several in London and will be some in regional centres) where they will interview you according to your job and position.

The service includes preparatory notes, the recording process, web page and password-protected URL for an initial three months, plus a CD ROM for potential employers or recruiters.

For details go to www.iteba.com/internet/control/TCV innovation or call 020 7841 3300.

Another route is DIY: use a web cam, a miniature camera (about £60) and a CD rewriter (around £100–400) to create your CV with the multimedia program included with the camera, type in any further information and then copy your CV to CD. You can also produce a video with text and pictures, but it could cost more. Go to www.winning-cvs.co.uk for help.

NOW TALK TO YOUR COMPUTER

If you want to dictate a release straight to your PC or get an instant print job in type you can do it with voice-recognition technology. You can start off with speech software such as Conversa Web (www.conversay.com), which you download to control and simplify access to web pages with voice commands. Unlike some specialist systems, you don't have to spend time 'training' the program to recognise your voice as it only has to 'understand' a few words. You install it and start talking.

More ambitious programs, such as IBM's ViaVoice (www-3.ibm.com/software/speech/) or Dragon's Naturally Speaking (www.scansoft.com/naturallyspeaking), are probably the better bet since they can control your PC with your voice and perform complex tasks without you having to touch the keyboard.

The programs are surprisingly inexpensive: the standard version of ViaVoice costs around £40, including a microphone headset, which is plugged straight into the sound card and integrates with Microsoft Word. Windows and Apple Mac versions cost slightly more. It has a vocabulary of about 100,000 words. The system is available in high street stores such as PC World or can be ordered online from Dabs (www.dabs.com) or Simply (www.simply.co.uk).

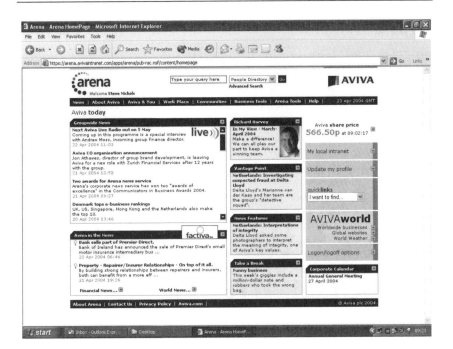

Figure 18.3 *CiB award winner Arena News Features in Best Writing for Electronic Media category. Credit: Steve Nichols, Infotech Communications, for Aviva plc*

AT A GLANCE

- Keep a consistent style for the language of the internet.
- There is no room for 'Weblish' in business communications.
- Don't allow over-informality in emails.
- Be clear about your target audience.
- Different writers may be needed for short and long stories.
- The key to a successful website is the design.
- Keep words to a minimum; use lively headings.
- Let the designer take charge.
- Agree policy on provision of media information.
- Aim for simplicity and ease of navigation.
- Choose typefaces carefully; no paragraph indents are needed.
- Ensure your website address is on all printwork.
- Keep voicemail messages brief, warm and welcoming.
- Investigate time-saving voice-recognition technology.

19

Tone – the linchpin of reputation

The one essential factor in any communication is its tone, or how the message is written and perceived by the reader. The tone must be appropriate for the audience: if it offends, smacks of officialdom, sounds harsh or patronising, or is full of unwarranted jest, then you have a public relations problem.

Tone of voice is the way we speak, how we talk. It displays our attitude to other people. A smiling face, a gracious greeting instead of a glum look and coarse voice do wonders for communication. The writer should try to put into words the warmth that exudes from a person who speaks in a relaxed and friendly way. Achieving an appropriate tone that is right for every audience is the difficult part, and must be tackled. A firm's overall tone of voice in words, speech and manner is as much the image of the company as any smart logo or snappy advertising campaign.

This chapter is mostly concerned with the written word; speech is covered in Chapters 16 and 17. The tone you adopt in writing will make all the difference between success and failure, no matter whether it's a corporate brochure, annual report, press release, leaflet or letter. Look now at your options and the possibilities of putting your company, your message in the best possible light, the right tone. After all, that is what public relations is all about.

BASIC PRINCIPLES OF TONE IN WRITING

What is tone in writing? The short answer is that it is the writer's attitude towards the reader and the subject of the message being delivered. The tone of a written message can affect the reader in the same way as tone of voice impinges on the listener's attitude and reactions to the speaker. So tone, whether in writing or speech, has a significant effect on how the message is perceived. It must therefore take a prime place in every organisation's communications strategy. But how is the writer to know the appropriate tone to adopt? That depends on the reason for writing a document or piece of print in the first place, its intended audience and whether a formal or informal tone is needed.

The chosen tone must not leave the reader feeling that the writing has jarred or is in any way unsettling. No matter whether it is a letter, mail shot, report or document, it needs the one quality that is so often missing: charm. As Drayton Bird describes in his *How to Write Sales Letters that Sell* (Kogan Page, 2002), the ability of the writer to adapt the tone will make letters *charming* (his italics). The adequate writers, he says, write in exactly the same way, but the outstanding ones disarm the reader just as a charming individual can disarm somebody he or she is trying to influence.

Making the reader comfortable

The overall tone for the written word must make the reader comfortable and at ease with what is said. This means, in pretty well every case, using I/we rather than the third person, as in XYZ company does this or that. It also means using 'you' instead of standing back and ignoring the reader as an individual. It means using the active voice, avoiding passive verb-phrases including am, is, was, were or been. For example, it is much better to write 'I make' than 'I am making'. And once you are in the habit of using constructions with participle *-ing* or *-ed* verb endings you make the copy stodgy and unpalatable, so off-putting to the reader.

It is crucial in adopting a suitable tone of voice to steer clear of discriminatory language that can offend. That means, for a start, avoiding sexist terms and such factors as race, religion, age, sexual orientation and any kind of disability.

In business communications it is hard to adopt an all-embracing tone when there are several audiences, for example in healthcare and financial services. In both, the tone needs to be warm, friendly and caring, yet authoritative and firm when the occasion demands, whether in correspondence or printwork.

TOWARDS A BETTER TONE

Write in a way that suggests you are helping the reader. You will need to stress the benefits of whatever product or service you are writing about, but you must avoid jargon and technical language that may not be widely understood. This is particularly important when the message is going to a variety of audiences, to shareholders, dealers and customers for instance. In such cases, it will probably be necessary to produce several versions of the same message. Internal budgets will usually decide whether or not this is worthwhile.

Adopt a friendly, warm style, even a chatty one provided it isn't overdone, but don't let it appear patronising. When the time comes for a negative message, use a tone that is gracious and understanding. For example, if it is necessary to tell someone their application for a loan must be rejected, don't sound officious and unhelpful. Put it so that the reader understands that your firm has its rules, and will do everything possible to help in the future. Again, if you have to write a letter to confirm someone's dismissal, write it in a considerate and caring way. You never know where that person will be employed next.

Don't try to bully the reader into believing something, as so many sales letters seem to these days. Don't be afraid to apologise if something goes wrong, say a delivery that went astray or failure on the part of your staff. Take the blame yourself and don't try to shift it to underlings.

It is necessary to strike a balance between a tone that is friendly but firm. There is the danger of over-informality: it kills credence, even authenticity. Write we will/would, not we'll/we'd, you are/have and not you're/you've. The shortened style is fine for ads, sales letters and mailshots, perhaps some letters, internal memos and emails, but is too sloppy for formal printwork.

The tone you take says something about you and what you and your company are like. Since it affects how your message is perceived, it is essential to get it right, no matter how much effort and time that might mean.

Tone for the public

Most firms dealing with the public and with many different audiences take tone seriously. A leading firm in the insurance sector has, for instance, issued its staff with a set of guidelines to give the company a distinctive tone. In correspondence and mailshots, for example, it's *you're* not you are, and using plain English with active verbs and superlatives where appropriate, but staying clear of slang words like 'fab' and 'cool'.

Rather than writing 'I'm in receipt of your letter' it's 'thanks for your letter' even though to some eyes this would appear over-informal, even slapdash. But the company's PR department says there is always room for personal expression when circumstances demand. It's all a question of combining figures and statistical information with human understanding. Everyday language is the company's watchword.

A caring tone can turn round a hostile and bitter audience. For example, the head of a city council's tax collections department at one time told bereaved families that they must pay the deceased person's remaining tax bill quoting 'chapter and verse' on how the tax must be paid without any expression of regret or sympathy. No apology was offered for making the demand in case of litigation. The council was seen as cold and uncaring, only interested in getting money out of taxpayers no matter what the circumstances. But the council's PRO says that once an apologetic acknowledgement of bereavement was given, a higher rate of tax collection resulted. 'By apologising and explaining, people paid up rather than ignoring the previous insensitive letter.' So here was a positive outcome from an improved and understanding tone.

Using a caring tone

The healthcare sector provides examples of how a friendly, yet authoritative, tone delivers a meaningful message to patients, as well as to health professionals and the wider public. For instance, a leaflet for the charity Healthy Heart UK, to raise awareness and increase understanding of the risk factors for coronary heart disease, is written in a clear, easy-to-follow style, but covering complex medical subjects. The leaflet, drafted by Ash Communications of London, explains a medical procedure in easy-to-follow steps, telling patients what they can expect from a new treatment procedure. It is printed in largish (18pt sans serif) type with a bright, cheerful cover.

Leaflets displayed in every doctor's surgery make extensive use of the personal pronoun 'you', 'we', and shortening *that is* to 'that's, *how is* to how's. Wide use of lower case for headings gives a softer, less harsh look than capitals. Such written and visual styles are the prime ingredients of a caring and positive tone, essential for effective communication to a range of audiences.

A study in 2004 by the National Consumer Council found that one in five people had trouble in understanding basic health information. 'Health literacy is essential for improving health and health services', says the NCC. Leaflets for patients should be written in plain, easy-to-understand language. Those presented in a question-and-answer format work well: for example, an NHS information pamphlet on immunisation against pneumoccoccal infection for the over-75s explains how infection is spread and what the symptoms are in an easy-read form. It is important not to downplay serious illnesses, but to give the facts without using medical terms and procedures that might not be understood.

A soft, warm tone of voice is essential for health messages. Phrases like 'you will understand/find that' is far preferable to 'you must do this or that', or 'you may feel a little uncomfortable' not 'you might/will feel pain'. Always write in a way that will leave patients feeling confident yet relaxed about any procedures they might have to undergo, and confident that the healthcare staff are there to help them at all times.

Sue Ash, managing director, Ash Communications, explains: 'The key is to pitch the message according to the audience. It is important not to be patronising, but to use straightforward language, avoiding jargon and finding a balance that will work for all levels of understanding.'

Tone in marketing communications

David Lowe, marketing consultant and lecturer, says that a consistent tone must be maintained in planning marketing communications, which today embrace an increasingly broad range of media. As well as the long-established mass media of TV and national press, posters, radio and cinema, there are the specialist press, direct mail and even the internet, which enable commercial messages to be targeted far more accurately at specific audiences.

He says that since marketing experts are now expected to justify their decisions by quantifying results in terms of enquiries and sales, there is a growing tendency to add more measurable communications media to the mix. The target audiences will therefore receive messages in a number of different ways. 'Sometimes the tone of these messages may vary with a consequent loss of overall impact', says David Lowe. 'One of the reasons for this is that rather than one agency being responsible for everything, specialist suppliers may be used to create material for their particular media and a consistent creative strategy is not followed. For instance, the website designer may have no knowledge of how the same message will be conveyed in a direct mail campaign. They in their turn are unaware of the work the agency is producing for the trade press.'

Another factor is that audiences don't necessarily fit into neat, self-contained 'boxes'. Customers may also be shareholders, employees or live close to the factory. In each of these roles, they may need to receive different types of information. But the tone must be consistent. 'To be effective, every piece of marketing communications should have the same tone, irrespective of the medium chosen. The organisation concerned has to establish clearly what tone is appropriate for its established corporate culture and brand identity, and then ensure that this is carried through in all its communications', says Lowe.

Developing an informal tone

Because you are writing a business letter or memo, or even a section for your company brochure or annual report, there is no need to be stiff and stodgy. Sentence structures with endless sub-clauses, perhaps running to 45 or even 60 words, fail to demonstrate anything other than the writer's ability to think up twice as many words as necessary.

The first thing to do is to use plenty of 'you' and 'your' and 'I' and 'we' pronouns. There is, however, danger in using too many 'I's, particularly for sentence starts. If you are talking about something your firm has done, or proposes to do, use 'we' and not XYZ company. But it would be egotistical to use 'I' in these circumstances, unless it is something that you have personally done or said.

The objective must be to make the communication sound natural and relaxed, but professional and authoritative at the same time. Be careful with the use of 'yourself' and 'myself', and make sure they don't sound self-effacing. Use everyday words and phrases, and don't try to be too clever by half and start talking about per annum, ad hoc and other familiar Latin terms. They don't sound friendly and can easily put off the reader who may not be as well educated as you are.

When it's time to be firm and formal

Useful tips on creating a formal tone will be found in Jo Billingham's handy book *Editing and Revising Text* in the Oxford 'One step ahead' series. The advice she gives can be summed up thus: use longer sentences than the recommended ones of 25–30 words; choose more complex words; number the points you want to make; omit softening phrases ('as you are aware' becomes 'as you know'); 'you should' becomes 'you must'.

Create a distance between writer and reader ('as you know' changes to 'readers will be aware'); long documents immediately appear more formal than short ones. And it's out with fashionable words like 'synergy' and jargon understandable to only a specialist audience. Treat the company as a single entity: XYZ company *is* not are doing something.

The best tone

The best tone is plain, unaffected, unblemished by superlatives. It neither talks down nor jazzes (nor sexes) up; it regards all readers as equal; it doesn't excuse or apologise unnecessarily; nor does it try to belittle the reader by showing how clever or sophisticated the writer is; it's not 'one-up' on the reader. It is warm and friendly if circumstances allow; it is enthusiastic about what you have to say. It is confident, yet courteous and sincere. And it demonstrates a helpful attitude coupled with an offer to overcome problems. The best tone can express disappointment but never anger.

The crux of the matter is to adapt and vary your tone according to the audience and whether the message is something you want the reader to do, or is simply for information. In a letter, for example, you would adopt a different tone to a supplier who had let you down to the one who is going to provide a special service that you desperately need.

Write with words that are similar to those you would use if you were speaking. You would write in a different way to junior members of staff instructing them to do something than you would to the managing director of a client company about a new contract. It's all a question of balance. Getting that balance right is the difficult bit.

AT A GLANCE

- How you say something is just as important as what you say: that's tone.
- Tone is the writer's attitude to the reader and subject of the message.
- The tone to choose depends on the reason for writing the document, what you are trying to convey.
- Decide whether a formal or informal tone is appropriate.
- Your chosen tone must not be jarring or unsettling to the reader.
- The tone used must make the reader feel comfortable and at ease with what is said.
- Use I/we not the third person; choose the active, not passive voice.
- Steer clear of discriminatory language.
- Avoid sexist terms, and terms that distinguish race, religion, age or any disabilities.
- Stress the benefits of products and services.
- Adopt a friendly, warm style but don't be patronising.
- Over-informality kills credence and authenticity.
- Use plain English; omit jargon.
- Ensure tone is consistent across all communications and audiences.
- Keep sentences short for an informal tone, longer for formal messages.
- Don't belittle the reader by showing how clever you are.

20

Reporting annually: chore or challenge?

There can be few public relations people who are not at some time in their careers involved with their organisation's annual report. Even if it's not their direct responsibility, PR practitioners will almost certainly be tasked with producing copy for it: perhaps a section on communications strategy, details of events and other functions, maybe even a draft of the chairman's statement. In the case of trade associations, they might possibly contribute an outline of a message from the president; or if a charity then it might be an appeal by the patron for funds from supporters.

But whatever the job, it is an important one, embracing anything from content and copy to design and delivery. In many cases, the annual report serves the dual purpose of providing an account of the year's activities and financial performance and a regularly updated corporate brochure lasting the year, thus avoiding the expense of a separate, expensive publication.

The annual report is a prime communications tool. It is the voice and tone of the organisation: it enables the chairman, chief executive and directors to make policy statements, and demonstrates corporate governance credentials and responsibility for corporate social responsibility issues. In fact, it is a critical and crucial arm of corporate strategy provided it communicates effectively.

But that is where many reports fall down and waste shareholders' or members' money, while sheltering under the excuse that the annual review is something that must be done, no matter what the expense, irrespective of its value as a communication medium. To some it can be a chore, but for all a challenge to get it right.

ESSENTIAL ASPECTS

Far too many annual reports are poorly designed, badly written and fail to achieve anything but an uplift to the chairman's ego with a big picture and a self-satisfied group of directors. Look now at what the annual report must, by law, provide for a company's shareholders or an organisation's members or supporters. Even if the legal rules and regulations are seldom the direct concern of PR professionals, you should at least be aware of the main legislation affecting your organisation and its annual report.

Statutory requirements

It is a requirement of the Companies Act that every company (whether limited by shares or guarantee) is required to produce a set of accounts and put to an annual general meeting for approval by shareholders or members, with a copy to the Registrar of Companies. The directors must prepare a directors' report and, for quoted companies, a directors' remuneration report. There are severe penalties for failure to comply with the Act (the only exemption to delivering accounts applies to unlimited companies).

There are strict rules covering the content and format of the annual report and accounts to give a 'true and fair view' of the company and its financial affairs. Every member or shareholder is entitled to receive a copy of the annual report and accounts; the Articles of the company may be amended (under the Electronic Communications Order) to allow the annual report to be sent to shareholders using electronic communications. Listed companies are allowed to issue summary financial statements to shareholders, instead of the full accounts, but the full accounts must be available as an option.

If the company is also a registered charity or if the organisation is a registered charity, an annual report and return should also be issued to the Charity Commission. Charities need to comply with SORP, the Statement of Recommended Practice. A number of industries are governed by separate legislation: for example banks, building societies, insurance companies and some businesses such as solicitors and accountants need to comply with the rules of their governing bodies. Trade associations are often in the form of limited companies and are governed by the Companies Act.

Operating and Financial Reviews

An Operating and Financial Review (OFR) will be a requirement for all UK quoted companies for financial years beginning in 2005. Guidance for directors has been published by the OFR Working Group.

The introduction of a mandatory OFR was a key recommendation of the Company Law Review, and endorsed in the government's White Paper *Modernising Company Law* in the summer of 2003. Full details are available on the Department of Trade and Industry website, www.dti.gov.uk, or by email to ofrworking-group@dti.gsi.gov.uk.

Further information

For companies: contact the Registrar, Companies House, www.companieshouse.gov.uk. For charities: contact the Commissioner, Charity Commission, www.charity-commissioner.gov.uk. See also 'Further reading' at the end of this book.

WHAT MAKES A GOOD ANNUAL REPORT?

The prime issue here is that what is good for one organisation may not be so for another. Depending on the number printed, size and design, an annual report could cost anything from a pound or two per copy to 20 or more times that. Many reports I have seen are clearly much longer than they need to be, are over-designed and are frankly a waste of shareholders' money. (Shareholders don't pay for them directly, but they eat up profits that would otherwise be attributable to them in dividends.)

Writing in *The Scotsman* in March 2004, Executive Editor Bill Jamieson says that some chairmen lavish tens of thousands of pounds and 'endless hours' of management time on the annual report, only to get no coverage whatever in the business press and at best a desultory response from shareholders. He says that 'almost all' of the dozens of reports he receives 'fail to explain clearly what the company does or makes, how it has done better or worse than last year and what the realistic outlook is for the year ahead'. His telling message for CEO and the PR department: 'I would say the bigger and more expensive the annual report, the more evident the failure.'

The chairman's statement, he says, is becoming 'formulaic': by the time it has passed through 'lawyers, spin doctors, and compliance officers he might as well have asked a machine to do the job'. It is time, he argues, that companies got a grip on annual reports and returned them to first principles: a full, clear, no-frills statement of the business and a frank assessment of current conditions.

As a first step, annual reports should be halved in size, and politically correct waffle removed; the environment would be better served by allowing the paper to 'remain on the trees'. But however well intentioned all that may be, it is easier said than done. Let's look now at the possibilities for making the annual report more readable, more creative and above all a more cost-effective communications vehicle.

An international view

Leading PR professional Toni Falconi, founding chairman of the Global Alliance for Public Relations and Communication Management, has long experience in producing annual reports for major companies. Signor Falconi, Immediate Past President of the Italian Public Relations Association (FERPI), says that the issue of reporting annually is at the very core of self-expression, its ability to tell a story of a company's achievements to influential publics.

He feels it is a mistake for PR executives to be only involved in their traditional roles of responsibility for design, format, distribution and promotion. Their skills would be much better employed if they were concentrated on content, with views on financial, social and environmental issues.

Signor Falconi gives substantial support to Bill Jamieson's views. 'In general, today's reports are not very useful as they are mostly written by experts who know more about the company than appears in print. They are not written for the influential publics.' The question of language, what the report says and how it is expressed, is crucial: the PR professionals should be capable of interpreting technical and specialised jargon, including financial terms and statements, and making it readable and understandable. Otherwise, he asks, what other purpose is there for the PR person? Since most PR people fail to understand properly an annual report's specialised content, they are less able to interpret it, and subsequently transmit the information in a way that satisfies neither the reader nor the company.

Returning to Jamieson's theme, he reiterates that reports should be much thinner and more readable. In-depth analysis, charts and specialised data should be left to the website for the experts to extract the information they need.

THE IMPORTANCE OF EFFECTIVE COMMUNICATION

An analysis of the annual reports of Europe's top 100 companies by Prowse & Co, *The Company Report Report 2004*, concludes that the majority failed to communicate effectively to the target audiences of shareholders, employees, suppliers, customers and analysts. 'Lacking innovation, poorly structured, woefully designed, the majority of this year's reports give the impression of being simultaneously under-resourced and undervalued.' This damning conclusion is given further weight by the impact of the Enron scandal, which resulted in companies cramming as much information into their reports as possible, to the detriment of the overall document.

According to the report's publisher, Peter Prowse, increasing regulation is encouraging a 'tick the box' approach to planning the content of annual reports. 'Many large companies are now including information about corporate and social responsibility, employment policies and directors' remuneration because they are obliged to. The manager or director responsible for the content of the annual report goes through a checklist of things that have to be done. The really important messages that the company should be delivering to stakeholders start to take a back seat. The result is a thick document that complies with all the regulations, but nobody

Figure 20.1 *This annual Prowse analysis is an invaluable guide to the communications effectiveness of annual reports from Europe's top 100 companies*

wants to read it. It looks like every other big company's annual report and communicates very little about the organisation's personality – what makes it different and where it's heading.'

The chairman's statement

Probably the most important part of any annual report is the chairman's statement. It sets the tone and, says the Prowse survey, is the one part readers will read and remember. It is the only section to be closely examined, for it is there to give an overview of the company's performance over the year and a forecast of future prospects.

For a trade association, the chief executive's or president's message serves a similar purpose to the chairman's statement for a company, and usually occupies a prime position early in the document.

BP plc is number two in the list of top reports identified by Prowse. 'Standing apart from the pack, this report has a strong, simple message on the front cover that is simply demonstrated in the content of the remainder of the document. It contains plenty of information which is both well presented and written.' The chair's statement reflects the changing role of the board of directors and the company's anticipation of these changes.

Among the questions affecting the score allocated in *The Company Report Report* to the chairman's statement in each annual report are: How intelligent is the writing? Is it too short or too long? Are statements backed up with evidence from the company's performance? Does it compare in quality with an article in *The Economist* or does it have the feel of being written by a committee? Are there allusions to the company strategy and how coherent are these?

Written by ghostwriters?

Too many of the chairmen's statements appear to have been written by ghostwriters, says the report. 'Lacking in personality and often underestimating the intelligence of the reader', the majority tended towards bland, uninspiring copy, full of banal statements. Some were overly long, with one of over 3,000 words. Others tended to criticise policies or legislation enacted by their national governments. But, asks the report, is this the right place for airing these statements? Since this appears to be a rare occur-

Figure 20.2 *A novel approach for the eight-page 2003 annual review of the Institute of Practitioners in Advertising: its huge A1 (594 × 841 mm flat sheet size) folds twice to A3. Designed and produced by Radley Yeldar, London. Difficult to handle, but an easy read*

rence, it is felt that it would be better to leave them out altogether than risk alienating the reader.

One conclusion to be drawn from this survey is that the chairman's statement and copywriting for the remainder of the annual report should be left to the PR professional. This confirms and endorses the views of Toni Falconi, summarised above.

Design and presentation

Most shareholders, and indeed the majority of all those who are sent annual reports, will look either for financial results and the dividend, or for photographs of people they know. Then they give up: in the bin goes the report that directors, accountants and PR people have slaved over for months. The stodgy report tightly packed with grey type unrelieved by headings and typographical tricks is the biggest turn-off of all time.

The effectiveness of a company's annual report as a means of communication to its publics depends largely on design and how the information is presented. The worst possible course is to dig out last year's copy, just change the date on the cover and print it in a different colour. Good design means high-level creative input that only comes at a price.

Something like £180 million is spent each year on printing the country's annual reports, says Tim Taylor, marketing director of annual report specialist Butler & Tanner. With an expenditure like this, much care and attention is needed on design and content.

High unit cost

A company can spend as much as a quarter of a million pounds on its annual report. A full-colour, square-backed print job on high-quality paper running to 100 or more pages for 50,000 copies could cost even more. If an optional summary report (or a corporate and social responsibility report) is produced as well, that could increase the price, since the full version will go to City analysts and institutions, to journalists and overseas investors. A cost of more than £10–15 a copy would not be unusual. The annual report might turn out to be a waste of money at 75p but be good value at a fiver or more, says one former PLC finance director. It all depends on its merit as a communications medium.

For trade associations and smaller companies, lower print runs can mean a far higher unit cost, particularly if expensive, quality materials are used. The relatively high cost per copy of a lavish production is often justified by using the report as a corporate brochure for the year, so saving the expense of regular updating and printing.

Indeed, the Prowse survey is critical of creativity and production values. Very little evidence exists, says the report, of design reflecting companies' claims for being innovative enterprises. 'Quality of design is poor and at times completely lacking.' For instance, the average number of photographs in reports has fallen from 57 to 44 over the last two years.

'In publishing the *Company Report Report*', says Peter Prowse, 'we are trying to show what works well and what doesn't. We hope that company chairmen will begin to recognise best practice. It doesn't have to cost more to produce an excellent report than it does to produce a mediocre one. Enlightened companies realise that they are saddled with having to produce a detailed document, so they might as well produce something that does the best possible job for them. Companies that are close to their markets tend to lead the way.'

WPP sets an example

Many companies spend substantial sums on making their reports attractive and readable documents. One of them is the WPP Group of advertising, marketing and public relations companies, which presents in its report and accounts for 2003 a mass of information in a succinct, easy-to-digest style using line illustrations and graphics, with a central theme carried through the entire document. Line drawings of executive officers rather than photographs are used to give an individualistic feel to the production. Shareholders are 'share owners' and are addressed thus.

The 150-page report opens with a six-minute 'fast read' section, an outline of the group structure, followed by reader-friendly sections headed, for example, by who we are, how we're doing, what we think. Then follow the directors' report and sections on corporate social responsibility and financial information, together with a list of contacts at the back. The creative theme is embodied in the documentation for the AGM, down to the plastic mailing wrapper, and repeated in the platform design and visual aids at the meeting.

Figure 20.3   *A contrasting design idea for the Advertising Association's annual report. Illustrations depict aspects of the AA's work. Design by Lawrence Cheung*

Figure 20.4 *Bright, cheerful design idea for Tesco's annual report and accounts. This style was followed for the annual review and summary financial statement*

The WPP report won a Platinum award from the League of American Communications Professionals (LACP), receiving 10 points out of 10 for first impressions, cover, letter to shareholders, narrative, report financials, creativity, message clarity and information accessibility. It was also ranked sixth overall out of 1,223 reports submitted across all categories.

PR benefits from good design

A well-produced annual report can provide immense PR benefits. For the communications department it demonstrates what they and their design team can do, and it can win them an award with attendant follow-up publicity. It gets the company talked about in the trade press. Above all that, it is the voice of the company and its employees to all its audiences. This means that it must be readable, attractive to look at and a key source of information for journalists, opinion-formers and analysts. The company's reputation depends on it.

All the elements that, put together, make an annual report readable – such matters as type size, headings, use of pictures and captions – are covered in earlier chapters. The principles of good design and layout should be followed rigorously, and with a level of creativity to make it stand out from the rest. The annual report is the most important document any organisation produces; it is its flagship. As such it should get all the attention it deserves.

Annual reports in an electronic age

Many companies, trade associations, charities and other organisations make their annual reports available online. Care must be taken to ensure that any information published in a printed report is given in the online version without any change whatsoever. While some readers prefer to read annual reports online, there are others who prefer them in a printed form. Despite the increasing popularity of online versions, communication strategies must be developed to allow all readers equal opportunity to access information, whether they read on screen or in print.

Most annual reports can be viewed on websites, and some companies ask shareholders for their email addresses so that they may request regular news and financial information. One such is the Management Consulting Group, which issues summary trading updates ahead of its interim and final results for the year, with the full updates on the 'Investor Relations Latest Company News' page of its website. It also confirms the results resolutions proposed at the AGM each year.

Conversely, those firms that rely on electronic technology to communicate with shareholders may fail to reach their readers as well as they could through the printed page. As the Prowse report puts it: 'What they want is something physical to hold and read.' However, the value of the printed annual report now appears to be in decline, even though there is a clear need for it among a significant number of shareholders and other recipients.

Therein lies a dilemma for chief executives and their public relations advisers: since the popularity of the online version continues to grow, a communications strategy allowing both the electronic and printed versions to benefit all readers is needed. And that, to a large extent, is in the hands of the technologist.

AT A GLANCE

- The annual report must communicate effectively; too many don't.
- The provisions of the Companies Act must be followed rigorously.
- Strict rules cover the content and format of accounts.
- The report and accounts must give a 'true and fair' view of the company and its affairs.
- Regulations for Operational and Financial Reviews (OFR) apply in 2005.
- Too many reports are longer than necessary, while others are over-designed.
- The first principle is to give a full, clear, 'no-frills' statement of the business.
- PR professionals must be involved with the content from the start.
- PROs must be able to interpret technical and specialised 'jargon'.
- The chairman's statement sets the tone: it's the one part that is read and remembered.
- Some reports, written by ghostwriters, lack personality and underestimate reader intelligence.
- Most chairmen's statements from Europe's top 10 companies are uninspiring, bland and banal.
- Reports can be expensive, but can be used as the corporate brochure for year.
- The most effective reports are creatively brilliant.
- Many PR benefits result from good design.
- Online versions must not differ from printed reports.

21

Is it legal?

Imagine this. You are opening the morning's post and there's an envelope with 'solicitors' after a set of names. Someone wants to sell us a service of some kind? If you could be so lucky. What you read will not be a good start to the day: it says that a press release you have just sent out has seriously maligned the reputation of a client's supplier, which is considering legal action and will be claiming damages.

Panic. It does not matter if a release is not published: it can still be the subject of a court action. If the damaging words are circulated to third parties, they could be defamatory even if they are not printed or broadcast in the media. And people talk in pubs and clubs. A release is out once you hit the 'send' key or once it is posted on your website. Phone calls to cancel it are a waste of time. Once it's out, it's out for good.

An action for defamation is just one of the perils any writer faces. Public relations practitioners must also be aware of legislation covering copyright, data protection, trade marks, competitions and price promotions. Besides these, there are several self-regulatory codes, mainly concerned with advertising, sales promotion and direct marketing, which must be followed. Legislation covering public relations and promotions is a complex subject, and it is not possible within the confines of this short chapter to give anything but a snapshot of the myriad laws and regulations impinging on our work. So here is a brief run-down of the main laws and rules that must be followed by PR and advertising practitioners alike.

WHAT IS LIBEL?

Libel is the publication, in 'hard copy', of a false statement which injures the reputation of a person by its tendency to 'lower him/her in the estimation of right-thinking members of society' or cause right-thinking members of society to shun or avoid that person. It can also apply to companies and organisations, in which case it is sometimes called trade libel. It is therefore essential to look out for any passage that could be libellous and delete it, or at least rewrite so that it is no longer open to challenge.

A libellous statement is defined as one made in a permanent form, such as in written documents, pictures or drawings. Malicious statements made in radio and television broadcasts, as well as distributed emails and messages on the internet, may also constitute a defamation. If the defamatory words are simply spoken, the defamation is called slander.

Among possible defences against a claim for damages are that the statement is not published, it is not defamatory, it's true, it was made on a privileged occasion, it is fair comment on a matter of public interest, and it was authorised by the complainant (that is, consent has been given). It is also possible to make a case for unintentional defamation, where a person who publishes a libel offers to make a suitable correction and apology; if this is not accepted, it is a defence to prove that the words were published 'innocently'.

If you are being sued, you can attempt to mitigate the amount of damages that may be awarded by means of an apology, a retraction, or by showing provocation.

Who is liable?

It is not only the author or writer of the statement who might be liable: if the statement appeared in a newspaper or periodical, the proprietor, editor, vendor or anyone placing the story can be sued. If a libellous statement is broadcast, the transmitting organisation or company, and the persons making the broadcast, could be held liable. Similarly printers are responsible, jointly with the publishers and authors, for all libels published in papers printed by them.

COPYRIGHT AND MORAL RIGHTS

As Philip Circus makes clear in his *Sales Promotion and Direct Marketing Law: A practical guide* (Butterworths LexisNexis, 2002), copyright is the right of the creator to control the reproduction of original material for as long as the material stays within copyright. It exists basically in every piece of literary, artistic, dramatic or musical work, and in sound recordings, films, television broadcasts, cable programmes and published material. An idea in itself is not copyright, and names, titles and slogans generally are not subject to copyright protection (although they can be protected by trade mark registration).

The copyright belongs to the creator of the work, with the exception that in the case of work created by employees in the course of their employment, the copyright belongs to the employer unless otherwise agreed. Copyright in literary, artistic, dramatic or musical works currently lasts for the life of the author plus 70 years from the end of the calendar year in which the author dies. For computer-generated works (work such as a table that has been created by computer software) it lasts 50 years from the end of the calendar year in which the work was made.

For IPR members, the basic positions on the duration and types of works attracting copyright protection are outlined in a copyright guide for PR practitioners, to be found in the legal centre pages of the Institute's website (www.ipr.org.uk). The guide has been produced for the IPR by Laytons Solicitors, tel: 020 7842 8000.

Obtaining copyright protection

Although copyright is automatically acquired immediately a work is written (or recorded in some other form such as on tape or computer disk) and there is no formal registration as such, it is advisable to establish evidence of the completion of the work, says the Society of Authors. One way of doing this is to deposit a copy of the script with a bank and get a dated receipt for it.

Moral rights of creators

The Copyright Designs and Patents Act 1988 creates two 'moral' rights, giving an author or creator of a work the right to be identified whenever that work is published, performed or broadcast, and to object to derogatory treatment of the work. The right to be identified does not apply unless it has been asserted in writing. Moral rights can, however, be waived by agreement.

Infringements

Civil remedies are available in the form of injunctions to prevent further abuse, and possible damages for past infringement by way of compensation or an account of profits. Copyright will not be infringed if it falls within exceptions provided for in the Copyright Act. The 'fair dealing exceptions' include research and private study, criticism, review and news reporting; others include use in education, libraries and archives, and the use of a typeface in the ordinary course of printing.

APPLYING FOR AN INJUNCTION

If you or your organisation are the ones whose copyright is being infringed, one option is to apply for an injunction to prevent further infringement. Nicola Solomon, Head of Publishing at Finers Stephens Innocent, writing in the *The Author* (the Society of Authors house magazine), explains that an injunction is an immediate court order preventing someone from taking certain steps, and a defendant who fails to obey it can be imprisoned for contempt of court. An injunction can be obtained in a 'matter of days or in urgent cases, a matter of hours', she says. But since it is urgent, it can be an expensive process. 'Your solicitor will have to drop everything to learn the facts, prepare witness statements and other documents, instruct a barrister and attend the application, which may mean a long day in court.' She warns that obtaining an injunction will therefore rarely involve legal costs of less than £10,000–20,000.

The Society of Authors says that a court would only award an injunction if the infringement was 'very damaging', and another deterrent is that the plaintiff would have to give a 'cross undertaking' meaning that if it loses, it guarantees to pay any losses the other party has incurred during the time of the interim injunction. So before taking such drastic action, think carefully before committing yourself to expenditure that may not, in the end, be recoverable.

GETTING PERMISSION

When quoting from copyright material, you need to obtain permission unless the copyright has expired (see above). This is normally obtained from the copyright holder or his/her agent: that is, from the creator and/or publisher. If you want to reproduce a quotation and it can be regarded as 'fair dealing' for purposes of criticism or review as defined in the Act, permission is not needed. But, says the Society of Authors in its *Quick Guide to Permissions* (available as a printed leaflet and also on the Society's website), the writer must ensure that either in the text itself or in an acknowledgement page, the title and the author of the work are given.

What is fair dealing?

It is not easy to say what constitutes 'fair dealing', but the CIPR legal service will advise on specific cases. The *Permissions* guide gives an example of the length of quotation that would fall within the context of 'criticism or review'. Some years ago the Society of Authors and the Publishers Association stated that they would usually regard as fair dealing the use of: (a) a single extract of up to 400 words or a series of extracts (of which none exceeds 300 words) to a total of 800 words from a prose work; (b) extracts to a total of 40 lines from a poem, provided that this did not exceed a quarter of the poem. The words must be quoted in the context of criticism or review.

'While this statement does not have the force of law, it carried considerable weight with a judge experienced in copyright in a leading infringement case. It does not mean, however, that a quotation for purposes of criticism or review in excess of these limits cannot rank as fair dealing in some circumstances.' The essential point to remember is that if you are quoting someone, regardless of length, you must always acknowledge the author and the source.

DATA PROTECTION

In a short guide to the Data Protection Act 1998 (available to CIPR members on its website), it is noted that a number of new measures were introduced in this Act to protect the rights of individuals (but not companies) about whom information is held and recorded and stored manually. The original data protection legislation was limited to electronic or automated processing, but that is no longer the case.

Among the data protection principles which must be observed are that personal data must be: fairly obtained; adequate, relevant and not excessive in relation to the purpose for which it is held; accurate and up to date; not kept longer than necessary; processed in line with the data subject's rights; secure; and not transferred outside the EU without adequate protection. Under the 1998 Act, there is a system of 'notification' to replace a registration procedure. If you control the processing of personal data, you must notify the Information Commissioner, saying where you obtained the data and what you intend to do with it.

The CIPR will advise

The CIPR legal centre will advise members on data protection issues; a guide for the CIPR has been produced by Lee & Pembertons Solicitors (tel: 020 7824 9111). Much useful advice will be found in question and answer form in Philip Circus's *Sales Promotion and Direct Marketing Law*. The Data Commissioner's website (www.dataprotection.gov.uk) gives much information, and there is a helpline on 01625 545745. This is a complex legal area, and action should only be taken after specific advice has been sought.

DEALING WITH TRADE MARKS

This is an area where great care must be observed, particularly in articles and news releases. Apart from the need to be careful to use an initial capital letter for proprietary names in everyday use such as Sellotape, Hoover and Xerox, and observe the rules under which trade mark registration is granted under the Trade Marks Act 1994, practitioners should be aware that the 1994 Act provided increased possibilities for registration. Sounds, shapes, slogans and smells can be registered. The Register of Trade Marks is kept at the Patent Office and can be searched online.

Philip Circus points out in his book that slogans can only be registered where they can be shown to be 'distinctive'. 'Most slogans are not distinctive because they are, to coin a phrase, here today and gone tomorrow.' He considers that it would be a waste of time and money to apply for trade mark registration if it is likely that a new slogan will not be in use by the time the procedural formalities have been completed.

Again, CIPR members can get advice on trade mark use and registration by visiting the Institute's website (www.cipr.co.uk), which also has information on the rules covering comparative advertising and public relations material.

COMPETITIONS AND PROMOTIONS

If you are planning a competition as part of a marketing programme for a client, be careful to follow the provisions of the Lotteries and Amusements Act 1976. A range of types of competition are unlawful under section 14 of the Act, and there are strict rules which must be followed under the requirements of the British Code of Advertising, Sales Promotion and Direct Marketing (the CAP code).

SELF-REGULATORY CODES OF PRACTICE

As well as legal requirements, there is a range of self-regulatory requirements which must be observed by PR practitioners. Prime among these is the IPR Code of Conduct, details of which are set out in the legal centre on the Institute's website. It is perhaps worth emphasising here that Clause 2.2. states that a member shall 'have a positive duty at all times to respect the truth and shall not disseminate false or misleading information knowingly or recklessly, and take proper care to check all information prior to its dissemination'.

Clause 4.1 states that a member shall 'adhere to the highest standards of accuracy and truth, avoiding extravagant claims or unfair comparisons and giving credit for ideas and words borrowed from others'. And Clause 4.3 states that a member shall not 'injure the professional reputation or practice of another member'.

There are also relevant provisions in the British Code of Advertising, Sales Promotion and Direct Marketing. (At the time of writing, the Advertising Standards Authority was due to take over the regulation of broadcast advertising from 1 November 2004.) It is important for all public relations practitioners to acquaint themselves with all statutory and self-regulatory codes of practice and to follow them to the letter. That will go a long way towards keeping out of the sights of lawyers and regulators.

DON'T FORGET THE IMPRINT

My collection of annual and interim reports from major companies includes 20 or so that do not give the printer's name and location – in other words their imprint. Failure to include it could mean a hefty fine: under the Printer's Imprint Act of 1961, the penalty is now up to £200 for every copy printed. Just try multiplying that with the print run and see what you get!

Although prosecutions are rare as proceedings can only be taken with the approval, and in the name of, the Attorney General or Solicitor General, or in Scotland the Law Advocate, within three calendar months after printing, its main purpose is to ensure that the person responsible for publication can be traced easily. There are exemptions for specific items such as business cards, price lists, catalogues and advertisements for goods and property for sale.

Election posters and leaflets must bear the address of the printer and publisher. Anyone contravening these provisions is liable on conviction to a maximum fine of £2,000.

Further information is available from the British Printing Industries Federation (020 7915 8300).

FURTHER INFORMATION

Additional sources of information available include: Advertising Standards Authority (www.asa.org.uk); Direct Marketing Association (www.dma.org.uk); Institute of Sales Promotion (www.isp.org.uk); Ofcom (www.ofcom.org.uk); Office of Fair

Trading (www.oft.org.uk); Philip Circus (www.lawmark.co.uk/philipcircus/). Register of Trade Marks (www.patent.gov.uk); Society of Authors (www.info@societyofauthors.org).

The CIPR provides a legal and business helpline for members. The legal service is offered by Croner Consulting.

AT A GLANCE

- Look out for possible defamation of a person or organisation.
- If sued, try to mitigate damages with apology.
- Copyright belongs generally to the creator of a work.
- For employees, it belongs to the employer if not otherwise agreed.
- A copyright guide is available to IPR members on its website.
- Check out the permissions guide from the Society of Authors.
- Ensure you are 'notified' with the Information Commissioner.
- Make sure you comply with the data protection principles in the Data Protection Acts.
- When writing about proprietary products, check whether you are using a registered trade mark, and acknowledge it if so.
- Only 'distinctive' slogans can be registered as trade marks.
- Strict rules apply for competitions and promotions.
- A failure to include an imprint notice on your publication could mean a substantial fine.

Appendix 1: English grammar – some definitions

WHAT IS IT? WHAT DOES IT DO?

Brief definitions of the terminology used in English grammar are given here as a help in using this book. Examples are shown in brackets where appropriate.

Abbreviation: A shortened form of a word or phrase, company name, product or service (*BBC, IPR, ad* for advertisement). No full stops between the characters nowadays.

Acronym: A word formed from a set of initials (*NATO*). NO full stops.

Active voice: Attributes action of a verb to a person or thing from which it logically follows (the ship *is* sinking, the man *hits* the ball). Intransitive verbs can only occur in the active voice (the client *laughs*). See entry for verbs.

Adjectival noun: An adjective used as a noun (the *young*).

Adjective: Describes or qualifies a noun (a *big* firm).

Adverb: A word that qualifies or modifies a verb (drove *quickly*), an adjective (*terribly* bad) or another adverb (*very* sadly). Care needed in use and positioning. See later entry for split infinitive.

Apostrophe: A mark to indicate the possessive case (the *firm's* staff, *men's* shirts) and the omission of a letter or letters (*shan't, can't*), or contractions of words (*'phone*).

Article: Definite article is the name for *the*; indefinite for *a* and *an*.

Bracket: Paired typographical marks to denote word(s), phrase or sentence in parenthesis, usually round ( ). Square brackets [ ] denote words inserted by someone other than the author.

Case: The role of a noun or noun phrase in relation to other words in a clause or sentence (in the *boy's* knees, boy is in the genitive case; similarly *boy* is in singular case, *boys* plural).

Clause: Part of a complex sentence usually with its own subject and verb; three main types – nominal clause when functioning like a noun phrase (*the name of the game*); relative clause like an adjective (the man *you love*); or adverbial (don't do it *unless you're sure*). Inferior to a sentence, superior to a phrase.

Collective noun: A noun referring to a group of people or animals (*audience, committee, family, herd, staff, team, majority, parliament, the clergy, the public*). Whether it takes a plural or singular verb depends on whether the group is considered as a single unit or as a collection of individuals (the audience *was* in its place but *were* clapping madly, the family *is* large; the board *is* meeting, but *are* going out to lunch).

Conjunction: A connecting word to join two clauses, or words in the same clause (*and, but, or*); also for introducing a subordinate clause (*although, because, since*).

Consonants: Letters of the alphabet other than the vowels *a, e, i, o, u*.

Count nouns: Nouns that can be used with numerical values (*book/books*), that can form a plural or be used with an indefinite article and usually refer to objects (*table, ship, pen*) as distinct from non-count nouns (*adolescence, richness, scaffolding*).

Dangling participle: Also called hanging participle, or dangler; a participle clause usually contains no subject and is unattached to the subject of the main clause. Considered ungrammatical rather than a style fault. (*Now broken, Fred Jones can remember what the teacup looked like.* Clearly, Mr Jones was not broken even though his memory was perfect.)

Determiners: Words that precede nouns to limit their meaning in some way (*all, both, this, every*).

Double negative: Two negative words in a sentence can confuse the reader. (I *haven't* got *nothing*; I *wouldn't* be surprised if they *didn't* come.)

Elision: Omission of speech sound or syllable as in *wrong*, lis*t*en, hym*n*. In each example the elided character is italicised.

Ellipsis: Omission of word or words from speech or writing usually recoverable from the context; useful in formal contexts for avoiding repetition. (We are as keen *to help* as you are.) Ellipsis of *to help* avoids duplication, aids flow and sharpens style.

First person: Pronouns and determiners denoting the speaker or writer in contrast to the addressee or others. (*I, me, myself, my, mine* in the singular; *we, us, ourselves, our, ours* in the plural.)

Gender: Nouns and pronouns representing natural distinctions of sex. The masculine gender denotes persons and animals that are *male*; feminine, those that are *female*.

Genitive: The case of nouns and pronouns indicating possession of something or close association of something (possessive case, the *cat's* paws).

Gerund: The *-ing* part of a verb when used in a partly noun-like way as in *No parking* as opposed to the *-ing* as used in a participle ending, *everyone was parking*. Sometimes called a verbal noun.

Headlinese: The grammar of newspaper headlines where articles and other words are omitted for reasons of space and where present tense verbs are used for past events (*soldier shoots terrorists*).

Hyphen: Mark to join words or to indicate word division, to separate figures or groups of figures. Many uses: in compound nouns as in *air-conditioning*, but *air force*; in compound adjectives as in a *two-page* report; with a prefix as in the votes have been *re-counted.*

Idiom: An expression with a meaning that cannot be guessed from the meaning of the individual words as in 'his mother *passed away* (died) this morning'. A peculiarity of expression or phraseology in language (*over the moon, under the weather*) which sounds natural to those born and bred in England, but incomprehensible to foreigners.

Indirect question: A question as reported in indirect speech. (*I asked when he could attend the meeting.*)

Infinitive: The form of a verb when used without direct relationship to time, person or number, often preceded by *to*. (*I wanted to laugh.*) See entry for split infinitive.

Interrogative: A word or sentence used to ask a question. (*What do you do?*)

Mass noun: Never takes the indefinite article *a* and seldom has a plural (*bread, capitalism, clothing, dust, equipment, leisure, traffic*).

Modal verbs: Auxiliary verbs to express mood (*can/could, may/might, shall/should, will/would, must*).

Modifier: Words which modify other words: *very* + badly (adverb); *really* + useful (adjective).

Noun: The name of a person, place or thing whether material or immaterial, abstract or concrete. Inflects for plural and functions as subject or object of a sentence. Common nouns (*cat/car*) are distinct from proper nouns or names (names of people, cities, months, days of the week and which carry a capital initial letter).

Number: Contrasts between singular and plural; in nouns (*girl/girls*), pronouns (*she/they*), verbs (*says/say; was/were*).

Object: The object of a sentence follows a verb and is normally a noun or noun phrase (the car hit the *wall*; the car hit the *wall, bricks and all*).

Paragraph: A short passage in text, at the start of a fresh line of thought, sometimes (but not always) indented. A unit of thought, not of length.

Parenthesis: A word, clause or sentence inserted as an afterthought and marked off with brackets, commas or dashes as in 'This is a useful book (*it should be kept for reference*).' Plural parentheses.

Participle: A form of the verb normally ending in *-ing* or *-ed*. Present participle (*being, doing/is going/looking*); past participle (*been/done/has gone/looked*).

Passive voice: Where the object of the sentence 'receives' the action of the verb (fast drivers *will be prosecuted*). Only transitive verbs can have passive forms. See entry for verbs.

Person: Classifies whether pronouns and verbs indicate the speaker, the addressee or a third party as first, second or third person, singular or plural. (First person: *I am/we are going to the theatre*; second: *you are going to the theatre*; third: *he/they are going to the theatre*.)

Phrase: A short expression, a group of words of lesser weight than a clause forming a unit in itself; part of a sentence that is not the subject (I refuse *to do it*).

Plural: More than one (*cats and dogs*, but *sheep and deer*).

Possessive: A word or case indicating possession or ownership; the possessive case of nouns is also called the genitive case (*John's hands, girls' fingers*).

Predicate: That part of a sentence that is not subject (I *decided what to do*).

Preposition: Words that relate word sets to each other and that generally precede the words they govern. Usually short words (*by, in, for, to, out, up*). Traditional prejudice against ending a sentence with a preposition is now fading, especially for informal contexts.

Pronoun: A word that replaces or stands for a noun without naming a person or thing already known from the context (*I/you/they* asked a question), and sometimes replaces a clause as in Why did you ask *that*?

Proper noun: A noun referring to a particular person, place, month, day of week, etc, and carrying a capital initial letter (*Smith, London, March, Monday*).

Second person: Denotes the person addressed as distinct from the speaker or writer or other person (*you, yourself, yourselves*, etc).

Sentence: The largest unit in traditional grammar; a set of words complete in itself containing subject and predicate (all that part that is not the subject). Usually contains a verb; starts with a capital letter and ends with a full stop, and also with question or exclamation mark, as in 'The client heard a presentation.' Here *the client* is the subject, *heard* the verb and *presentation* the object.

Singular: A word or form referring to a single person or thing.

Split infinitive: Where an adverb is placed between *to* and the infinitive form of a verb (*to boldly go*). Nowadays it's considered a myth that *to* must never be detached from the verb. Generally, it is better not to split but avoidance can sometimes cause awkward constructions. ('Do you want *to* really help them?' is preferable to putting *really* before *to*, impossible after *help*.)

Subject: That part of the sentence which usually comes first and governs the verb, often defined as the 'doer' of the verbal action. See entry above for sentence.

Syllable: Unit of pronunciation; a word or part of a word uttered with a single pulse of the voice and usually containing one vowel sound with or without consonant(s) preceding or following it. *Pro/nun/ci/a/tion* has five syllables.

Synonym: A word or phrase having the same meaning (or virtually the same) as another. Some synonyms for *care* are (nouns) *anxiety, caution, charge, burden*; (verbs) *be anxious, be disposed, have regard.*

Tense: A form taken by the verb in a sentence to indicate the time at which the action is viewed as occurring. Past (something that *has happened*), present (*is happening*) and future (*will happen*) tenses. In media usage, present tenses can refer to the past (PRO *resigns*).

Third person: Denotes the person or persons spoken or written about as distinct from the addressee, speaker or writer (*he, him, they, theirs*, etc).

Verb: The core of a sentence or clause, the 'doing' or 'action' word. Major types are transitive, intransitive, auxiliary. Using a transitive verb, the meaning passes from subject to the object of the sentence (he *built* the house); using an intransitive verb the meaning is complete without the addition of an object (she *laughs*). Auxiliary verbs form tenses, moods and voices of other verbs (*be, do, have*) and modals (*may, might*, etc). Verbless, or incomplete, sentences are common in sports commentaries and in broadcasting (*And now the news*).

Voice: Mode of inflecting verbs as being active or passive (the cat *ate* the food; the food *was eaten* by the cat).

Vowels: Letters of the alphabet producing simple vocal sound by continuous passage of breath (*a, e, i, o, u*). All English words contain at least one vowel.

Note: Source material for Appendices 1 and 2 has been drawn largely from the 1994 edition of the *Oxford Dictionary of English Grammar* and from the 1974 edition of the *Concise Oxford Dictionary* by permission of the Oxford University Press.

Appendix 2: Confusing pairs of words

LOOKALIKES: DIFFERENCES AND DISTINCTIONS

Many pairs of words look and sound alike, but some are exact opposites, while others have different shades of meaning. Get them wrong and you could have a verbal disaster on your hands: at best an embarrassing telephone call to rectify what is really meant, at worst a press release or print job that has to be corrected and reissued. Here are some of them.

Adaption/adaptation: While both mean the same thing, adaptation is preferred. Adaption is eventually expected to supplant adaptation which is slowly on the way out.

Adverse/averse: Close in meaning. Adverse suggests being hostile or contrary to somebody or something, while averse means being opposed or disinclined to do something.

Adviser/advisor: Both spellings acceptable, but most style guides recommend -er. The -or variant has a pretentious, self-important ring to it.

Alternate/alternative: Alternate as a verb means interchanging one thing with another; as a noun it means things of two kinds coming one after the other. Alternative as an adjective means offering choice between two things; as a noun denotes an option to choose between two or more things.

Biennial/biannual: Biennial means once every two years, biannual twice a year or, if preferred, twice yearly. Similarly, bimonthly means every two months, not twice a month. With this pair, it is often better to write it out in full rather than risk ambiguity.

Brochure/pamphlet: A brochure is normally taken to mean a wire-stitched or square-backed, illustrated colour-printed production used for promoting an organisation's products, services or activities. There is little difference between a pamphlet, usually just a folded sheet produced in larger numbers at low cost, and a leaflet.

Complement(ary)/compliment(ary): The former means completing, supplying a deficiency, two or more things complementing each other; the latter an expression of regard or praise as in 'with compliments'.

Compose/comprise: Compose means to constitute, to form or make up a list by putting two or more things or parts together; comprise means to include or contain the items on the list.

Continual/continuous: A close pair. Continual means frequently happening and without cessation, again and again; continuous means joined together, or going on non-stop without interruption.

Counsel/council: Counsel is usually taken to mean giving advice to someone; council is a body of people or an authority.

Delusion/illusion: A delusion denotes a false idea, impression or belief as a symptom of insanity, someone who is genuinely convinced of what is not the case (*a delusion of grandeur*); an illusion denotes a false impression as to the true nature of an object, a misapprehension of a true state of affairs (*an optical illusion*).

Derisive/derisory: Derisive means mocking, scoffing; derisory equals ridiculous, laughingly inefficient.

Especial(ly)/special(ly): Little difference. Especial the adjective now replaced by special without much trouble; especially/specially the adverbs expected to survive in contexts where *in particular*, or *even more* is meant.

Disinterested/uninterested: The former suggests impartial or unbiased while the latter means indifference. Most writers prefer to write 'lack of interest' rather than disinterested.

Effect/affect: Effect means to accomplish something; affect means to have an influence upon something. The difficulty is compounded by the fact that both can be used as nouns and verb, although *affect* is more commonly used as a verb and *effect* as a noun.

Flout/flaunt: To flout means to violate a rule, show a contemptuous disregard; to flaunt means to show off, to make an ostentatious or defiant display.

For ever/forever: For ever (two words) is for always; forever means continually.

Forgo/forego: To forgo is to abstain from or do without; to forego is to precede in place or time.

Fortuitious/fortunate: Fortuitous means by accident or chance; fortunate equals lucky.

Imply/infer: To imply is to hint or state something; to infer is to draw a conclusion from what has been implied. A useful rule to remember is that the writer or speaker *implies*, while the reader or listener *infers*.

Inapt/inept: The former means not apt or unsuitable, the latter unskilful.

Less/fewer: The distinction between these words is often lost: *less* goes with singular 'mass' nouns (population/difficulty) while *fewer* with numbers or quantities capable of being counted or listed (people/things).

Magazine/journal: Both are periodicals, but a journal is usually the more serious, professional publication, like the IPR's magazine, *Profile*.

Masterful/masterly: Masterful means domineering, wilful; masterly means executed with superior skill.

Militate/mitigate: To militate against something is to have a significant effect against it; to mitigate is to create conditions for reducing the severity of something.

Number/amount: These two words are very close in definition, but be careful to distinguish between them: the distinction is whether they go with 'count' or 'mass' nouns, as in the *number* of releases sent out compared with the *amount* of work in writing. As in this example, *number* is usually constructed with a plural.

Practical/practicable: Practical (suitable for use) and practicable (able to be done). What, for example, is practical is to mail 100 news releases before the office closes, but not necessarily practicable in that there may not be the staff to do it.

Refute/deny: Both verbs dispute the truthfulness of a statement; deny says it is false, refute proves that it is.

Regretfully/regrettably: The former means an expression of regret, the latter something to be regretted, unwelcome, worthy of reproof.

Scotch/Scottish: Scotch is for whisky made in Scotland (-ey for varieties made in Ireland and the United States); Scottish for those from north of the Border.

That/which: Again close and often interchangeable pronouns. The important distinction between them is that *which* can never refer to people. That defines as in 'the PR firm that was formed', while *which* describes as in 'the PR firm, which was formed in 1990, is still operating profitably'. The careful observer will note that *which* usually follows a comma, while *that* doesn't need one before it.

Under/underneath: While there is a slim distinction between them, the simplest way to show it is to write *underneath* meaning 'directly covered by' while *under* means below or beneath. A sentence can end with *underneath* far more easily than it can with *under*.

Note: Further examples of confusing pairs will be found in the *Oxford Guide to English Usage*.

Appendix 3: Glossary and jargon buster

INFORMATION TECHNOLOGY

ADSL: Asymmetric Digital Subscriber Line, a new modem technology, converts existing twisted-pair telephone lines into access paths for multimedia and high-speed data communications.

Bluetooth: Short-range (10–100 metres) digital communication without connection by cables or wires.

Broadband: Communication network carrying a large amount of data, including voice and visual information.

Byte: Unit of measurement of digital data.

CD ROM: Stands for Compact Disc Read Only Memory.

CD RW: CD rewritable. CDs that can be recorded over and over again.

Convergence: Combining personal computers, telecommunications and television.

Domain name: Name of an internet website, or web address, the URL (uniform resource locator).

Download: Transfer of data from computer to computer, ie from internet to PC.

DVD: Once stood for Digital Versatile Disc but now does not stand for anything. Popular way to view movies, giving higher quality picture and sound than video.

e-tailing: Electronic shopping or teleshopping using programmes within television schedules.

Ethernet: Name of local area network and accompanying technical specifications and products.

Freeware: Software that can be downloaded or distributed free of charge although under copyright.

FAQ(s): Frequently asked question(s).

FTP: File Transfer Protocol. Means of transmitting via the internet or local area network from computer to computer.

GIF: Graphics Interchange Format.

HTML: HyperText Markup Language. For creating a document on the internet.

HTTP: HyperText Transfer Protocol. Means of sending web pages across the internet.

ISDN: Integrated Services Digital Network. For speedy transfer of digitised information by digital lines. Ideal for transferring graphics and text and fast downloading of internet files.

ISP: Internet Service Provider. Examples: Freeserve, AOL.

Java: Computer language.

Link: Takes the user from one point on a website to another.

Log-on: Synonym for going online, or connecting to the internet or to a network operating system.

Megabyte: MB (abbr). Unit of data storage (a million bytes).

Multimedia: Combination of computerised data from, eg audio, video, text, CD ROM.

Netiquette: From internet and etiquette – a standard code: eg, no messages in capitals, users should check with FAQs before asking a question.

Newsgroup: Discussion group on the internet.

Online: Being connected to the internet.

Portal: Term for a website used as a 'gateway' or starting point for those planning to enter the internet.

RAM: Random Access Memory measured in Megabytes (MB). Used to store data and details of programmes currently being run.

Server: Powerful computer storing digitised information for websites and emails.

Shareware: Software sent through the internet free of charge or included on CD ROM disc distributed free with printed publications. Can also be downloaded from the internet.

Smiley: Also called an emoticon, a contraction of emotion and icon. Smileys are read sideways: eg :-) for smiling, :-(for sad.

STB: Set-top box. Enables an ordinary TV set to receive cable, and all digital transmissions.

Upload: Reverse of download. Transfer data from PC to internet website, another PC or server or to wide area network.

URL: Uniform Resource Locator. The address of a website.

Voice recognition: Technology that permits copy to be voice-recognised and set in type.

WAP: Wireless Application Protocol. Connects a mobile phone to the internet. Hence WAP phones.

Webcam: Miniature, low-cost camera mounted on top of a TV set or computer monitor to capture images for digital transmission.

PRINTING AND PUBLISHING

Author's: Corrections to copy after it has been set in type; usually charged extra.

Bleed: When images, usually illustrations, extend beyond the trimmed edge of a sheet; allowance must be made for this when sizing photographs to be bled off the page.

Crosshead: Small heading placed in text, to liven the page (and fill space).

Display type: Type used for headings, in larger size than text.

Draw-down quote: Significant phrase or statement from a quote used within the page as a heading. Useful for filling space and enhancing look of the page.

Halftone: Printing term for continuous tone artwork such as a photograph; reproduces as series of dots of various sizes.

JPEG: Joint Photographic Experts Group (jpg for short). A format for graphics computer files.

Lower case: Small characters of a typeface, abbreviated to l.c.

Makeup: Arrangement of type and illustrations on a page.

Measure: Width of typesetting, or line length, usually expressed in ems or picas (one em = 0.166044 in).

Moiré (pattern): When halftone images, usually photographs, are printed over one another, a moiré pattern can occur through different screen angles used; can occur, for example, if a newspaper photograph is screened for use in a magazine which uses paper needing a different screen angle.

OCR: Optical Character Recognition. The scanning of text for subsequent typesetting.

Overlay: Transparent covering for artwork for instructions or corrections to avoid spoiling original images.

Overset: More text set in type than is needed for a given space.

Page proof: Proof of a page for OK before printing.

PDF: Portable Document Format (usually shown as pdf).

Point (size): Printer's unit of measurement, used principally for designating type sizes. There are 12 points to a pica, approximately 72 points to the inch; 1pt = 0.013837 in or 0.351 mm.

Printer's error: Mistake by the printer. Should not be charged to the customer.

Progressives: Progressive proofs, sometimes called progs, made from separate plates in colour work, showing the sequence of printing and the result after the application of each colour.

Ragged left: In typesetting, where the left-hand edge is ragged and the right-hand edge is aligned.

Ragged right: Reverse of ragged left: here the type is aligned on the left.

Ream: Five hundred sheets of paper. Paper for short-run work is normally bought by the ream.

Register: When two or more printing images are printed in exact alignment with one another they are said to be in register.

ROP: Run of Paper. Material printed in a magazine or newspaper as part of the main text.

Running head: A title repeated at the top of each page of a magazine or book.

Serif: Short lines at the ends of main letter characters in some typefaces. Typefaces without them are sans serif types.

Set-off: This occurs when the ink of a printed sheet rubs off and marks the next sheet.

Sidebar: Panel of text, usually in colour or white reversed out of black, alongside feature article giving supporting detail or illustrations.

Small caps: Small capital letters, about the same size as lower case characters.

Showthrough: Where the printing on one side of the sheet shows through to the other side.

Stock: Another word for paper or printing material. Also called substrate.

Subhead: Inferior to main headline.

Transpose: When a letter, word or line is exchanged in position for another.

Trapping: Where a wet ink film is printed over a previously printed ink, or where dry ink is used over a wet ink. When the colour is held then trapping has occurred.

Web press: Printing press which prints on reels of paper, as used in long-run newspaper and magazine printing.

Appendix 4: When you're lost for words

OVERCOMING WRITER'S BLOCK

You can't get going, your insertion point keeps blinking. If you've typed a few words, they're rubbish and you delete them. The screen's blank again, the trash can is full, the waste bin is brimming with scraps. You've got word freeze. You're brain dead. What do you do?

Several things. First, don't panic. Walk around the office, talk to colleagues, have a drink (but no alcohol), snatch today's paper. Grab your firm's annual report, and look for salient points. Study recent correspondence or documents on the subject. Anything to get going.

For the moment, forget the computer keyboard: just jot down in bullet-point form, as two to three-word headings, the essential thoughts and ideas you want to get over. Concentrate on facts and figures, the human angle. Put your points in logical sequence. If it's a release or article, think up some possible quotes that can be cleared later. You are halfway to your first draft.

Now switch on your computer or word processor. Even if you can't get everything organised the way you want, just get typing. Start with something easy, say the main facts you want to communicate. After that, subsidiary points will follow naturally. If you're still unhappy with your efforts, read out what you have got to a colleague. It may mean a rewrite, but you're getting there, albeit slowly. Now's the time to get the grammar and style right. Get rid of clichés and verbiage. Polish again. You're on the way.

And what should you never do if the words won't come? If there's a chance of doing something else, don't take it. If all else fails, dictate your thoughts into a tape recorder. Play back and see what they sound like. That might help, but you're back to square one.

CONTROLLING YOUR NERVES ON STAGE

An outline of measures to combat nerves at the microphone is given by speaking coach Roy Topp in Chapter 17. Here are some additional points for dealing with stress on stage, given by Sarah Dickinson in her *Effective Presentation* (Orion Business Books). Release tension with exercises to relax the body and to develop the voice. 'Practise your text ... tape yourself speaking at [a slow] pace. You may be surprised at how some of it sounds perfectly normal.' It is important, she emphasises, to realise that what is eaten and drunk before a performance will dramatically affect how the speaker feels. And the better he or she feels, the better the presentation.

Your nerves will be controlled much more easily if you are relaxed, confident that the technical arrangements for visual aids, microphone and sound checks have been made, that you have a copy of your speech in your pocket and that any props are easy to reach. You should know who's in the audience and that the press handouts are ready. And of course you have rehearsed and rehearsed. You can't have enough of it.

After that it's up to you.

Further reading

Aitchison, James (1994) *Cassell's Guide to Written English*, BCA by arrangement with Cassell, London.

Allen, RE (1990) *The Oxford Spelling Dictionary*, Oxford University Press, Oxford.

Allen, RE (1996) *The Oxford Writers' Dictionary*, Oxford University Press, Oxford.

Allen, R (ed) (1999) *Pocket Fowler's Modern English Usage*, Oxford University Press, Oxford.

Amis, Kingsley (1997) *The King's English, A Guide to Modern Usage*, HarperCollins, London.

Apsey, Linda (2000) *The Jobsearch Manual*, Management Books, Cirencester.

Bickerton, Anthea (ed) (2001) *American English/English American*, Abson Books, London.

Billingham, Jo (2002) *Editing and Revising Text*, Oxford University Press, Oxford.

Bird, Drayton (2002) *How to Write Sales Letters that Sell*, Kogan Page, London.

Bryson, Bill (1984) *Penguin Dictionary of Troublesome Words*, Penguin, London.

Burchfield, RW (ed) (1998) *Fowler's Modern English Usage*, Oxford University Press, Oxford.

Circus, Philip (2002) *Sales Promotion and Direct Marketing Law: A practical guide*, Butterworths LexisNexis, London.

Crone, Tom (2002) *Law and the Media*, Focal Press, London.

Cutts, Martin (2004) *Oxford Guide to Plain English*, Oxford University Press, Oxford.

Dent, Susie (2003) *The Language Report*, Oxford University Press, Oxford.

Dickinson, S (1998) *Effective Presentation*, Orion Business Books, London.

Dorner, Jane (2002) *Writing for the Internet*, Oxford University Press, Oxford.

Dummett, Michael (1993) *Grammar & Style for examination candidates and others*, Duckworth, London.

Evans, H (2000) *Essential English for Journalists, Editors and Writers*, revised by Crawford Gillan, Pimlico Random House, London.

Economist Style Guide (1993) Hamish Hamilton in association with Economist Books, London.

Farkas, Anna (2002) *Oxford Dictionary of Catchphrases*, Oxford University Press, Oxford.

Garner, Bryan A (2003) *Garner's Modern American Usage*, Oxford University Press, Oxford.

Gowers, Sir Ernest (1987) *The Complete Plain Words*, Penguin, London.

Hornby, Robert (1965) *The Press in Modern Society*, Muller.

Kahn, John Ellison (1985) *The Right Word at the Right Time*, Reader's Digest Association, London.

Kahn, John Ellison (1991) *How to Write and Speak Better*, Reader's Digest Association, London.

Lowe, D (1999) *Creating Web Pages for Dummies*, IDG Books, USA.

Marsh, David and Marshall, Nikki (2004) *The Guardian Style Book*, Guardian Books, London

Marshall, Susie B (1991) *Collins Gem Dictionary of Spelling and Word Division*, HarperCollins, London.

Montague-Smith, Patrick (1992) *Debrett's Correct Form*, Headline Book Publishing, London.

Partridge, Eric (1973) (ed Janet Whitcut 1994) *Usage and Abusage*, BCA by arrangement with Hamish Hamilton, London.

Partridge, Eric (1978) *A Dictionary of Clichés*, Routledge, London.

Prowse, Peter (ed) (annually) *Company Report Report*, Prowse & Co Ltd, Leatherhead.

Ritter, R M (ed) (2000) *Oxford Dictionary for Writers and Editors*, Oxford University Press, Oxford.

Ritter, R.M. (ed) (2003) *Oxford Style Manual*, Oxford University Press, Oxford.

Robertson, Geoffrey (1992) *Media Law*, Penguin Books, London.

Sealy, John (2003) *Law in Everyday Life*, Oxford University Press, Oxford.

Seigels, D (1997) *Creating Killer Web Sites*, Hayden Books, Hemel Hempstead.

Smith, Bud E and Bebak, Arthur (2002) *Creating Web Pages for Dummies*, Wiley, Sussex.

Society of Authors Quick Guide to Permissions, Society of Authors, London [online] http://www.societyofauthors.net/publications/index.html (accessed 9 November 2004)

Soule, Richard (1991) *The Penguin Dictionary of English Synonyms*, Penguin, London.

Stittle, John (2003) *Annual Reports: Delivering your corporate message to stakeholders*, Gower Press Publishing, London.

Strunk, William and White, EB (1979) *The Elements of Style*, Allyn and Bacon, Needham Heights, Mass.

Studner, Peter K (2000) *Super Jobsearch*, Management Books, Cirencester.

The Times Guide to English Style and Usage (1999) Times Books, a Division of HarperCollins, London.

Truss, Lynne (2003) *Eats, Shoots and Leaves*, Profile Books, London.

Waterhouse, Keith (1993) *Waterhouse on Newspaper Style*, Penguin, London.

Weiner, EDS and Delanhunty, Andrew (1994) *The Oxford Guide to English Usage*, Oxford University Press, Oxford.

Note: There are very many books and guides available on style, including several published by newspapers for their own staff, for the reader to consult. The titles in this bibliography, and others mentioned and acknowledged, form a selection recommended by the author to be of special interest and use in day-to-day writing and editing.

Index

NB: page numbers in *italic* indicate figures